DEVOTIONS UPON
EMERGENT OCCASIONS

JOHN DONNE

DEVOTIONS
Upon Emergent Occasions

Edited, with Commentary, by
ANTHONY RASPA

MCGILL-QUEEN'S UNIVERSITY PRESS
Montreal and London 1975

© McGill-Queen's University Press 1975
ISBN 0 7735 0194 0
Legal Deposit Fourth Quarter 1975
Bibliothèque nationale du Québec

This book has been published with the help of a grant
from the Humanities Research Council of Canada
using funds provided by the Canada Council.

Design by Anthony Crouch MGDC
Printed in Great Britain by William Clowes & Sons, Limited
London, Beccles, and Colchester

*This book has been typeset in
Monotype Bembo and letterpress
printed on Abbey Mills Cream
Antique Laid paper.*

Pour Christiane, Valérie et Benoît

Contents

Preface

The editor must express his thanks to a number of individuals and organizations for their help, which was indispensable in the preparation of this edition of Donne's *Devotions*.

Of particular note in this respect are the Canada Council, which supported me from start to finish; Millar MacLure and Hugh MacCallum of the University of Toronto, for their academic advice which partly inspired this volume; Anthony Camps, now the Master of Pembroke College in Cambridge, for consultations about Donne's classical allusions and other things; and Janice Houghton and Peter Gautery in the Anderson Room (rare books) of the Cambridge University Library.

A number of libraries and individuals in Britain allowed their copies of *Devotions* to be sent either to the Bodleian Library in Oxford or the Cambridge University Library, for collation and consultation. These include John Sparrow, the former Warden of All Souls College, Oxford; Sir Geoffrey Keynes; Dr. Williams Library, London; the Sheffield University Library; the Aberdeen Public Library; St. Andrews University; Magdalen and Worcester Colleges in Oxford, and St. Johns and Pembroke Colleges in Cambridge.

The Oxford University Press must be thanked for permission to quote Simpson's edition of Donne's *Essays* and her *Study of the Prose Works of John Donne*, and Grierson's edition of his *Poetical Works*; and the University of California Press for quotations from Potter's and Simpson's edition of Donne's *Sermons*.

ix

PREFACE

I cannot forget my former colleagues at Dalhousie University in Halifax, N.S., who supported me with time, effort and money, and a friend who found me a room with a view in the McGill University Library, Montreal, to put this edition together.

Université du Québec à Chicoutimi
November 1974

Abbreviations

The Renaissance works referred to in the Introduction are listed in the Bibliography. Meanwhile, the following are editions of Donne and major criticisms of his work quoted repeatedly in the Introduction and the Commentary. The former will be referred to as *Essays, Conclave, Letters, Poetical Works, Pseudo-Martyr, Sermons* (1640) and *Sermons*; the latter as Bald, Keynes, and Simpson, *Study*.

I DONNE'S WORKS

Essays in Divinity. Edited by E. M. Simpson.
    Oxford, 1952.

Ignatius His Conclave. Edited by T. Healy.
    Oxford, 1969.

Letters to Several Persons of Honour. London
    [1651], 1654.

Poetical Works, II Vol., edited by H. J. C. Grierson.
    Oxford, 1958.

Pseudo-Martyr [First edition]. London, 1610.

LXXX Sermons. London, 1640.

Sermons. Edited by G. R. Potter and E. M. Simpson.
    Los Angeles, 1958.

II CRITICAL AND BIBLIOGRAPHICAL WORKS

R. C. Bald. *John Donne: A Life*. Oxford, 1970.

Sir Geoffrey Keynes. *Bibliography of Donne*.
    Cambridge, 1958.

E. M. Simpson. *A Study of the Prose Works of
    John Donne*. Oxford, 1962.

Introduction

Donne's *Devotions upon Emergent Occasions* does not rate as the most lucid or the most representative of his prose works. However, it is a striking example of his theory of literature in the service of his theology and his view of creation. The work synthesizes his ideas about metaphysics and literature, medicine and cosmology, and the relationship of man to God. Its genre is devotional and, more specifically, meditative, though the nature of the meditative and devotional traditions he was following is not readily apparent.

Devotions is an autobiographical work too. It develops Donne's thoughts on a variety of topics in a series of meditations related very specifically to the events surrounding his illness in late November and early December, 1623. Written during his convalescence, in some of the longest, weightiest sentences Donne ever composed, the work uses one incident in his life to pursue the significance of its whole. By the chance occurrence of a bout with death, Donne is brought to investigate the nature of his relationship with God. The occasion of his illness fused in Donne's imagination the mysteries of the pre-modern cosmos with their concrete expressions in the vicissitudes of human health. *Devotions upon Emergent Occasions* is a straightforward work reflecting without contrivance, but with natural complexity, the experience of a lifetime in the exigencies of a moment.

I

The Illness and the Occasion

Donne does not make clear in his text what the illness was that brought him to the verge of death, and he has not written elsewhere about its nature, if in fact he knew. But modern scholarship has shown that there are two fairly certain possibilities. These are typhus and the seven-day or relapsing fever. Both these illnesses have been suggested to explain the epidemic fever that swept London between late October of 1623 and January of 1624.[1] That Donne caught the epidemic virus is beyond doubt. If the epidemic was typhus, it accounts for the full period of his illness. Simpson and Lander estimate this period as three weeks, the time that it takes typhus to run its course.[2] If we accept the diagnosis of typhus, we must take seriously Walton's statement in the first edition of *Lives* that Donne's fever was accompanied by a cough, a symptom of typhus, but are led to question his reasons for dropping the phrase in the second edition. Of course, the problem of Walton's differing accounts is irrelevant if typhus is not at stake.

On the other hand, Donne may have been suffering from relapsing fever, which ran from five to seven days at the most.[3] If so, he suffered first from another illness such as the 'rewme', a severe cold, to account for the length of his sickness and the symptoms that he describes. In this case, he passed into the epidemic fever in a state weakened by the earlier illness.[4] The first diagnosis of typhus, however, is not to be dismissed out of hand. We do not know how accurate Donne's record of his symptoms is, as he weaves his description of it in and out of his meditations. But one is more attracted to the possibility of relapsing fever preceded by another disease, than to that of typhus, for a number of reasons. Walton's description of Donne's malady need not be reliable. The fact that he altered his account indicates that he was unsure of his evidence. Moreover, Donne himself never mentions delirium or the cough symptomatic of typhus;[5] and he describes two sets of contradictory symptoms. Contemporary medical manuals attributed these contradic-

1. The argument for relapsing fever is made by I. A. Shapiro, 'Walton and the Occasion of Donne's *Devotions*', *Review of English Studies* (1958), NS 9: 20; and for typhus by Clara Lander, 'Per Fretum Febris', Diss. University of Manitoba 1968, pp. 1, 263.

2. Simpson, *Study*, p. 243; Lander, pp. 34–35.

3. Shapiro, *RES*, p. 21.

4. The symptoms of the rewme were 'hot fever', inflammation of the lungs supposedly cured by julep medicine, and the congestion of head and breast, by the herb agaric. The rewme is discussed by Elyot, *The Castle of Health*, 78, 78ᵛ, and its fever by Barrough, *The Method of Physick* (1613), pp. 239, 244.

5. Shapiro, *RES*, p. 21.

tory symptoms to diseases of internal and external origins, like the 'rewme' and contagious fevers.

Whether Donne suffered from one or two diseases in a row, his condition was not due, as Gosse suggests, to an attack of the sickness that killed him in 1631.[6] This illness has been fairly certainly diagnosed as cancer of the stomach.[7] Modern science shows that cancer of the stomach does not last eight years, and Donne's description of his illness in *Devotions* stresses the vapours and moving bodily heats that contemporary medical manuals associated with fevers and not with cancer. Moreover, Donne in the ninth Meditation identifies canker knowledgeably according to its contemporary categories of cancer, wolf, and polypus. There is, in addition, no reason to doubt the word of John Chamberlain, the letter writer, that Donne had fallen victim to the current epidemic and was one of the few to survive.[8] Donne's illness was also unconnected with his sickness of 1625, two years later. This illness was consumption, and Donne mentions none of the symptoms of consumption in *Devotions*. Walton confused the two illnesses and attributed them to a single sickness in 1625. In an attempt to clear up this confusion, he appears to have eliminated his reference to the symptom of the cough in the second edition of *Lives*, but in doing so, he also eliminated the validity of his evidence for typhus.[9]

Donne's reason for failing to identify his illness in *Devotions* is difficult to imagine. The problem also occurs in the four letters he sent with complimentary copies of the work to friends. His symptoms may have been too complicated for him to describe in polite letters sent with presentation copies. But he may also have expected the 'rewme' or cold and seven-day fever to be evident to his reader. In the fourth and sixth Expostulations, Donne describes medicine and symptoms associated with

6. Sir Edmund Gosse, *The Life and Letters of John Donne* (London, 1899), II, 181.

7. Simpson, *Study*, p. 242; Gosse, *Life*, II, p. 374.

8. John Chamberlain, *Letters*, edited by N. E. McClure (Philadelphia, 1939), II, 531.

9. In the first edition of his *Lives* (1640), Walton described Donne's illness of 1625 as one 'which turned to a spotted Fever, and ended in a Cough'. He dropped this clause in the second edition (1658), perhaps on the advice of Henry King (see Shapiro, *RES*, p. 22, n. 1) and continued to attribute *Devotions* to 1625 (p. 21): Walton, *The Lives* (London, 1927), World's Classics Series, p. 57.

severe cold, namely, 'simples' and 'suffocation', and, in the first of these, he suggests that he has already been sick seven days; in the thirteenth Meditation, he discovers the spots of the epidemic on his body; in the fourteenth Expostulation, he indicates that he has been sick yet another seven days; and, in the last Meditation, he talks about his doctor's fear of a relapse.

In the light of Chamberlain's comment, the spots of the illness and the doctor's fear seem to point out beyond argument that the current epidemic was relapsing fever, and that Donne had caught it. However, his other, earlier symptoms must be explained. At first, Donne did not seem to be suffering from anything so serious as the epidemic fever. Calling the doctor is not referred to until the fourth devotion, when he suggests that his illness is already a week old. The time factor, which dominates all attempts at identifying the illness, excludes seven-day relapsing fever as the only possibility. Nor can we assume that Donne suffered from two successive bouts of relapsing fever. He writes in the twenty-third Expostulation that his doctors feared a relapse, but never suggests that he had one.

If Donne was not taking absolute licence with the symptoms of his fever and stretching them out for purposes of devotional speculation, his bout with the epidemic was preceded by another less severe fever. This secondary fever possessed all the symptoms of the 'rewme'. Gosse's suggestion that Donne caught influenza walking through tor-rential rain from Westminster to St. Paul's on the occasion of a Sargeants' Feast, may therefore be correct. It at least deserves to be taken more seriously than it has been in recent scholarship.[10] One doubts that it would have taken Donne's doctor more than a week to suspect he had caught the spotted fever if it had been raging in London for a month and took only seven days to run its course. The doctor would also have hastened to call for outside advice for a diagnosis, unless the first symp-toms clearly suggested something else. Only when they fear an attack

---

10. Gosse bases his assumption, *Life*, I, 181, 183, on Chamberlain's report in another letter, that numerous guests at the feast walked bareheaded in the rain, *Letters*, II, 518. Shapiro (p. 19) rejects Gosse's view.

by 'venom' do the medical authorities in charge of Donne begin to treat him for contagious disease.[11]

Donne describes his first symptoms as due to inner disturbances which suggest 'rewme' fever. In the medical allusions of the first and seventh Meditations, vapours move up to his head from his entrails, rather than attack him in plague form from the outside. He suffers from a hot fever typical of the 'rewme' rather than the fever of a venomous illness. He is fed cordials which medical manuals stipulated for the cold, before he is given the purgative treatments they recommended for the harsher ravages of a virus. In a condition weakened by cold, Donne may have easily passed from one illness to another, with or without cause and effect. The possibility of successive illnesses is supported by his statements elsewhere in *Devotions*. He is aware of one illness resulting from another in the fourth Meditation when the doctor is first called. And in fact if Donne did suffer from 'rewme' before relapsing fever, this explains why one of his physicians, probably Dr. Simeon Fox who attended him in his last illness in 1631,[12] ordered medicines that contradict one another in the treatment of a single sickness. It also accounts for the two contradictory developments of the illness Donne describes. Renaissance medical manuals made rigid distinctions between diseases originating inside and outside the body according to the movements of vapours, and Donne indicates that he suffered from both.[13]

During the illness Donne may have jotted down notes about his spiritual reactions to his physical state, which he later incorporated into *Devotions*. In a letter, unfortunately undated, which he sent with the printer's sheets to Sir Robert Ker, he writes that he used the leisure time of his convalescence 'to put the meditations had in my sicknesse, into some such order, as may minister some holy delight'.[14] But he perhaps should not be taken literally. Elsewhere, he indicates that he was so weak, even in his convalescence, that he was forbidden to read.[15] In

11. Heading to the eleventh devotion.
12. Bald, pp. 452, 525.
13. Eleventh Prayer and twelfth Meditation.
14. *Letters*, pp. 249–50.
15. Perhaps to the Earl of Dorset: quoted in Gosse, II, 208.

addition, he hastened the wedding of his daughter, Constance, at Camberwell, to 3 December, because he anticipated the possibility of death.[16] By 6 December, however, Donne was out of danger: Chamberlain's letter discussing his survival is dated that day.[17] By the end of the month, the work was written, and it was in the hands of a publisher very early in January.[18] In the letter Donne sent to Ker with the printer's sheets, he asked him if *Devotions* was a suitable work to dedicate to Prince Charles.[19] Presumably, he wrote the dedicatory address to Charles quickly after the sheets came back to him with Ker's affirmative reply. Another letter by Donne dated 1 February indicates that the work, in that brief time, was already published.[20] His activity in his weakened state was phenomenal.

Donne relished *Devotions*. He sent at least four complimentary copies with letters: to James I's daughter, the unfortunate Elizabeth of Bohemia, alone in exile in Holland; to one of Elizabeth's unidentified court ladies to whom he entrusted both the volume and letter for the Princess; to the Duke of Buckingham; and to an unidentified lord, who Gosse suggests was the Earl of Dorset.[21] The names of the second and fourth recipients do not appear in the letters.

Donne asked Elizabeth her indulgence for the personal character of the work: 'In the hearing of me deliver my messages to God, I can hope for the continuance of your Majesty's patience.' She had already started reading *Devotions* when she answered him: 'For what I have already read I give you hearty thanks . . . I will not fail upon any good occasion to acknowledge the courtesy.' Meanwhile, in the letter to Buckingham, Donne plumbed the nature of the work a little more than his royal address to Elizabeth allowed him: 'And as the reading of the actions of great men may affect you for great actions, so for this our necessary

16. Bald, p. 450.

17. Chamberlain, *Letters*, II, 528.

18. On 9 January, 1623–24, it was entered in the Stationer's Register: *A Transcript of the Registers of the Company of Stationers of London, 1554–1640 A.D.*, IV, 110, p. 72.

19. *Letters*, pp. 249–50.

20. To Princess Elizabeth, the Queen of Bohemia, cited in Gosse, *Life*, II, 205.

21. Ibid., pp. 205, 206, 207, 208.

defect of dying . . . you may receive some remembrances from the *Meditations and Devotions* of your Grace's devoted servant.'

In the letter to the last recipient, Donne talked about *Devotions* critically at greatest length. In the style typical of the work, he used the image of the parenthesis appearing in the fourteenth Meditation: 'To make myself believe that our life is something, I use in my thoughts to compare it to something. . . . And, as in some styles there are open parentheses, sentences within sentences, so there are lives within our lives. I am in such a parenthesis now (in a convalescence) . . . God . . . showed me high Jerusalem upon so high a hill as that He thought it fit to bid me stay and gather more breath. This I do by meditating, by expostulating, by praying.' The personal, visionary nature of Donne's experience with illness found a natural analogy for him in literary effort.

II

Meditation and Metaphysics

The nature of Donne's *Devotions upon Emergent Occasions* hinges on the meaning of two recurrent terms in his text, *word* and *type*. The first of these refers to the Divine Word of God copied down by his amanuenses, the prophets, in the Scriptures. The second term, *type*, has less general connotations than the first. It refers to the historical events described by God's written scriptural word.[22] The written types of the Bible were exemplary for the Christian.[23] They provided him with the prototypes for judging the moral character and mystical meaning (as opposed to mere literal empirical fact) of history in the present.[24] It is with these ideas about word and type that Donne proceeded to write *Devotions*. It is a literary record of a contemporary experience that found its meaning in scriptural types.

Donne, of course, did not consciously set out to write *Devotions* as a

22. *Essays*, p. 18.
23. Ibid., p. 8.
24. Seventh Prayer.

new elaboration of a theology of word, type, and copy. In his thinking, these terms had already been long developed in the three metaphoric books in his system of theology. The section on the Bible in his *Essays in Divinity* of 1615, nine years earlier, describes the books in detail.[25]

In the ninth Expostulation of *Devotions*, Donne develops the same ideas about the three books as in *Essays*, but now in the context of his illness:

If your *consultation* determin in *writing*, if you refer mee to that which is *written*, you intend my recovery: for al the way, *O my God*, (ever constant to thine owne wayes) thou hast proceeded *openly, intelligibly, manifestly, by the book*. From thy first *book*, the book of *life*, never shut to thee, but never throughly open to us; from thy second *book*, the *booke* of *Nature*, wher though subobscurely, and in shadows, thou hast expressed thine own *Image*; from thy third *booke*, the *Scriptures*, where thou hadst written all in the *Old*, and then lightedst us a candle to read it by, in the *New Testament*.

The three books played an interconnected role in Donne's theology. The first, the Register of the Elect, also called the First Book of Life, was the metaphoric list of saved souls in eternity. By contrast, the second, the Book of Creatures, was the created historical world of space and time through which the saved souls in the Register of the Elect passed for a while. The third, the Bible, sometimes called the Second Book of Life, was saving knowledge. For the Christian in his progress to the New Jerusalem, the Bible recorded exemplary incidents of history in the Book of Creatures. These incidents possessed a literal meaning that obviously revealed their mystical significance in the spiritual world of the Register of the Elect.

Donne's use of word and type, and their influence on the nature of *Devotions* and his attitude to his frightful illness, were therefore moulded years before November, 1623. A middle-aged divine at 51, under the care of King James' famous court doctor, Sir Theodore de Mayerne, he wrote *Devotions* with a clear idea of the nature of his experience and of its relationship to theology and literature. In the sixteenth Expostulation he says:

I know I cannot have any better *Image* of *thee*, than thy *Sonne*, nor any better *Image* of *him*, than his *Gospell*: yet must not I, with thanks confesse to thee, that

25. *Essays*, pp. 6–7.

some *historicall pictures* of his, have sometimes put mee upon better *Meditations* than otherwise I should have fallen upon? I know thy *Church* needed not to have taken in from *Jew* or *Gentile*, any supplies for the exaltation of thy *glory*, or our *devotion*; of *absolute necessitie* I know shee needed not; But yet wee owe thee our thanks, that thou hast given her leave to doe so, and that as in making us *Christians*, thou diddest not destroy that which wee were before, *naturall men*, so in the exalting of our religious devotions now we are *Christians*, thou hast beene pleased to continue to us those *assistances* which did worke upon the affections of *naturall men* before.

As a literary work, then, *Devotions upon Emergent Occasions* is the fruit of a Christian's spiritual quest inspired by a struggle with a dangerous illness. The quest itself is fully understood by him at its start as a response to history and biblical message. The quest stops short of its logical conclusion in death, but Donne's experience is not the less valid. The experience has made the Bible's truth more vivid to him. For all these reasons, the work is both typical of Donne and unique among his writings. *Devotions* is typical in the sense that it says nothing new and respects the theological principles Donne has stated before. However, it is unique (perhaps 'curious' as Simpson calls it)[26] in that it relies on what he has already said elsewhere to create a literary effect without a close parallel in either his poetry or the rest of his prose. Donne used the literary techniques of both his poetry and his anterior prose under the pressure of an intense personal experience, to create a new meditative form of literature unique among his works.

The style emerging from the literary techniques of *Devotions* is complex, stimulating, and consistently powerful. The factors that went into the making of its aesthetic qualities are the elements that characterized the rest of Donne's literary output. The sentences are loose, Senecan, and 'periodic', and the language is marked by the puns, paradoxes, and forced contrasts associated with the Metaphysical mode of poetry. The so-called Senecan style and the Metaphysical use of language were not normally conjoined in the prose of the seventeenth century. But they are so wedded in Donne's meditative work.

Donne's long, flowing sentences in *Devotions*, constructed of delicately balanced phrases and clauses, are jarred by the Metaphysical

26. Simpson, *Study*, pp. 241, 251, 254.

imagery that he used to illustrate his thought. The natural movement of his sentences is diverted by the elaborateness of his figurative language. The resulting effect is original to the Donne of *Devotions*, and there are only occasional hints of it in the sermons. The use of Metaphysical mode and Senecan style creates what Nelly (writing about his imagery), described as an individual sort of dialectics in some of his sermons and in *Devotions*.[27] Metaphysical pun, paradox, contrast, and enigma become integral parts of the series of balanced phrases and clauses of the Senecan style. The Metaphysical mode associated with poetry conditions the 'periodic' cadence of Donne's sentences and the method of his argumentation.

Donne's style in *Devotions* supports the development of the figure of the 'conservative "I"' that Webber identifies at the core of its narration.[28] The style bestows its literary qualities on the narrator, John Donne, at the same time that it derives them from him as a man. If, as Webber believes, the 'conservative' and 'Anglican' narrator of *Devotions* is ambiguous, meditative, anti-historical, obscure, and symbolic,[29] the reason is that Donne, the man, has transferred his personal qualities to the work. The Metaphysical mode of his prose style recreates the narrator's qualities of obscurity and ambiguity, and the Senecan style recreates the elements of his meditative temper. The style of *Devotions* is consequently functional in terms of both Donne's sensibility and the devotional nature of his work. It incorporates into a single form of narrative expression a number of diverse elements. At the same time, the style of *Devotions* is faithful to the broadest reaches of Donne's views on the nature of both literature and the Bible.

Devotions, like the Bible, has levels of literal and mystical meaning. Mueller has described the development of these levels in *Devotions* as a kind of 'figurative exposition' of its subject matter. *Devotions* is an exploration of both these levels.[30] Its narrator, Donne, relives the stages of illness just past and writes as did Hezekiah, his prototype, whom he

27. Una Nelly, *The Poet Donne, A Study in His Dialectic Method* (Dublin, 1969), p. 104.
28. Joan Webber, *The Eloquent 'I'* (Madison, Wisc., 1968), p. 5.
29. Ibid., p. 7.
30. Janel M. Mueller, 'The Exegesis of Experience, Dean Donne's *Devotions*', *Journal of English and Germanic Philology* (1968), 67: 12.

invokes in his dedication to Prince Charles. The work's purpose is to reveal to the writer the visionary significance of the illness besetting him in his very spirit. *Devotions* is more representative of the deepest reaches of Donne's thought than more topical volumes like *Ignatius His Conclave* and *Pseudo-Martyr*. It is more personally revealing, too, than Donne's sermons of the same year, and the exegetical parallels it shares with them.[31] The structure of *Devotions* supports his theology, theories of literature, and self-revelation.

On the surface of things, the structure of *Devotions* is rather simple. The work is composed of a eulogistic personal introduction in the form of a dedicatory address to Prince Charles, later King. Next come the Latin *Stationes* or table of contents in the shape of a poem, as Joan Webber points out,[32] listing the titles of the twenty-three devotions that follow in the main body of the work.

Each of these devotions is divided into three parts, a Meditation, an Expostulation, and a Prayer. And each tends to develop a group of related images coherently through all three parts. The first Meditation discusses the first symptoms of an illness in images of dissolution, decomposition, dismay, and melancholy; the same images recur in different forms in the metaphors of dust and ashes of the Expostulation, and at the beginning and end of the Prayer.[33] Similarly, the tenth Meditation describes the movement of Donne's illness towards his heart in images of primogeniture and motion among the bodily organs, derived from contemporary manuals of psychology and physiology. The Expostulation adapts these images to describe the filial relation of Donne to God the Father; and the Prayer adapts them in turn to illustrate the presence of God in the world of men. Only in one instance does the imagery— that of bells—introduced by the sixteenth Meditation, persist for three whole devotions, and that is because in each, Donne is dealing with one of the three tolling bells in the Anglican service for the dying and the

31. On Psalms 6, 8, 9, and 10, dated by Simpson, VI, *Sermons*, pp. 1–3, discussed by Mueller, Exegesis of Experience', *JEGP*, pp. 8–9.

32. *Eloquent 'I'*, pp. 19–20.

33. N. J. C. Andreason, 'Donne's *Devotions* and the Psychology of Assent', *Modern Philology* (1964–65), 62: 213, says the recurrent imagery is the principle of unity in the work.

dead. So structurally the work hangs together by its treatment of the historical event of Donne's illness. Its imagery gives coherence to each devotion, binding its three parts cogently without turning the work into an imagistic whole.

The devotions proceed chronologically in a plain way. They sometimes display a homeliness of imagery that came into the *Devotions* out of the tradition of homilies that Donne shared as preacher.[34] They move title by title, list the stages of his illness, beginning with his observation of the first physiological changes of his body, and end with his convalescence.

Between these extremes of affliction and convalescence, the devotions deal superficially with the patient taking to his bed; elsewhere, with his physician calling for a pigeon treatment; and later with the pronouncement that the patient is out of danger. At this purely medical level, the work is not dramatic. Its interest is the light it throws on Donne's knowledge of current medicine, astrology, alchemy, cosmology, and the natural world, for he uses images of these abundantly to describe his physical state. In the fourteenth Devotion, he draws very knowledgeably on the most subtle and difficult concepts of the crisis point of the year in astrology, and in the twelfth Devotion, he compares the symptoms of his fever to the second of the three kinds of smoke known to emanate from coal mines. Structurally, in the sense of suggesting the obvious disposition of the parts of the work, *Devotions upon Emergent Occasions* hangs upon such images. In other senses, the structure of the work is open to dispute and exploration.

The grounds for dispute lie in the current tendency to discuss the devotional works of Donne and the other Metaphysical poets, prose and poetry alike, in terms of formalized meditation. Is Donne's *Devotions* a formal meditation, perhaps along the lines of the *Exercises* of the Spanish mystic, Ignatius Loyola, or is it not? If *Devotions* is not such an exercise, what is it? Does it have to be anything at all other than what is suggested by its obvious structure of twenty-three sections each split up into

34. Joan Webber, 'The Prose Styles of Donne's *Devotions Upon Emergent Occasions*', *Anglia* (1961), 79: 139.

three parts, describing a medical case in 1623, and the thoughts about life and death it prompted in Donne's mind?

The number of suggestions about the formal meditative character of the work in recent years continues to proliferate rather than abate, and it speaks for a seemingly unanswerable side to the question. The number of these suggestions is itself symptomatic of the malaise of modern critics. Critics find it difficult to consider *Devotions* outside the field of disciplined seventeenth-century meditative practices. The fairly rigid division of each of the twenty-three devotions into three characteristically recurrent parts has been criticized adversely by some and praised by others, but it has been consistently recognized as too regular to be described as undisciplined. This regularity and the meditative quality of the devotions cannot be ignored. In *Contrary Music*, for example, Webber finds the 'pattern' of *Devotions* 'bolder and more daring than the ordinary spiritual exercise', but cannot deny that it has 'some connection with meditational organization'.[35]

Martz and Gardner represent the poles of opinion about the influence of formal meditation on Donne. Sometimes these opinions refer directly to *Devotions*, and at other times to his other works, but in all cases they are relevant to the meditative character of the work. Martz believes that the tripartite meditative structure of Loyola's *Spiritual Exercises* was indigenous to Donne's way of thinking,[36] a result of his training as a young Catholic both at the hands of his Jesuit uncle, Jasper Heywood,[37] and in the private classrooms of the English recusant church. He suggested his theory for Donne's devotional poetry, and Van Laan took up his argument for the *Devotions*, comparing details of Ignatius' *Exercises* to details of *Devotions*, such as the titles of its parts.[38] At the opposite pole from Martz and Van Laan's position, has been Gardner's opinion that

35. Joan Webber, *Contrary Music* (Madison, Wisc., 1963), p. 184.

36. Louis Martz, *The Poetry of Meditation* (New Haven, 1954), p. 38.

37. Ibid., p. 38. Most critics support Martz, including M. P. Ramsay, *Les Doctrines Médiévales Chez Donne* (London, 1924) pp. 35–36, and W. F. Mitchell, *English Pulpit Oratory* (London, 1932), p. 183, while Bald, p. 39, denies that Donne could have had a Jesuit upbringing.

38. Thomas Van Laan, 'John Donne's *Devotions* and the *Jesuit Spiritual Exercises*', *Studies in Philology* (1963), 60, 197.

there is no formal meditative pattern discernible in Donne's work; she concedes at most that the *Exercises* may 'lie behind' poems like the Holy Sonnets; Donne's devotional tone, when it exists, is in the general current of seventeenth-century Anglican piety.[39] Taking up this point of view, Mueller found the real explanation for the nature of *Devotions* not in Ignatius, but in Donne's practice of biblical exegesis in his sermons.[40]

Running through these discussions are several recurrent issues. These concern the respective roles of biblical exegesis, Ignatius Loyola, Anglican piety, and the three metaphoric books of Donne's theology. The question at stake seems to be the extent of the contribution of each of these elements to the making of Donne's devotional tone, particularly in *Devotions*.

To answer this question, two important things must be kept in mind. First of all, there was more than one way in which, devotionally, Ignatius could leave his indelible trace on Donne. Next, the question of biblical exegesis in Donne is basically inseparable from the metaphysics underlying the three books in his system of theology. It is possible that the Jesuit-inculcated Donne brings the meditative mentality induced by the *Exercises* to bear on the vision of his metaphysics. If so, *Devotions upon Emergent Occasions* is a literary fusion of this metaphoric vision in the discipline of the meditative mentality. It conforms in every way to the general requirements of late Renaissance Anglican piety. The metaphysical vision and the Ignatian mentality are the elements that circumscribe Donne's individuality within the Anglican tradition, rather than force him outside it.

An examination of the metaphysical vision and the Ignatian mentality reveals the unique elements of Donne's devotional tone. The metaphysics into which Donne projects the meditative qualities of his mind in *Devotions* are exegetical in character and distinctly seventeenth-century by nature. Classical metaphysics is the study of being, essence, and the nature of nature; and Donne's statement in *Essays* and *Pseudo-*

39. Helen Gardner, '*The Poetry of Meditation*. By Louis Martz', *Review of English Studies* (1957), n.s. 8, 197; 'Introduction', Donne's *The Divine Poems* (Oxford, 1964), p. liv.

40. Mueller, 'Exegesis of Experience', *JEGP*, p. 7.

Martyr,[41] as well as in *Devotions*, is that the reality of being, existence, essence, and nature is understandable metaphysically in terms of the three metaphoric books of his theology. The books somehow cover all forms of existence. Donne writes, in the nineteenth Expostulation,

Neither art thou thus a *figurative*, a *Metaphoricall God*, in thy *word* only, but in thy *workes* too. The *stile* of thy *works*, the *phrase* of thine *Actions*, is *Metaphoricall*. The *institution* of thy whole *worship* in the *old Law*, was a continuall *Allegory*; *types* & *figures* overspread all; and *figures* flowed into *figures*, and powred themselves out into *farther figures*; *Circumcision* carried a *figure* of *Baptisme*, & *Baptisme* carries a *figure* of that *purity*, which we shall have in *perfection* in the *new Jerusalem*. Neither didst thou *speake*, and *worke* in this *language*, onely in the time of thy *Prophets*; but since thou spokest in thy *Son*, it is so too.

The outstanding thing about nature in the material world of Donne's theology, is that it was created. A creature in the Book of Creatures is, in the very sense of the noun, the dependent subject of its maker. Nature was made from nothing by a God who imagined and created his materials for it, namely, space, time, and tangible matter, out of selfless love for himself. For Donne, the thinking man does not find the ultimate meaning of the reality of creatures in the metaphysical disputations of the medieval philosophers and of the Greeks, nor in human intellection. Rather he discovers it in the First Book of Life, the Register of the Elect. From this, it is not necessary to assume that Donne is a strict 'literalist' for whom all the philosophical categories of the Ancients and of medieval Christian tradition were valueless. He cites Aquinas often enough as an authority, for example in *Essays*, to suggest the opposite. But his approach to traditional speculation is effectively circumscribed by the principles of his metaphysical typology.[42]

In Donne's thinking, the Register, in the topmost position of this typology, is a kind of statement that explains the nature of the Book of Creatures. The Register is itself comprehended intuitively by the inspired conscience rather than by the sensory experience of a three-dimensional world,[43] and its message is that those who are saved know

41. *Essays*, pp. 7–8, 20–21; *Pseudo-Martyr*, p. 365.
42. *Essays*, p. 20.
43. Opening of seventeenth Prayer; *Essays*, p. 7; *Pseudo-Martyr*, pp. 83–84.

it, and the knowledge of this salvation is the answer to the question of the nature of all being. For it is by salvation that man, for whom the rest of the world was made, fulfils the purpose of the whole Book of Creatures, to give love to God. The nature of being is intelligible, therefore, only in terms of its end, that is, the divine purpose—reciprocal love—which makes beings subsist. Where the medieval scholastic and the Greek Ancient arrived at the reality of being by speculation, syllogism, and argument, the Christian, according to Donne, reached it by responding to the curiosity of the heart. To pursue metaphysical impulses was a question of sensibility which the pursuit itself broadened, deepened, and made more exact by suggesting certain issues for consideration, and rejecting others. To the searching Christian heart, the Register of the Elect provided a humanly discoverable mystical meaning to the metaphoric words, letters, lines—in sum, to the images in the Book of Creatures.

The Book of Creatures conformed to the significance of the Register of the Elect. It was an eternal God's love poem to himself in time. For the man who cared to read his poem, metaphysics was the art of practical criticism. Man understood the poetry of God's creation by using Donne's metaphysics to explicate its images. Donne says several times in *Devotions* that he and others try to 'read' historical events. In the seventh Prayer he reads it 'as a *mercy*' that he is sick, and in the ninth Meditation his doctors 'are gon to read upon me' to draw a medical conclusion for which he eventually finds some religious significance.

By way of contrast, Donne's description of the reading of nature altered the term 'Book of Creatures' as Saint Augustine devised it and as Raymond of Sebund, Donne's authority,[44] later used it. Augustine invented the term in the closing pages of the *Confessions* as a device to help him correlate the poetic account of creation in Genesis with its apparent contradictions in the real world.[45] Donne employed it more strictly to limit the scope of metaphysics itself. He made the Book of Creatures the matter for his metaphysical speculation about the temporal world. He thus altered the meaning of the term 'Book of Creatures' as it

44. *Essays*, p. 7.
45. *Confessions*, XIII, 15, p. 309.

appears in Sebund's writing too, because Sebund used it to make the objects of intellection clear to the human mind.[46] Donne adapted the term to restrict human speculation to the issues suggested by the Register of the Elect.

The role of the Bible, the Second Book of Life and the last of the three book's in Donne's theology, in turn conformed to his descriptions of the Book of Creatures and the Register of the Elect. The Bible bridged the gap between the limited understanding that man could get out of the Book of Creatures, and the mystical knowledge that was available to fallen man in the Register. The Bible was 'saving knowledge' which unfallen man had not needed[47]. It put a stop to, and in fact made unnecessary, the metaphysical speculation of the medievals and the Greeks. It was a work that told of the happenings in the spiritual world of the Register of the Elect, which the unfallen world of the Book of Creatures had once made wholly evident to the human mind. The Scriptures were an indispensable supplement, as it were, to the volume of the Book of Creatures partly outdated by original sin.

This bridge, the Bible, between the Book of Creatures and Register of the Elect was a work directly inspired by God. In Donne's thought, God had it written by his amanuenses. In one case, to Moses, he dictated directly, and in all other instances he spoke indirectly by visions as to Enoch and Elias.[48] The amanuenses wrote by prototype and copy. At God's command they recorded historical incidents occurring in biblical times that he considered exemplary for future generations of men. Man could use these incidents to identify the meaning of history in the present for the benefit of his salvation. The whole Bible was made of telling facts, with a significance readily identifiable by the inspired heart in the spiritual world of the Register of Elect.

For Donne, the inspired heart's technique for grasping the meanings of the Bible was the one used by the amanuenses of God in its writing. The Old Testament writers made prophecies on the basis of events in

46. Raymond Sebon, *La Théologie Naturelle de Raymond Sebon. Traduite ... par ... Montaigne* (Paris, 1612), aiii^v, aiiii.

47. *Essays*, pp. 92–93.

48. Ibid., pp. 11, 92.

current history, which the writers of the New Testament described as fulfilled in the history of Christ's day. There were means open to New Testament writers to recognize this fulfilment from Old to New Testament, from Abraham to Christ, from Babylon to the corrupt Jerusalem. These means were, firstly, the prototypes and copies of the Bible itself, and secondly, the techniques such as parables that both the prophets and Christ had used to interpret the events recorded in the Scriptures. The Christian used the same means to interpret the moral character of history in the contemporary world. The Old Testament served as the prototype for its copies fulfilled prophetically in the New Testament; and both Testaments served as prototypes for the Christian to find living copies in the world of the seventeenth century.

The system of the three books in Donne's theology conditioned his thinking profoundly. It drew upon all the areas of his thought and mingled traditional ideas in a novel way. The system combined the visionary character of creation in Augustine's thought with the traditional scholastic approach to the universe. Donne looked at nature with the eyes of a poet. That is, in the tradition of the last books of Augustine's *Confessions* and as though by intuition, he saw creation as fundamentally typological, made up of two levels, material and spiritual.[49] But the things on the material level of this typology, such as he described in *Essays*, he saw as intelligible in scholastic terms.[50] Under the pressure of his vision of the created universe, Donne understood the mystical nature of things in terms of personal revelation. However, the material nature of things he understood in terms of scholastic forms, causes, categories, and essences.

This peculiar fusion of philosophies concerning the three books in Donne's system of theology distinguishes him in the current of contemporary thought. It involved few ideas in comparison to the wide traditions of Augustinian and Thomistic thought on which Donne drew. However, we do not find the fusion in the thinking of other contemporary English writers. One thinks of Browne discussing the 'books'

49. *Essays*, pp. 15–16.
50. Ibid., p. 33.

from which he 'collected' his 'divinity' in *Religio Medici*,[51] and of Bacon describing the mystical books of knowledge in *The Advancement of Learning*.[52] In Donne, the fusion of personal revelation and scholasticism pervades all areas of his thought. At the end of the 'The Second Anniversary', commemorating the death of Elizabeth Drury, Elizabeth is like a piece of scroll written on both sides (l. 504). On one side is inscribed the record of her material existence, intelligible in purely historical terms, and on the other side is written her mystical significance in the Register of the Elect. Similarly, in the *Essays in Divinity*, Donne writes that things in the material universe may be described metaphysically according to scholastic terminology of forms and essences. But their mystical significance is intelligible metaphorically by a kind of philosophical contemplation.[53] Then, again, in *Ignatius His Conclave*, the standard by which Donne measures the victims of his satire combines the Augustinian and scholastic elements in question in his system of theology. He attacks a Roman Catholic use of the word 'imaginarie' in a description of the Scriptures, preferring to evaluate the Scriptures according to their historical implications. But his point of view relies heavily on a visionary appreciation of the significance of history.[54] Finally, in 'A Nocturnall upon S. Lucies day', Donne describes the material universe in scholastic terminology (quintessence, privations, and absences, ll. 15, 16, 26), but his insight into the spiritual significance of this universe is visionary and metaphoric.

Against this metaphysical, theological, and literary backdrop, the formative influence of Ignatius' *Exercises* on Donne's *Devotions* was decisive. How, rather than if, they influenced *Devotions* is the question at stake. The influence of the *Exercises* could take one of the three shapes imputable to them. First of all, there is the tripartite Ignatian division of Martz's criticism, Prelude, Meditation, and Colloquy, conducted by a toughly logical mind.[55] Secondly, there is Van Laan's suggestion of

51. Thomas Browne, *Religio Medici*, in vol. I, *The Works*, ed. G. Keynes (London, 1963), pp. 24–25.

52. Francis Bacon, *The Advancement of Learning* (London, 1954), pp. 41–42.

53. *Essays*, pp. 24, 20.

54. *Conclave*, p. 31.

55. Martz, *Poetry of Meditation*, p. 27.

the five-part Ignatian division found elsewhere in the *Exercises* of a Prayer, two Preludes, a Meditation, and a Colloquy, each developed according to an ascending scale of intensity by the faculties of the mind, namely, memory, understanding, and will.[56] Thirdly, there is the meditative experience which can be described as the terminal stage of the Ignatian use of the mind. The use of the mind was developed by Ignatius in the *Exercises* by synthesizing certain ideas about psychology, philosophy, and the universe. This third influence is the one that prevailed on Donne.

The meditative experience in this third category is not intelligible in terms of the structure of the *Exercises* in the first two. It is, rather, a kind of private experience of a baroque universe. The origins of this experience can be attributed to Ignatius' view of the relationship between the three powers of the mind (the memory, understanding, and will) and a universe charged with the force of suprahuman affections like love. To Ignatius, the meditative experience and the structure of the *Exercises* were different things. He structured the *Exercises* to accommodate the meditative experience. He did not develop the experience to fit the structure. Donne brings the cast of mind indigenous to this Ignatian experience to the writing of *Devotions*, without being bound by the structure. The Ignatian approach to things left him free to devise a meditational structure of his own choosing, conforming to his theology and the tenets of his church.

The meditative experience at the basis of the *Exercises* was complex and original, but clear to Ignatius' readers. It drew on scholastic traditions familiar to them. The experience consisted of three stages, the Prelude, the *evacuatio sensuum*, and the *applicatio sensuum*.[57] These stages made up the structure of an experience for controlled sensation, and must be distinguished from the steps of the exercise singled out by Van Laan and Martz. Rather than constituting a series of chronological steps in a strict sense, the stages in the Ignatian experience suggested the movement of the mind through certain clearly defined uses of the five

56. Van Laan, 'Donne's *Devotions*', *SP*, pp. 194–95.

57. St. Ignatius Loyola, *The Spiritual Exercises*, edited by Henry Keane, S.J. (London, 1952), p. 45.

senses, the three powers of the soul, and the imagination. The Ignatian meditator was conscious that these sensory and mental powers made up a cosmology in the inner man. In this analogy, the powers of a man in meditation were the constellations of his private cosmology. This inner cosmology was a meeting point between the outer world of time and space and the eternal world of divine love and satanic hate. It was wholly manipulable for meditation between these two emotional poles of attraction—of love and hate, of God and Satan. The inner cosmology, geared to the meditation of the *Exercises*, appears to be the indelible residual effect of Donne's upbringing in the Jesuit-dominated English recusant church of his boyhood. Donne had the Ignatian self-consciousness of the inner man as the seat of willed experience, capable alone of uniting the earth of his origin below with the heaven of his desires above.

Of course, if Donne retained the sense of the inner cosmology of the Ignatian meditation of his boyhood, because of training, conviction, or both, he did not necessarily accept the path of every one of its planets. Some of Ignatius' ideas forbade it. A number of elements in the meditative application of the powers of the mind and body in the Ignatian inner cosmology prevented Donne's full commitment to the rules of the *Exercises*. Each of the powers of the mind in scholastic tradition had two functions, and Ignatius used each of these functions in a particular way. According to the general currents of scholastic tradition, the memory, the first power, brought about the recall of an idea suitable for meditation, and it also had the task of restoring to the consciousness the memories of experiences. The understanding, for its part, had a visionary side and also a speculative, logical side to its operations. Finally, the will was the highest emotive faculty: it enabled a man to experience eternal love, and it was charged with forcing the body to obey the commands of the rational mind. Donne used the first functions of all three powers to further the ends of the Ignatian sensibility for willed experience. But he rejected Ignatius' use of their second functions.

The reasons for Donne's rejection were complex but clear. The Prelude of the *Exercises* offended his sense of metaphysical realities in the

Book of Creatures. It contradicted his idea of historicity. The Prelude required that one wipe clean the screen of one's imagination. That is, an exercitant erased the images of the senses which present time was continually flashing on his imagination (according to its description in scholastic tradition) in the normal course of sensation. On the blank screen the exercitant, by willed effort rather than by sensory spontaneity, projected images of past experiences. He plucked these images out of the storehouse of his mind, sensory, memorative, and Augustinian in character, rather than Thomistic and pictorial. He designed these experiences, as though giving them a second lease on life, into an emotive pattern suitable for the object of his meditation. Out of past experiences, the exercitant thus created the blueprint for a new one. The choice of past experiences themselves was governed by the suitability of the things originally associated with them in the senses.

Donne could not accept the imaginative picture in the original Ignatian Prelude and satirized it brutally in *Ignatius His Conclave*.[58] The picture which the exercitant of the *Exercises* created was a fictional image that dangerously subsumed the function of the prototypes of the Bible as the sufficient staple of salvation. But the art of the Ignatian Prelude was acceptable to him—with certain alterations.

Donne could replace the fictional picture of Ignatius with the copies of the prototypes of the Bible in contemporary history. He writes in the sixteenth Expostulation of the funeral bell of another man as an object of meditation for his personal life: 'And this continuing of ringing after his *entring*, is to bring him to mee in the application'; and in the seventh Expostulation: 'We take *S. Luke* to have bin a *Phisician*, & it admits the application better, that in the presence of one good *Physician* we may be glad of more'. In Donne's substitution, the activity of the understanding in the Ignatian cosmology was restricted to copies of biblical prototypes in nature. The two prototypes in the above examples show this substitution taking place without destroying the original Ignatian aim of creating a willed experience.

To effect this substitution, Donne developed the Meditation of each

58. *Conclave*, p. 5, and in the poems satirizing the counterpart of the Ignatian withdrawal of the senses in Jesuit poetry, on pp. 7, 63–65, 97.

devotion as an historical picture.[59] Each stage of his illness became exegetically and historically his material for understanding his spiritual state. Each Meditation introducing one of these stages is noteworthy for establishing a purity of content which the whole devotion maintains. Every step in Donne's illness is isolated with care from the dross of distracting experience by a rigid choice of words. There are not only practically no references to sources outside the Book of Creatures in the twenty-three Meditations of *Devotions*;[60] there are hardly any even to the Bible. The Meditation of each of Donne's devotions is not an Ignatian Prelude, but its frugal number of references bespeaks the discipline of the Ignatian understanding in the Preludes. The Meditation shows the logical intelligence of a mind at work, intensifying a piece of knowledge to achieve a depth of felt comprehension. In the rest of each devotion, the Expostulation and Prayer do not relax the discipline of the Meditation. They merely amplify in their own way the experience that it initiates. Like all parts of the Ignatian exercise, all parts of each of Donne's devotions are directed towards the central experience.

Donne rejected the Ignatian *evacuatio sensuum* as he rejected the Prelude, and for the same reasons. He nevertheless preserved the intensity of the original experience through all parts of each devotion. Donne's satire on the voiding of the senses in *Conclave*, described in the dream state of his fictional narrator, is an attack on a departure from the historicity of the Book of Creatures. It is not, however, an attack on intense experience. The picture of Donne's illness in *Devotions* does not provoke a less vivid experience, it does not suggest a less striking picture to the reader, through its relentlessly mounting number of literary metaphors, paradoxes and antitheses, than does an Ignatian exercise:

Stil when we return to that Meditation, that *Man is a World*, we find new *discoveries*. Let him be a *world*, and him self will be the *land*, and *misery* the *sea*. His misery, (for misery is his, his own; of the happinesses even of this world, hee is but *tenant*, but of misery the *free-holder*; of happines hee is but

59. Mueller, 'Exegesis of Experience', *JEGP*, pp. 4, 6; Webber, 'Prose Styles', *Anglia*, p. 142.

60. In Mueller's observation, the majority of the Biblical quotations are in the Expostulations: 'Exegesis of Experience', *JEGP*, p. 3.

the *farmer*, but the *usufructuary*; but of misery, the *Lord*, the *proprietary*) his misery, as the *sea*, swells above all the hilles, and reaches to the remotest parts of this earth, *Man*; who of himselfe is but *dust*, and coagulated and kneaded into earth, by *teares*; his *matter* is *earth*, his *forme*, *misery*. In this *world*, that is *Mankinde*, the highest ground, the eminentest *hils*, are *kings*; and have they line, and lead enough to fadome this *sea*, and say, My misery is but this deepe? (Eighth Meditation).

Donne rejected the Ignatian withdrawal of the senses because it produced a fictional picture in the exercitant's imagination. For him, the evacuation induced a false dream state. The exercitant appeared to conduct the withdrawal to intensify an artificial sensation. But Donne's replacement in the Meditations of the Book of Creatures for the exercitant's fictional picture, his taut rhetorical references to the Bible in the Expostulations, and his dramatic discussion of the connection between Meditation and Expostulation in each of his Prayers achieve the intensity of the Ignatian exercise. His prototypes, rhetoric, and dramatic monologues depend on the inner cosmology of the *Exercises*, and they sustain the Ignatian awareness of a religious truth by sensation. In the three parts of each devotion the Ignatian control of the understanding and the will dominates, because of Donne's choice of imagery, topic, and prose style. This control is present side by side with the development of an aesthetic literary experience that seems to contradict it. It gives *Devotions* a sustained paradoxical character more vivid than the intensity of the work's accumulated images.

The Expostulation of each devotion, therefore, clearly fulfils a role that respects both the mental cosmology of the *Exercises* and Donne's metaphysics. It is the variation of an experience, but not a new structural part of that experience. Into a literary medium, the Expostulation fuses scriptural prototypes in the shape of biblical quotations[61] with the historical incidents of Donne's illness. The biblical references are not merely illustrative or authoritative, but broadly rhetorical. Donne fuses the contemporary appreciation of rhetoric as the experience of felt truth with Ignatius' aim of comprehension through sensual depth. The biblical passages abound, one on top of the other; about half of them are

61. Ibid.

not even annotated in the marginalia (most of Donne's seemingly confusing italics[62] are uncredited scriptural quotations or paraphrases, identified here in the Commentary). Such passages do not so much prove Donne's statements as rhetorically confirm them. Donne is not conducting an exegesis of the Bible in his work, nor, say, an exegesis of experience in general. He is creating by style and structure a meditative experience of a specific exegetical character. Donne's Expostulations declare the affinity of his illness and of the lot of mankind to their biblical prototypes by persistent rhetorical statement.

The rhetorical prose of the Expostulation fulfils the emotive end of the *Exercises*, that of withdrawing the mind wholly into itself. The Expostulation is never far from its original Latin meaning of vehement request. Donne tells God that his eighteenth Expostulation is almost too bold a literary process for him to use, and he excuses himself on the ground that it is the only literary correlative to wonder at a religious truth that he can think of. In the fifth Expostulation he fears that his emotional pitch resembles the 'murmuring' of the Israelites against God. However, he persists.

Because it prevents the possible degeneration of the Expostulation into mere plaint, the Prayer at the end of each devotion preserves the meditative aim. The Prayer shifts the devotion from the declaratory tone of its preceding parts to a less urgent statement and sustains the taut exegetical character of the Meditation and Expostulation without slackening the vividness of the reader's experience. The meditator reposes in the typology of his devotional experience, accustomed to the intensity of its vision, while the experience itself remains unbroken. Where the Meditation sustained the emotional experience of the devotion by taut historical description, and the Expostulation by biblical exegesis, the Prayer sustains it by its affirmative tone. Each Prayer affirms that some aspect of Donne's illness represents historically a moral value already stated in the Bible. This value is invariably universal in its implications:

How much oftner doth he [thy Sonne] exhibit a *Metaphoricall Christ*, than a *reall*, a *literall*? This hath occasioned thine ancient *servants*, whose delight it

62. Webber, 'Prose Styles', *Anglia*, p. 139.

was to write after thy *Copie*, to proceede the same way in their *expositions* of the *Scriptures*, and in their composing both of *publicke liturgies*, and of *private prayers* to thee, to make their accesses to thee in such a kind of *language*, as thou wast pleased to speake to them, in a *figurative*, in a *Metaphoricall language*; in which manner I am bold to call the comfort which I receive now in this sicknesse, in the *indication* of the *concoction* and *maturity* thereof, in certaine *clouds*, and *residences*, which the *Physitians* observe, a discovering of *land* from *Sea*, after a long, and tempestuous *voyage*. (Nineteenth Expostulation).

In the Prayers of *Devotions*, one no longer senses literary effort. The meditator feels the universal affection, the emotion of love, which the arguments of the Meditations and Expostulations have already projected indirectly. The meditator rejoices overtly in an experience which he has had as completely in each Meditation and Expostulation. The Prayer reminds us of the Ignatian *applicatio sensuum* (the inward application of the senses to the picture in the imagination) a little more than do the earlier parts of each devotion: it brings the love relationship between man and God directly to the fore of the discussion. However, it recalls the *applicatio* because it achieves the same end, and not because it shares structural similarities with it. In each Prayer, God and man openly participate in an eternal emotive reality in the exegesis of the new experience of the meditator. The reader of the Prayers is made to understand the images of the Book of Creatures lovingly in the immediate light of their biblical types. He caps the experience of comprehension and love in the Meditations and Expostulations by concentrating on the affection alone.

While it is tempting to identify the three parts of each of Donne's devotions with the three stages in the Ignatian experience, no such parallel is really possible. Without entering into a discussion of how private Donne intended *Devotions* to be, the work is a literary one, and as such it contradicts the original ascetic character of the Ignatian experience. It was meant to be read by people, and to that extent its meditative experience is aesthetic. The first two stages of the Ignatian experience were preparatory, while no such preparatory steps are possible in a literary experience, meditative or not. The *Spiritual Exercises* was a text on how to induce a meditative experience, but Donne's *Devotions* is a work eliciting from the reader an experience simultaneous with his reading. Though one may sometimes draw a few superficial parallels between the mental cosmology of Ignatius and the tripartite sections of Donne's *Devotions*, the real meditative qualities accruing to the Ignatian use of the powers of mind and body are present in all parts of the work at once. Otherwise these meditative qualities and all other factors related to meditative experience would not be present in the work at all. Donne's discussion of meditation in *Devotions* must be distinguished from the actual development of this experience in the reader of his book. Donne at first describes a meditation as a kind of biblical exegesis, and later he refines his view in the light of the relevance of the typological levels of this exegesis to the body and soul of the meditator.[63] But the exegesis in question is present in the literary structure of his work from its first to last lines. It is not something that occurs only when he openly discusses it.

Donne's tripartite structure, for which we may mistakenly find a parallel in formal seventeenth-century methods of devotion, is original with him. He devised it because he needed such an argumentative structure to satisfy the dialectical cast of his mind. We see this dialectical character at work elsewhere in his writings, in the argumentative structure of 'Love's Growth' and of so many of his other poems. In *Devotions*, this structure reconciles the aim of Ignatian meditation to Donne's understanding of the two Books of Life and the Book of Creatures. The division of Meditation, Expostulation, and Prayer in his devotions enabled him to expose, develop, and resolve his material according to his concept of devotional literature. It permitted him to create a literary work fusing biblical prototypes and their copies in the Book of Creatures into a literary form that had an aesthetic effect on the reader akin to the ascetic experience of Ignatius.

The exegetical character of *Devotions* and the experience of its reader were not typical of Anglican devotional literature in the seventeenth century.[64] There is no other work even remotely like *Devotions* in that

63. Twenty-third Meditation.

64. Helen C. White, *English Devotional Literature [Prose], 1600–1640* (Madison, Wisc., 1931), pp. 247–48.

tradition, and Donne never used its structure again. The originality of *Devotions* is that Donne employed the ideal quality of memories, the visionary power of the understanding, and the emotive power of the will, in the Ignatian cosmology of the inner man, to create an exegetical work, and that this work was meant to repeat its exegetical character in the experience of the reader.

The reader of *Devotions* was supposed to achieve a meditative typological vision. For Donne, devotional literature was a work that inspired this vision, and, as such, it accomplished the ends of the general current of Anglican devotion. By forcing his reader to use his memories (of the Book of Creatures), Donne's *Devotions* made him probe the eternal; by engaging his understanding, it inspired deep comprehension of spiritual things; such comprehension, in turn, invariably led the reader to the exercise of the will for love. Through such kinds of probing, inspiration, and love, *Devotions* fulfilled the criterion of meditation of Donne's contemporary, Bishop Hall. Hall's description of meditation represents the pith of the seventeenth-century tradition of Anglican devotion to which *Devotions* conforms: 'Divine Meditation is nothing else but a bending of the mind upon some spiritual object, through divers forms of discourse, until our thoughts come to an issue'.[65] *Devotions* is one of the most singular examples of this tradition, even if it does not share the details of the kinds listed by Hall.

III

Seventeenth-Century Copies

The following is a list by date of the known extant copies of the seventeenth-century editions of *Devotions*. A copy referred to in the Apparatus, Commentary, or Introduction is followed by the abbreviation of its location. Not all locations have standard abbreviations in bibliographies. For the abbreviations, preference was given to the following sources in this order:

65. Joseph Hall, *Works*, VI (Oxford, 1837), 48.

STC (Pollard), STC (Wing), and Union Catalogue of the Library of Congress, or to my own abbreviation when none existed. The copies without abbreviation were not consulted.

I *Devotions* 1624(1)   STC 7033, Keynes 34

1. All Souls College, Oxford, O⁹
2. Bodleian Library, Oxford, O
3. British Museum, L
4. Cambridge University Library, C
5. Chapin Library, Williams College, Mass., CH
6. Christ Church, Oxford, O³
7. Clarke Library, University of California, Los Angeles, CLC
8. Dr. Williams Library, London, L³
9. Folger Shakespeare Library, Washington, D.C., Folg
10. Harvard College Library, HD
11. Henry E. Huntington Library, California, HN
12. Johns Hopkins University, Garrett Library, BJ
13. Sir Geoffrey Keynes, GK
14. Magdalen College, Oxford, O¹²
15. Peterborough Cathedral Library (Cambridge University Library), P
16. Robert S. Pirie, Hamilton, Mass., Pir
17. Saint Andrew's University, St. A
18. John Sparrow, S
19. Robert Taylor (Princeton University), PN
20. Trinity College, Cambridge, C²
21. Worcester College, Oxford, O⁶
22. Yale University Library, Y

II *Devotions* 1624(1)   STC 7033a, Keynes 35

   1. Henry E. Huntington Library, California, HN

   2. Sir Geoffrey Keynes, GK

III *Devotions* 1624(2)   STC 7034, Keynes 36

   1. Bodleian Library, Oxford, O

   2. Cambridge University Library, C-1

   3. Cambridge University Library, C-2

   4. Christ Church, Oxford, O³

   5. Folger Shakespeare Library, Washington, D.C., Folg-1

   6. Folger Shakespeare Library, Washington, D.C., Folg-2

   7. General Theological Seminary, New York City, NNG

   8. Hartford Seminary Foundation, Conn., CtHC

   9. Harvard College Library, HD

  10. Henry E. Huntington Library, California, HN

  11. University of Indiana Library, InU

  12. Sir Geoffrey Keynes, GK

  13. Lambeth Palace Library, L²

  14. Newberry Library, Chicago, Ill., N

  15. Norwich Public Library, NPL

  16. Robert S. Pirie, Hamilton, Mass., Pir

  17. Saint Paul's Cathedral Library, L¹⁵

  18. Victoria and Albert Museum, L¹⁸

  19. Worcester College, Oxford, O⁶

  20. Yale University Library, Y

IV *Devotions* 1626   STC 7035, Keynes 37

   1. Bodleian Library, Oxford, O

2. British Museum, L

3. Brown University Library, RPB

4. Dartmouth College Library, Hanover, N.H., NhD

5. Folger Shakespeare Library, Washington, D.C., Folg

6. Harvard College Library, HD

7. University of Illinois Library, Urbana, Ill., IU

8. Sir Geoffrey Keynes, GK

9. Lincoln Cathedral Library, Linc

10. Robert S. Pirie, Hamilton, Mass., Pir-1

11. Robert S. Pirie, Hamilton, Mass., Pir-2

12. Princeton University Library, PN

13. John Sparrow, S

V *Devotions* 1627   STC 7035a, Keynes 38

1. Bodleian Library, Oxford, O

2. Corpus Christi College, Oxford, O^5

3. Exeter Cathedral Library, O^{10}

4. Folger Shakespeare Library, Folg

5. Harvard College Library, HD

6. Sir Geoffrey Keynes, GK-1

7. Sir Geoffrey Keynes, GK-2 (very imperfect)

8. Marsh Library, Dublin, D^2

9. Robert S. Pirie, Hamilton, Mass., Pir

10. Princeton University Library, PN

11. Saint Andrew's University, St. A

12. Sheffield University Library, Shef

13. John Sparrow, S

14. Yale University Library, Y

VI *Devotions* 1634   STC 7036, Keynes 39

1. Boston Public Library
2. Folger Shakespeare Library, Washington, D.C.
3. Harvard College Library
4. Sir Geoffrey Keynes, GK
5. Pembroke College, Cambridge, C^{15}
6. Robert S. Pirie, Hamilton, Mass.
7. John Sparrow
8. Trinity College, Cambridge, C^2
9. Worcester College, Oxford, O^6
10. Yale University Library

VII *Devotions* 1638   STC 7037, Keynes 40

1. Aberdeen Public Library, Aber
2. National Library of Scotland (Advocates'), Edinburgh, E
3. British Museum, L
4. Cambridge University Library (Bassingbourne Parish), C
5. Chethams Library, Manchester, M^2
6. Folger Shakespeare Library, Folg
7. Henry E. Huntington Library, California, HN
8. Sir Geoffrey Keynes, GK
9. Robert S. Pirie, Hamilton, Mass., Pir
10. Saint John's College, Cambridge, C^5

IV

The Editions

Devotions went through five editions in the seventeenth century. The first three, 1624(1), 1624(2), and 1626–27, printed in Donne's lifetime, interest us because they throw light on the text of the work. The other two, 1634 and 1638, contain revealing editorial corrections, but are evidently derived from previous editions. They continue to repeat certain errors of the earlier printings, and make flagrant new errors that could never have come from Donne's manuscript (obviously incorrect and incomplete footnotes, for example, are conveniently dropped).[66]

There are no editions of *Devotions* in the eighteenth century. There were three in the nineteenth century by, respectively, Alford in 1839, Pickering in 1840, and Talboys in 1841; and four in the twentieth, by Sparrow in 1923, Draper in 1925, Hayward in his *Complete Poetry and Prose* in 1929, and the University of Michigan Press Reprints in 1959. Of these, only Alford's and Sparrow's editions have critical pretensions.

Of the first three editions in the seventeenth century, the first two are textually good, with reservations. Donne's request to Sir Robert Ker to read the sheets of the first edition may have resulted, fortunately, in Ker's occasional judicious editorial correction.[67] For its part, the second edition, like the first, appears to have lacked Donne's personal proof-reading, at least in any evident way. However, it was printed with care. Meanwhile, the third edition inaugurates a whole series of new textual mistakes. It was set by a compositor particularly poor at Latin, although it carries out certain indisputable editorial corrections.

The first edition was entered in the Stationers Register on January 9, 1624, by Thomas Jones[68] who was active in the bookselling trade in London between 1600 and 1637.[69] Its collation reads 12°, A⁶, B-Z, Aa-Dd¹², Ee⁴, in 312 leaves; and C2 is a cancel. The Register records that the work was submitted to the Stationers on Jones' behalf by 'Master Doctor Wilson', the official licencer, and by 'Master Bill warden'. It

66. With the fifth edition following suit, the fourth edition dropped these notes, most of them incomplete in earlier editions; Deu. 33.33, D8ᵛ; Buxdor, F7ᵛ; Augustus, G5ᵛ; Job, H6; Josephus, 13ᵛ; Amos, 4.14, K4; Val. Max, Lᵛ; Ardoinus, L3; Magius, O4; Antwerp and Roan, O4ᵛ; Roccha, O5ᵛ; Psa. 31.5, P8ᵛ; Apoc. 8.9, R11; August., S5ᵛ; Galen, recurring three times on S11ʳˑᵛˑ and S12 respectively; and Tertull., Y5; and introduced this error, Ecc. 5.7, T10ᵛ.

67. *Letters*, pp. 249–50.

68. *Stationers' Register*, IV, 110, p. 72.

69. *A Dictionary of Printers and Booksellers in England, Scotland, and Ireland, and of Foreign Printers of English Books, 1557–1640*, edited by R. B. McKerrow (London, 1910), p. 160.

also records the three subdivisions of its title page and Donne's name.[70] The title page of the vast majority of the known surviving copies of this edition (STC 7033) gives information that the Register does not. It indicates that the edition was 'Printed by A. M.', or Augustine Mathewes, the printer active in London between 1619 and 1653.[71] Mathewes' initials appear again in the second and fifth editions, and his name is spelled out in the fourth.

The absence of Mathewes' initials on the title page of two known surviving copies of the first edition[72] poses a problem about its publication. While a number of hypotheses are possible, including Keynes's theory that there were two issues of the edition, clearly there was only one issue. The inclusion of Mathewes' initials is a variant of the title page of this issue rather than an indication of a whole new printing. Keynes also suggests more accurately that the initials might have been slipped into the title page after a number of copies of the sheet on which it appeared had already been printed.[73]

Two editorial facts support this argument. First, there are no distinct errors common to the surviving copies of the edition without Mathewes' initials to suggest a separate issue. Secondly, collation reveals that all words in the title pages of both hypothetical issues were printed by exactly the same letters in the printer's frame. The only difference is that the initials appear in the one and not in the other. In the second to last line of the page with the initials, the words 'for Thomas' were pushed over to the right hand margin to make room for 'by *A. M.*', and 'Iones' was slipped to the next line and centred with the date. The exclusion of Mathewes' initials appears to have been an oversight rectified during publication.

The first edition came out under normally propitious circumstances. Mathewes, who held the printing rights on all five editions, but not the actual copyright until the fourth, probably printed the book on his press in Cow Lane near Holborn Circus where he appears to have been

70. *Stationers' Register*, IV, 110, p. 72.
71. McKerrow, *Dictionary*, p. 188.
72. 1624, STC 7033a: HN, GK.
73. Keynes, p. 66.

situated in 1624.[74] *Devotions* would have come from the same press as Mathewes' other releases of 1624, such as *Divers Epigrams* of William Andrewes and *The Watchmans Warning*, a sermon preached by William Proctor at Paul's Cross that year.[75] Jones who, for his part, held selling rights on the book, had already been in charge of the distribution of other works by Donne, namely, the Sermon on John X. 22 the year before, the sermon on Acts 1. 8 in 1622, and yet a third sermon in 1624 itself.[76] He was a dealer mainly in religious literature with headquarters from 1622 onwards at the sign of the Black Raven (mentioned in the colophon of the second edition) near St. Clement's Church,[77] where Anne Donne was buried in 1617.[78] Jones assigned all his copyrights, including those of the *Devotions* and the three sermons mentioned above, as well as another two by Donne, to Mathewes in 1633.[79]

Of the three copies of the first edition that form the base copy of the present edition, only the Cambridge University Library copy has its original binding. The binding is in contemporary vellum and, like the rest of the volume, is in excellent condition. Each of its boards is decorated with a frame made by a gilt fillet intersecting at the corners, and its spine is decorated with four triple fillets that flank rosettes, with the royal coat of arms imprinted in the centre of both boards. The binding does not seem to have been affected by the insertion of end papers at the front and back during its repair.

The watermarks of the paper indicate that Mathewes, like all reputable printers in the period, imported his sheets from the north of France. The French produced the linen for the rag content of good paper, while the English, faced with recurrent inclement weather, produced wool materials suitable for warm clothes but not fit for paper.

74. McKerrow, *Dictionary*, p. 188.

75. *Stationers' Register*, IV, 127, p. 89, and 129, p. 91.

76. Ibid., 13 June, 1623, IV, 99, p. 61; 28 November, 1622, IV, 86, p. 48; 31 October, 1622, IV, 84, p. 46.

77. McKerrow, *Dictionary*, p. 160.

78. Bald, pp. 324–25.

79. *Stationers' Register*, IV, 307, p. 281. The editors refer the reader in square brackets to the sermons for April, 1625, entered 23 April, IV, 138, p. 100, and for 24 February, 1626, IV, 116, p. 154.

The marks depict an orb-like crown with a number of inwrought curves suggesting the repetition of the design of the fleur-de-lys according to some indefinite plan. The initials 'J C', sometimes looking like 'J G', appear in a box below the crown. This watermark is the only one in the Cambridge copy, while it is interspersed with another recurring French watermark, a crown much like the first with the initials 'A B' fixed in a device beneath it, in the copy in the Trinity College Library, Cambridge. Both watermarks recur in 1624(2), C-2, accompanied by yet a third French water-mark.

The text of the first edition indicates that Donne quoted the King James' version of the Bible published only a brief fourteen years before the composition of *Devotions*. The vocabulary of his biblical paraphrases almost invariably echoes the King James' version, rather than, for example, the Geneva Bible. He uses 'thy' of Psalms 26.8, 'be not negligent' of Ecclesiasticus 38.9, and 'healed Babylon' of Jeremiah 51.9, of the King James' Bible, instead of 'thine', 'faile not', and 'cured Babel', in the Geneva Bible. Where the numbering of the King James' version is in competition with the Geneva Bible, Donne follows the former (as in Ecclesiasticus 18.8 and 18.7 rather than 18.7 and 18.6 of the Geneva version), except in one case, where he rejects 1 Sam. 24.14 of King James' for 24.15 of Geneva.

The second edition appeared only months after the first in the same year, with the collation 12°, A–Bb[12], in 300 leaves. Its rapid publication after the first edition attests to the public interest in the work. The edition appears to have been a large one, if its 20 extant copies is an indication of the number printed, and it seems to have been disseminated widely. One copy, probably delivered to Oxford in sheets and bound with another work[80] in its present Oxford binding, is in excellent condition and has interesting variants valuable for determining the original text.

The edition, however, begins the process of corruption in the copy text represented by the first edition. It contains many unjustified changes in punctuation and a number of other errors. It also repeats most of the errors of the first edition, except those signified in its *errata*

80. *Of the Fabrique of the Church*, London, 1604.

list. Besides punctuation, the major corruptions are on the whole restricted to the marginalia, while its text, like that of the first remains relatively pure.

Many obvious errors in pagination occur that a diligent editor would have caught. They suggest that the second edition was put out in a hurry. Some of these errors appear singly but others in groups in signatures I, M, and S.[81] An interesting variant is the correct pagination of page 7 in the excellently preserved volume, O, and in HD, N, Pir, Folg-1, Folg-2, L[15], and InU, which appears as page 10 in other copies. This error suggests that these copies are late ones which the compositor tried to correct during the press run.

The second edition adds a colophon. It reads: 'London/Printed for Thomas/Jones, and are to be/sold at the black Ra-/ven, in the Strand./ 1624.' The black Raven was Jones' motto and must have hung on a sign outside his shop in the western end of the Strand. In addition, the edition was printed on two lots of paper differing greatly in thickness, the finer, thin one of 1624(2), O and C-2, and the coarser, thicker paper of other copies like 1624(2), C-1, which failed to withstand age so well.

The third edition, the last of the three *duodecimo* editions in the century, appears to have been a rather rapidly executed reprint of the second edition, with the same collation, and a colophon updated to 1627. The title pages of the first and second parts of the edition are respectively dated 1626 (STC 7035) and 1627 (STC 7035a), but are otherwise identical. As Keynes suggests, the edition was very likely put out in a single issue over the new year, and the date on its title page was changed during publication.[82] This theory is borne out by the appearance of 1627 on the colophon of even those copies bearing 1626 on the title page. It is not possible, moreover, to ascribe a separate issue to each title page, because the textual errors occur among the surviving copies without pattern.

81. Pages 7, 183, 186, 187, 190, 191, 194, 195, 198, 199, 202, 203, 206, 259, 262, 263, 266, 267, 270, 271, 274, 275, 278, 400, 401, 404, 405, 408, 409, 412, 413, 416, 417, 420, 421, 424, 448, and 567, appear as 10, 159, 162, 163, 166, 167, 170, 171, 174, 175, 178, 179, 182, 289, 292, 293, 296, 297, 300, 301, 304, 305, 308, 376, 377, 380, 381, 384, 385, 388, 389, 392, 393, 396, 397, 324, 338 and 467.

82. Keynes, p. 67.

The errors in the marginal notes and the Latin *Stationes* at the beginning of the third edition are constant throughout the copies. However, its errors in pagination vary interestingly. Page 422, for example, reads correctly in 1626, O, S, Linc, and IU, and 1627, D², HD, Y, PN, O⁵, GK-2, and Shef, but incorrectly as page 398 in 1626, PN, Folg, HD, GK, and L, and 1627, O, Folg, and GK-1. Then, 1627, O, alters the numbering of page 530 to page 503, an error which does not occur in 1627, Shef. The sheets of all copies of the edition were evidently printed in a single run and assembled without respect to the differing title pages.

Though their textual authority is doubtful, the fourth and fifth editions of *Devotions* are romantically interesting as volumes.

The fourth edition changed the size to 24° in twelves, with collation A-Y¹² in 264 leaves, without pagination, and its new holder of sale rights was Charles Greene. It introduced the celebrated frontispiece engraving by William Marshall of Donne in death, his bearded head surmounted by a crown protruding through his shroud, set in a baroque niche beneath a skull, with two cameos on either side depicting biblical scenes. Marshall was the prolific seventeenth-century engraver of book illustrations and title pages for booksellers like Greene and Humphry Moseley. He also designed the frontispiece of the eighteen-year-old Donne for the edition of his *Poems* in 1635 (and of Milton, aged 21, in his *Juvenile Poems*).[83] The copies of the edition would have been disseminated out of Greene's shop at the sign of the gun in Ivy Lane in London, his headquarters between 1631 and 1648.

The new partnership of Mathewes and Greene may have come about for financial reasons. Greene had obtained the rights for the sale directly from Mathewes, to whom the copyright had by now passed from Jones. He and Mathewes would have prepared to print and sell the first posthumous edition of a popular work by a leading man of the realm recently dead, describing his bout with a nearly fatal illness ten years earlier. The addition of the frontispiece suggests their consciousness of the sale value of *Devotions*. Greene was a seller chiefly of popular plays and romances, and the lower level of seriousness of the volumes

83. *Dictionary of National Biography*, edited by Sidney Lee (London, 1893), xxxvi, 251.

1

that he handled compared to those of Jones may account in part for the corruption of Donne's text in this edition.[84]

For the fifth edition four years later, Mathewes transferred the sale rights to Richard Royston in Ivy Lane. Royston was a peculiar choice because, while he published Jeremy Taylor's works, he was notorious and several times arrested for purveying scandalous books.[85] The collation of this edition reads 24° in twelves like the fourth edition, and A^1–T^{12} in 228 leaves, without pagination.

The frontispiece of the 1634 edition appears in some copies of the fifth edition, updated to 1638. However, it may be a variant of the last edition of the century rather than the rule. The frontispiece is prefixed to 1638, Folg, HN, M^2, and E, but appears never to have been attached to the original end sheets in Pir, C, L, and possibly C^5. The end sheets in 1638, Aber, were replaced years ago, and with them the frontispiece removed, if it existed. The colophon of the edition is new, reading: 'Novemb. 23./1637./Imprimatur. Guil./Bray', indicating that its publication, like that of the third, began late in one year and ended in the next, although its title page, unlike the 1626–27 edition, is consistently dated 1638.

Of the three nineteenth-century editions, Alford's, in volume III of his *Dr. Donne's Works* (London, 1839), is the most ambitious. A number of its editorial suggestions have been incorporated in this edition, and credited in the textual apparatus with the letter *A*. Pickering's edition relocates all the marginalia to footnotes, without textual apparatus or commentary, while the publication of Talboy's edition with elaborate designs, in the following year, derives its inspiration largely from the Gothic revival.[86]

Of the four twentieth-century editions, the last, the Michigan Press Reprint, is a reproduction of the first edition in modern pagination; Hayward's is a selection in an anthology of Donne; Draper's is an uncritical edition in the Abbey Classics; and Sparrow's (Cambridge

84. *A Dictionary of the Booksellers and Printers Who Were at Work in England, Scotland and Ireland From 1641 to 1667* (London, 1907), edited by Henry R. Plomer, p. 85.

85. Ibid., pp. 158–59. Royston published the first edition of *Eikon Basilike* in 1648.

86. Keynes, p. 69.

University Press) contains editorial revision and commentary, to which the present edition acknowledges its many debts in its textual apparatus with the letter *S*.

V

The Text

Since there are no manuscripts of *Devotions*, the first edition from which all other seventeenth-century editions were derived, must also serve as the copy text of a modern edition. The text of this edition was fortunately put to press with care, even though its marginalia are replete with errors. Its proofreading appears to have ended at about page 185 with the last item in the errata.[87] It does not appear to have been thorough, since even the pages covered by the errata contain errors that careful checking would have caught. But the text remains generally reliable, though its individual problems are by no means simple. The copies serving for the master text of the present edition are STC 7033, L (shelf mark C.III.B.8), and C (Syn.8.62.69), and STC 7033a, HN (53918).

The first edition served as the copy text for the second edition. The third edition, in turn, was set from the second, the fourth edition from copies of the second and perhaps the third, and the fifth edition from copies of the third and fourth. None of the editions after the first gives evidence of having been set with the aid of a manuscript.

The marginalia of the first edition are in a poor shape, in that they contain some sixty errors and incomplete notes. We may surmise that Donne, still in a convalescent state when he submitted the manuscript for publication, wrote his notes from memory without checking them, and was often wrong. Either that or, less plausibly, the notes were considerably garbled by Mathewes' compositors, who otherwise seem to have remained faithful to the body of his text. Elsewhere, the

---

87. The proofreading did not include the systematic correction of wrong pagination. It may have ended with the last leaf of Sig. I on p. 192.

replacement for the cancel C2 (pp. 27–28) shows editorial care. The re-setting of the page appears to have covered lines 12–15 on C2^v.[88]

The second edition was evidently set from a copy of the first edition. It reproduces its errors with the exception of the errata, which it corrects, and except for a limited number of editorial revisions. The edition could not have been set from the same manuscript as 1624(1), because one would have to assume a number of humanly impossible typesetting situations. The typesetter of 1624(2) would have had to make exactly the same errors as the typesetter of 1624(1), in addition to making his own.

The second edition was therefore set from a copy of 1624(1), and, yet more specifically, from one of a group with a corrected note, Daniel 7.9 (p. 340, HN, BJ, Pir, PN, Folg, GK, C^2, P, CH, CLC, HD), which other copies of the edition print wrongly as Daniel 7.6 (C, Y). The second edition also produced seven new errors in the marginalia (Genesis 28.16, missing, p. 13; Maa., p. 154; Mat. 8.14, p. 355; 1 Sam. 21.29, p. 493; Ma. 9.6, p. 525; Deu. 23.12, p. 575, and Ecc. 1.21, p. 587), and a number of other new mistakes including *stignate* for *stigmate*, and 11 for 18, in the *Stationes* listing the devotions.

The third edition appears to have been printed from a copy of 1624(2), for much the same reasons that 1624(2) seems to have come from 1624(1). It recreates its errors, including its seven new marginal inaccuracies, as well as the errors of 1624(1) found in 1624(2). It attempts to correct Maa. on page 154 wrongly with Mar. The third edition also reproduces the errors in the Latin *Stationes* of the 1624(2), including *stignate* and 11, which basic proofreading would have caught. Interesting if not con-clusive evidence of the paternity of the second edition for the third, is that 1626–27 is set in identical pagination with similar printing. There is only the odd minor printing difference in the layout of the two editions, like the catchword 'knowes' for 'knows' (p. 19), and 'it' at the beginning of the fourth line rather than at the end of the third on page 21. Other-wise, the collation of the two editions is the same.

The fourth edition was set from a copy of 1624(2) with limited refer-

88. E. M. Simpson, 'A Bibliography of Dr. John Donne', *Review of English Studies* (1933) 9, 107–8.

ence, if any, to 1626–27. It contains the errors of the second edition, but avoids thirteen[89] of the eighteen marginal errors, and all four of the mistakes in *Stationes* (*incubitus*, *iungitur*, *obstrepera*, and *sonita*), which the third edition introduced.

Meanwhile, the fourth edition more or less shares with the third five marginal errors which may not have been derived from it.[90] Of these errors, the fourth edition drops completely (L3) the faulty 'Ardinus' of 1626–27, and, although it makes the same error as the third of Mar. 25.31 (F9ᵛ), its typesetter did not have to be copying from it. Both alike may have simply been guessing in correcting the Maa of 1624(2) to Mar. instead of to the Mat. of 1624(1). The three remaining errors in question, Lev. 13.49 (D10ᵛ), Mat. 27.49, 50 (T9), and Mar. 1.70 (Y6) may have crept into the fourth edition from variants of lost copies of 1624(2) rather than from the third edition itself. This possibility is supported by the occurrence of variants in other editions, such as the reference to Daniel 7.6 in 1624(1), Y and C, and to a variant in copies of the third edition. Three copies of 1626 (STC 7035; S, NhD, and IU) and two copies of 1627 (STC 7035a; D², Shef) appear to read Numbers 15.4 (p. 577) because of a broken number 2, while all other copies of the edition clearly read 25.4. If variants in unknown copies do not account for the remaining errors, the compositor of 1634 appears to have set his text from 1624(2) and to have relied curiously on a copy of the third edition of 1626.

The editor of the fifth edition attempted to prepare a sound text from copies of the third and fourth editions, hopefully but unsuccessfully. His task was doomed because both of his copy texts derived a great number of errors from their common source, the second edition, Surviving copies of the fifth edition indicate its origins clearly. The Bassingbourne copy includes a number of correct marginal notes (Mat. 13.16, A9; Joel 2.30, K3ᵛ, and Job 9.30, K10) originating in the third edition, completely missing in the fourth edition (A10ᵛ, L5, L12ᵛ), and

89. Apoc. 21.21, p. 156; Mat. 13.30, p. 329; 2 Pet. 2.8, p. 334; Sap. 143, p. 465; Psa. 162.12, p. 498; Joh. 11.14, p. 517; 2 Sam. 23.14, p. 519; I Sam. 26.15, p. 523; 2 Chro. 26.52, p. 523; Jere. 67, p. 548; Eph. 4, 2.2, p. 550; 2 Cor. 5.7, p. 550; Num. 15.4, p. 577, in 1627, Shef; on pp. F10, M11ᵛ, N, R9, S12, T8, T9, T11 (twice), V12, Xᵛ (twice), and Y3, of 1634.

90. On pp. 280, 154, 101, 518, and 581 in 1626-7 Shef.

it also reproduces a number of notes (namely, Mat. 23.30, L7^v; Sap. 14.3, P11^v; Psalms 106.12, Q12^v; Mat. 9.6, R10^v; Eph. 4.22 and 1 Cor. 5.7, S8) derived from the fourth edition (M11^v, R9, S12, T12 and X^v twice), to change or correct the third (pp. 329, 465, 498, 525 and 550). But the fifth edition records the references to Joel and Job above wrongly as 'Jo'. (K3^v, K10); it includes another twenty marginal errors which the fourth edition invented; and prints eight errors (Apoc. 21.21, F2; 2 Pet. 2.8, L9; John 11.14, R7; 2 Sam. 23.14, R8; 1 Sam. 26.15, R9^v; 2 Chron. 26.25, R10; Jer. 67, S7; and Num. 15.4, T6) originating in 1626–27 (pp. 156, 334, 517, 519, 526 twice, 598, and 577) not found in the fourth edition.

Though the fifth edition is the only one to correct the first edition, its emendations indicate the passing revisions of a knowledgeable editor, rather than of a methodical corrector. They do not suggest that the editor was working from the manuscript of 1624(1). The revisions are 1 Tim. 1.19 (T10^v) and 1 Thes. 5.5 (L7) for Tim. 1.19 and 2 Thes. 5.8, in all previous editions. The edition also emends 'place' in the second Meditation to 'pace' (A11^v), a change adopted independently by Sparrow (p. 6); but elsewhere it follows 1626–27 and corrupts the text with 'houses' for 'places' (A7).

In the light of the seventeenth-century editions of *Devotions*, the present edition changes the text of 1624(1) independently only where it is absolutely necessary. It preserves its punctuation, except in cases of obvious error, and follows the corrections of these errors in 1624(2) and 1626–27, if they are in accord with the practice of the first edition. There is no reason to suppose that the textual strength of the first edition does not extend to its punctuation.

All textual changes in the present edition are recorded in the apparatus, and, where necessary, dealt with at greater length in the Commentary. The apparatus also records the significant variants between the first and two subsequent editions in Donne's lifetime, but makes no note of insignificant changes in spellings by ligatures and lengthening of words with extra letters, by typesetters, to fill out their lines. The edition standardizes the long s, the v and u, and j and i, and all ligatures according to modern usage. It refers to the editions in

Donne's lifetime as 1624(1), 1624(2), and 1626. The Bible used for the present edition is the Cambridge University Library copy of the first edition of the King James version (Shelf Mark Young 40).

DEVOTIONS
UPON

Emergent Occasions, and severall
steps in my Sicknes:

DIGESTED INTO

1. MEDITATIONS *upon our Humane Condition.*
2. EXPOSTULATIONS, *and Debatements with God.*
3. PRAYERS, *upon the severall Occasions, to him.*

By JOHN DONNE, Deane of *S. Pauls,*
London.

LONDON
Printed by A.M. for
Thomas Jones
1624

6 *Condition.* 1624(2), 1626: *Condition:* 1624(1)

TO THE
MOST EXCEL-
lent Prince, Prince
CHARLES.

Most Excellent Prince,

I *Have had three* Births; *One,* Naturall, *when I came into the* World; *One* Supernatural, *when I entred into the* Ministery; *and now, a* preternaturall Birth, *in returning to* Life, *from this* Sicknes. *In my* second Birth, *your* Highnesse Royall Father *vouchsafed mee his Hand, not onely to sustaine mee in it, but to lead mee* to it. *In this* last Birth, *I my selfe am borne a* Father: *This* Child *of mine, this* Booke, *comes into the world, from mee, and* with mee. *And therefore, I presume (as I did the* Father *to the* Father) *to present the* Sonne *to the* Sonne; *This* Image *of my* Humiliation, *to the lively* Image *of his* Majesty, *your* Highnesse. *It might bee enough, that* God *hath seene my* Devotions: *But* Examples *of* Good Kings *are* Commandements; *And* Ezechiah *writt the* Meditations *of his* Sicknesse, *after his* Sicknesse. *Besides, as I have liv'd to see, (not as a* Witnesse *onely, but as a* Partaker) *the happinesses of a part of your* Royal Fathers *time, so shall I live, (in my way) to see the happinesses of the times of your* Highnesse *too, if this* Child *of mine, inanimated by your gracious* Acceptation, *may so long preserve alive the* Memory *of*

Your Highnesse

Humblest and

Devotedst

JOHN DONNE.

14 Highnesse 1624(2), 1626: High nesse 1624(1)   17 *liv'd*] lived 1624(2), 1626
19 *live,*] live 1624(2), 1626   24 Devotedst] Devotedst, 1624(2), 1626

Stationes, *sive* Periodi
in Morbo, *ad*
quas referuntur Meditationes
sequentes.

5   1 Insultus *Morbi primus*;

    2 *Post*, Actio laesa;

   3 Decubitus *sequitur tandem*;

    4 Medicusque *vocatur*;

   5 Solus *adest*;   6 Metuit;

10   7 Socios *sibi iungier instat*;

   8 *Et* Rex *ipse suum mittit*;

    9 Medicamina scribunt;

   10 Lentè *& Serpenti satagunt occurrere Morbo.*

   11 *Nobilibusque trahunt, a cincto corde, venenum,*

15 Succis, *& Gemmis; & quae Generosa, ministrant,*

  Ars, & Natura, *instillant*;

    12 *Spirante* Columbâ,

  Suppositâ pedibus, revocantur ad ima vapores;

   13 *Atque Malum Genium, numeroso* stigmate, *fassus,*

20 *Pellitur ad pectus, Morbique*

  Suburbia, Morbus:

   14 *Idque notant* Criticis, *Medici, evenisse* diebus.

   15 *Interea insomnes* Noctes ego duco, *Diesque*:

   16 *Et properare* meum, *clamant, e turre propinqua*

25 Obstreperae Campanae, aliorum *in funere, funus.*

   17 *Nunc* lento sonitu *dicunt*, Morieris;

   18 *At inde,* Mortuus *es, sonitu* celeri, pulsuque

  agitato.

5 Insultus] Incubitus 1626 10 *iungier*] *iungitur* 1626 15 *ministrant, Ed.: ministrant* 1624(1 &2); *ministrant.* 1626 17 Columbâ] Columba 1624(2), 1626 18
Suppositâ] *Supposita* 1624(2), 1626 19 stigmate] stignate 1624(2), 1626 22
Medici,] *Medici* 1624(2), 1626 24 *clamant,*] *clamant* 1624(2), 1626 25 Obstre-
perae] Obstrepera 1626 27 18] 11 1624(2), 1626 27 *sonitu*] sonita 1626

19   Oceano *tandem emenso, aspicienda resurgit*
　　 Terra; *vident, iustis,* Medici, *iam* cocta *mederi*
　　 Se posse, indiciis　　　　　　 20　　 Id agunt;
　　　　 21　　 *Atque annuit* Ille,
　　 Qui per eos *clamat, linquas iam* Lazare *lectum*;　　　　　　　　　　 5
22　　 *Sit* Morbi Fomes *tibi* Cura;　　　　　　 23　　 Metusque Relabi.

I. Insultus Morbi primus;

The first alteration, The first grudging of the sicknesse.

1. MEDITATION

5 Variable, and therfore miserable condition of Man; this minute I was well, and am ill, this minute. I am surpriz'd with a sodaine change, & alteration to worse, and can impute it to no cause, nor call it by any name. We study *Health*, and we deliberate upon our *meats*, and *drink*, and *Ayre*, and *exercises*, and we hew, and wee polish every

10 stone, that goes to that building; and so our *Health* is a long & a regular work; But in a minute a Cannon batters all, overthrowes all, demolishes all; a *Sicknes* unprevented for all our diligence, unsuspected for all our curiositie; nay, undeserved, if we consider only *disorder*, summons us, seizes us, possesses us, destroyes us in an

15 instant. O miserable condition of Man, which was not imprinted by *God*; who as hee is *immortall* himselfe, had put a *coale*, a *beame* of *Immortalitie* into us, which we might have blowen into a *flame*, but blew it out, by our first sinne; wee beggard our selves by hearkning after false riches, and infatuated our selves by hearkning after false

20 knowledge. So that now, we doe not onely die, but die upon the Rack, die by the torment of sicknesse; nor that onely, but are preafflicted, super-afflicted with these jelousies and suspitions, and apprehensions of *Sicknes*, before we can cal it a sicknes; we are not sure we are ill; one hand askes the other by the pulse, and our eye

25 askes our own urine, how we do. O multiplied misery! we die, and cannot enjoy death, because wee die in this torment of sicknes; we are tormented with sicknes, & cannot stay till the torment come, but pre-apprehensions and presages, prophecy those torments, which induce that *death* before either come; and our *dissolution* is

30 conceived in these *first changes*, *quickned* in the *sicknes* it selfe, and *borne* in *death*, which beares date from these first changes. Is this the honour which Man hath by being a *little world*, That he hath these *earthquakes* in him selfe, sodaine shakings; these *lightnings*, sodaine

2 *alteration*] altercation A   5 Man;] Man, 1624(2), 1626   6 surpriz'd] surprized 1624(2), 1626   11 all, overthrowes all,] all; overthrowes all; 1624(2), 1626   16 God;] God, 1624(2), 1626   25 urine,] urine 1624(2), 1626   33 shakings;] shakings, 1624(2), 1626

flashes; these *thunders*, sodaine noises; these *Eclypses*, sodain offuscations, & darknings of his senses; these *blazing stars*, sodaine fiery exhalations; these *rivers of blood*, sodaine red waters? Is he a *world* to himselfe onely therefore, that he hath inough in himself, not only to destroy, and execute himselfe, but to presage that execution upon 5 himselfe; to assist the sicknes, to antidate the sicknes, to make the sicknes the more irremediable, by sad apprehensions, and as if hee would make a fire the more vehement, by sprinkling water upon the coales, so to wrap a hote fever in cold Melancholy, least the fever alone shold not destroy fast enough, without this contribution, nor 10 perfit the work (which is *destruction*) except we joynd an artificiall sicknes, of our owne *melancholy*, to our natural, our unnaturall fever. O perplex'd discomposition, O ridling distemper, O miserable condition of Man.

1. EXPOSTULATION 15

If I were but meere *dust* & *ashes*, I might speak unto the *Lord*, for the *Lordes* hand made me of this *dust*, and the *Lords* hand shall recollect these *ashes*; the *Lords* hand was the wheele, upon which this vessell of clay was framed, and the *Lordes* hand is the *Urne*, in which these *ashes* shall be preserv'd. I am the *dust*, & the *ashes* of the *Temple* of the 20 *H. Ghost*; and what Marble is so precious? But I am more then *dust* & *ashes*; I am my best part, I am my *soule*. And being so, the *breath* of *God*, I may breath back these pious *expostulations* to my *God*. *My God, my God,* why is not my *soule,* as sensible as my *body*? Why hath not my *soule* these apprehensions, these presages, these changes, 25 those antidates, those jealousies, those suspitions of a *sinne*, as well as my body of a *sicknes*? why is there not alwayes a *pulse* in my *Soule*, to beat at the approch of a tentation to sinne? why are there not alwayes *waters* in mine eyes, to testifie my spiritual sicknes? I stand in the way of tentations, (naturally, necessarily, all men doe so: for 30 there is a *Snake in every path,* tentations in every vocation) but I go, I run, I flie into the wayes of tentation, which I might shun; nay, I

8

breake into houses, wher the plague is; I presse into places of tentation, and tempt the *devill* himselfe, and solicite & importune them,
who had rather be left unsolicited by me. I fall sick of *Sin*, and am
bedded and bedrid, buried and putrified in the practise of *Sin*, and all
5 this while have no presage, no pulse, no sense of my *sicknesse*; O
heighth, O depth of misery, where the first *Symptome* of the sicknes
is Hell, & where I never see the fever of lust, of envy, of ambition,
by any other light, then the darknesse and horror of *Hell* it selfe; &
where the first Messenger that speaks to me doth not say, *Thou*
10 *mayst die*, no, nor *Thou must die*, but *Thou art dead*: and where the
first notice, that my *Soule* hath of her sicknes, is *irrecoverablenes*,
irremediablenes: but, *O my God, Job did not charge thee foolishly*, in his
temporall afflictions, nor may I in my spirituall. Thou hast imprinted
a *pulse* in our *Soule*, but we do not examine it; a voice in our con-
15 science, but wee doe not hearken unto it. We talk it out, we jest it
out, we drinke it out, we sleepe it out; and when wee wake, we doe
not say with *Jacob, Surely the Lord is in this place, and I knew it not*: but   Gen. 28.16
though we might know it, we do not, we wil not. But will *God*
pretend to make a *Watch*, and leave out the *springe*? to make so
20 many various wheels in the faculties of the Soule, and in the organs
of the body, and leave out *Grace*, that should move them? or wil *God*
make a *springe*, and not *wind* it up? Infuse his first *grace*, & not
second it with more, without which, we can no more use his first
grace, when we have it, then wee could dispose our selves by *Nature*,
25 to have it? But alas, that is not our case; we are all *prodigall sonnes*,
and not *disinherited*; wee have received our portion, and misspent it,
not bin denied it. We are *Gods tenants* heere, and yet here, he, our
Land-lord payes us *Rents*; not yearely, nor quarterly, but hourely,
and quarterly; *Every minute he renewes his mercy*, but wee *will not*   Mat. 13.15
30 *understand, least that we should be converted, and he should heale us.*

1. PRAYER

O eternall, and most gracious *God*, who considered in thy selfe, art a
Circle, first and last, and altogether; but considered in thy working

1 houses,] houses 1624(2), 1626   1 places] houses 1626   8 selfe;] selfe 1624(2),
1626   11 notice,] notice 1624(2), 1626   11 *irrecoverablenes*,] *irrecoverablenes*
1624(2), 1626   *Margin* Gen.28.16] *missing* 1624(2), 1626   28 *Rents*;] *Rents*,
1626   *Margin* Mat. 13.15 *Ed.*: Mat. 13.16 all edd.

upon us, art a *direct line*, and leadest us from our *beginning*, through all our wayes, to our *end*, enable me by thy *grace*, to looke forward to mine end, and to looke backward to, to the considerations of thy mercies afforded mee from the beginning; that so by that practise of considering thy mercy, in my beginning in this world, when thou 5 plantedst me in the *Christian Church*, and thy mercy in the beginning in the other world, when thou writest me in the *Booke of life*, in my *Election*, I may come to a holy consideration of thy *mercy*, in the beginning of all my actions here: That in all the beginnings, in all the accesses, and approches of spirituall sicknesses of *Sinn*, I may 10 heare and hearken to that voice, *O thou Man of God, there is death in the pot*, and so refraine from that, which I was so hungerly, so greedily flying to. *A faithfull Ambassador is health*, says thy wise servant *Solomon*. Thy voice received, in the beginning of a sicknesse, of a sinne, is true health. If I can see that light betimes, and heare that 15 voyce early, *Then shall my light breake forth as the morning, and my health shall spring foorth speedily*. Deliver mee therefore, O my God, from these vaine imaginations; that it is an overcurious thing, a dangerous thing, to come to that tendernesse, that rawnesse, that scrupulousnesse, to feare every *concupiscence*, every offer of *Sin*, that 20 this suspicious, & jealous diligence will turne to an inordinate dejection of spirit, and a diffidence in thy care & providence; but keep me still establish'd, both in a constant assurance, that thou wilt speake to me at the beginning of every such sicknes, at the approach of every such *Sinne*; and that, if I take knowledg of that voice then, and flye to 25 thee, thou wilt preserve mee from falling, or raise me againe, when by naturall infirmitie I am fallen: doe this, O *Lord*, for his sake, who knowes our naturall infirmities, for he had them; and knowes the weight of our sinns, for he paid a deare price for them, thy *Sonne*, our *Saviour, Chr: Jesus, Amen*. 30

2 Reg. 4.40

Prov. 13.17

Esa. 58.8

11 *there is*] *ther's* 1626   14 received,] received 1624(2), 1626

2. Actio Laesa.

*The strength, and the function of the Senses, & other
faculties change and faile.*

2. MEDITATION

5 The *Heavens* are not the lesse constant, because they move continually, because they move continually one and the same way. The
Earth is not the more constant, because it lyes stil continually,
because continually it changes, and melts in al the parts thereof.
Man, who is the noblest part of the *Earth,* melts so away, as if he
10 were a *statue,* not of *Earth,* but of *Snowe.* We see his owne *Envie*
melts him, hee growes leane with that; he will say, anothers *beautie*
melts him; but he feeles that a *Fever* doth not melt him like *snow,*
but powr him out like lead, like yron, like brasse melted in a furnace:
It doth not only *melt* him, but *Calcine* him, reduce him to *Atomes,*
15 and to *ashes*; not to *water,* but to *lime.* And how quickly ? Sooner
then thou canst receive an answer, sooner then thou canst conceive
the question; *Earth* is the *center* of my *body, Heaven* is the *center* of my
Soule; these two are the naturall place of those two; but those goe
not to these two, in an equall pace: My *body* falls downe without
20 pushing, my *Soule* does not go up without pulling: *Ascension* is my
Soules pace & measure, but *precipitation* my *bodies*: And, even
Angells whose home is *Heaven,* and who are winged too, yet had a
Ladder to goe to *Heaven,* by steps. The *Sunne* who goes so many miles
in a minut, The *Starres* of the *Firmament,* which go so very many
25 more, goe not so fast, as my *body* to the *earth.* In the same instant that
I feele the first attempt of the disease, I feele the victory: In the
twinckling of an eye, I can scarce see; instantly the tast is insipid, and
fatuous; instantly the appetite is dull and desirelesse: instantly the
knees are sinking and strengthlesse; and in an instant, sleepe, which
30 is the picture, the copy of death, is taken away, that the *Originall,*
Death it selfe may succeed, and that so I might have death to the life.

1 2.] 3. 1624(2)   4 2.] 3. 1626   6 way. 1624(1)L, 1624(2), 1626: way:
1624(1) HN   8 changes,] changes 1626   13 lead...yron...brasse] *lead*...
yron...brasse 1624(2), 1626   15 *ashes;*] ashes, 1624(2), 1626   18 of those *S*:
of these 1624(1&2), 1626   19 two,] two 1624(2), 1626   19 pace *S, A, P*:
place 1624(1&2), 1626   24 The *Starres*] the *Starres* 1624(2), 1626

It was part of *Adams* punishment, *In the sweat of thy browes thou shalt eate thy bread*; it is multiplied to me, I have earned bread in the sweat of my browes, in the labor of my calling, and I have it; and I sweat againe, & againe, from the brow, to the sole of the foot, but I eat no bread, I tast no sustenance: Miserable distribution of *Mankind*, where 5 one halfe lackes meat, and the other stomacke.

2. EXPOSTULATION

1 Sam. 24.15
2 Sam. 9.8

David professes himself a *dead dog*, to his *king Saul*, & so doth *Mephibosheth* to his king *David*: & yet *David* speaks to *Saul*, and *Mephibosheth* to *David*. No man is so little, in respect of the greatest 10 man, as the greatest in respect of *God*; for here, in that, wee have not so much as a *measure* to try it by; *proportion* is no measure for *infinitie*. He that hath no more of this world but a grave, hee that hath his grave but lent him, til a better man, or another man, must bee buried in the same *grave*, he that hath no *grave*, but a *dung-hill*, 15 hee that hath no more *earth*, but that which he carries, but that which hee is, hee that hath not that *earth*, which hee is, but even in that, is anothers slave, hath as much proportion to *God*, as if all *Davids Worthies*, and all the *worlds Monarchs*, and all *imaginations Gyants* were kneaded and incorporated into one, and as though that one were the 20 survivor of all the sonnes of men, to whom God had given the world. And therefore how little soever I bee, as *God calls things that are not, as though they were*, I, who am as though I were not, may call upon *God*, and say, *My God, my God*, why comes thine anger so fast upon me? Why dost thou melt me, scatter me, powre me like water 25 upon the ground so instantly? Thou staidst for the first world, in *Noahs* time, 120 yeres; thou staidst for a rebellious generation in the wildernesse 40 yeares, wilt thou stay no minute for me? Wilt thou make thy *Processe*, and thy *Decree*, thy *Citation*, and thy *Judgement* but one act? Thy *Summons*, thy *Battell*, thy *Victorie*, thy *Triumph*, all 30 but one act; & lead me captive, nay deliver me captive to death, as soon as thou declarest mee to be *enemy*, and so cut me off even with

13 grave,] grave; 1624(2), 1626   27 120] 129 1626   31 nay] nay, 1624(2), 1626

the drawing of thy sword out of the scabberd, and for that question, *How long was he sicke?* leave no other answere, but that the hand of death pressed upon him from the first minute? *My God, my God,* thou wast not wont to come in *whirlwinds,* but in soft and gentle
5 ayre. Thy first breath breathed a *Soule* into mee, and shall thy breath blow it out? Thy breath in the *Congregation,* thy *Word* in the *Church,* breathes *communion,* and *consolation* here, and *consummation* heereafter; shall thy breath in this Chamber breathe *dissolution,* and *destruction, divorce,* and *separation?* Surely it is not thou; it is not thy
10 hand. The devouring sword, the consuming fire, the winds from the wildernes, the diseases of the body, all that afflicted *Job,* were from the hand of *Satan*; it is not thou. It is thou; Thou *my God,* who hast led mee so continually with thy hand, from the hand of my Nurce, as that I know, thou wilt not correct mee, but with thine own hand.
15 My parents would not give mee over to a *Servants* correction, nor my *God,* to *Satans.* I am *fallen into the handes of God* with *David,* and 2 Sam. 24.14 with *David* I see that his *Mercies are great.* For by that mercy, I consider in my present state, not the haste, & the dispatch of the disease, in dissolving this body, so much, as the much more hast, &
20 dispatch, which my *God* shal use, in recollecting, and reuniting this *dust* againe at the *Resurrection.* Then I shall heare his *Angels* proclaime the *Surgite Mortui, Rise yee dead.* Though I be dead, I shall heare the voice; the sounding of the voice, and the working of the voice shall be all one; and all shall rise there in a lesse *Minute,* then any one dies
25 here.

2. PRAYER

O most gracious *God,* who pursuest and perfitest thine own purposes, and dost not only remember mee by the first accesses of this sicknes, that I must die, but informe me by this further proceeding therin,
30 that I may die now, who hast not only waked mee with the first, but cald me up, by casting me further downe, and clothd me with thy selfe, by stripping me of my selfe, and by dulling my bodily senses,

5 Thy] The 1626   7 *communion,*] communion 1626   16 *handes*] *hand* 1626
27 pursuest] pursuest, 1624(2), 1626

to the meats, and eases of this world, hast whet, and sharpned my spirituall senses, to the apprehension of thee; by what steps & degrees soever it shal please thee to go, in the dissolution of this body, hasten *O Lord* that pace, and multiply *O my God* those degrees, in the exaltation of my *Soule*, toward thee now, & to thee then. My tast is 5 not gone away, but gone up to sit at *Davids* table, *To tast, & see, that the Lord is good*: My stomach is not gone, but gone up, so far upwards toward the *Supper of the Lamb*, with thy *Saints* in *heaven*, as to the *Table*, to the *Comunion* of thy *Saints* heere in *earth*: my knees are weak, but weak therfore that I should easily fall to, and fix my selfe 10 long upon my devotions to thee. *A sound heart is the life of the flesh*; & a heart visited by thee, and directed to thee, by that visitation is a sound hart. *There is no soundnesse in my flesh, because of thine anger.* Interpret thine owne worke, and call this sicknes, correction, and not anger, & there is soundnes in my flesh. *There is no rest in my* 15 *bones, because of my sinne*; transferre my sinnes, with which thou art so displeased, upon him, with whome thou art so well pleased, *Christ Jesus*, and there will be rest in my bones: And, *O my God*, who madest thy selfe a *Light* in a *Bush*, in the middest of these *brambles*, & *thornes* of a sharpe sicknesse, appeare unto me so, that I may see thee, 20 and know thee to be my *God*, applying thy selfe to me, even in these sharp, and thorny passages. Doe this, *O Lord*, for his sake, who was not the lesse, the *King of Heaven*, for thy suffering him to be *crowned* with *thornes*, in this world.

Psa. 34.8

Prov. 14.30

Psa. 38.3

Ibid.

3. Decubitus sequitur tandem.   25

The Patient takes his bed.

3. MEDITATION

Wee attribute but one priviledge, and advantage to Mans body, above other moving creatures, that he is not as others, groveling, but

2 thee; *Ed.*: thee, all edd.   4 *Lord* . . . multiply . . . *God*] *Lord* . . . multiply, . . . *God*, 1624(2); *Lord*, . . . multiply, . . . *God*, 1626   6 *tast*,] *tast* 1626   23 *Heaven*,] *Heaven*; 1626   27 3. 1624(1) *errata*, 1624(2), 1626: 2. 1624(1)   28 priviledge,] priviledge 1626

of an erect, of an upright form, naturally built, & disposed to the
contemplation of *Heaven*. Indeed it is a thankfull forme, and recom-
pences that *soule*, which gives it, with carrying that *soule* so many
foot higher, towards *heaven*. Other creatures look to the *earth*; and
5 even that is no unfit object, no unfit contemplation for *Man*; for
thither hee must come; but because, *Man* is not to stay there, as
other creatures are, *Man* in his naturall forme, is carried to the con-
contemplation of that place, which is his *home*, *Heaven*. This is *Mans*
prerogative; but what state hath he in this *dignitie*? A fever can fillip
10 him downe, a fever can depose him; a fever can bring that head,
which yesterday caried a *crown* of gold, five foot towards a *crown* of
glory, as low as his own foot, today. When *God* came to breath into
Man the breath of life, he found him flat upon the ground; when hee
comes to withdraw that breath from him againe, hee prepares him to
15 it, by laying him flat upon his bed. Scarse any prison so close, that
affords not the prisoner two, or three steps. The *Anchorites* that
barqu'd themselves up in hollowe trees, & immur'd themselves in
hollow walls; That perverse man, that barrell'd himselfe in a Tubb,
all could stand, or sit, and enjoy some change of posture. A sicke
20 bed, is a grave; and all that the patient saies there, is but a varying of
his owne *Epitaph*. Every nights bed is a *Type* of the *grave*: At night
wee tell our servants at what houre wee will rise; here we cannot
tell our selves, at what day, what week, what moneth. Here the head
lies as low as the foot; the *Head* of the people, as lowe as they,
25 whome those feete trod upon; And that hande that signed Pardons,
is too weake to begge his owne, if hee might have it for lifting up
that hand: Strange fetters to the feete, strange Manacles to the hands,
when the feete, and handes are bound so much the faster, by how
much the coards are slacker; So much the lesse able to doe their
30 Offices, by how much more the Sinnewes and Ligaments are the
looser. In the *Grave* I may speak thorough the stones, in the voice of
my friends, and in the accents of those wordes, which their love may
afford my memory; Here I am mine owne *Ghost*, and rather
affright my beholders, then instruct them; they conceive the worst
35 of me now, and yet feare worse; they give me for dead now, & yet

19 posture 1624(1) *errata*, 1624(2), 1626: pasture 1624(1)   20 grave;] grave,
1624(2), 1626   23 the head] the the head 1624(2)   24 they,] they 1626

wonder how I doe, when they wake at midnight, and aske how I doe to morrow. Miserable, and, (though common to all) inhuman *posture*, where I must practise my lying in the *grave*, by lying still, and not practise my *Resurrection*, by rising any more.

3. EXPOSTULATION   5

My God, and *my Jesus, my Lord*, and *my Christ, my Strength*, and *my Salvation*, I heare thee, and I hearken to thee, when thou rebukest thy *Disciples*, for rebuking them, who brought children to thee; *Suffer little children to come to mee*, saiest thou. Is there a verier child than I am now? I cannot say with thy servant *Jeremy, Lord, I am a* 10 *child, and cannot speake*; but, *O Lord*, I am a sucking childe, and cannot eat, a creeping childe, and cannot goe; how shall I come to thee? Whither shall I come to thee? To this bed? I have this weake, and childish frowardnes too, I cannot sit up, and yet am loth to go to bed; shall I find thee in bed? Oh, have I alwaies done so? The bed is 15 not ordinarily thy *Scene*, thy *Climate*: *Lord*, dost thou not accuse me, dost thou not reproach to mee, my former sinns, when thou layest mee upon this bed? Is not this to hang a man at his owne dore, to lay him sicke in his owne bed of wantonnesse? When thou chidest us by thy *Prophet* for lying in *beds of Ivory*, is not thine anger vented? not 20 till thou changest our *bedds of Ivory*, into beds of *Ebony*; *David* sweares unto thee, *that hee will not goe up into his bed, till he had built thee a House*. To go up into the bed, denotes strength, and promises ease; But when thou saiest, *That thou wilt cast Jesubel into a bed*, thou mak'st thine own comment upon that, Thou callest the bed *Tribula-* 25 *tion*, great *Tribulation*: How shal they come to thee, whom thou hast nayled to their bed? Thou in the *Congregation*, & I in a solitude: when the *Centurions* servant lay sicke at home, his *Master* was faine to come to *Christ*; the sicke man could not. Their friend lay sicke of the *Palsey*, and the four charitable men were faine to bring him to 30 *Christ*; he could not come. *Peters* wives mother lay sicke of a fever, & *Christ* came to her; shee could not come to him. My friends may

Mat. 19.14

Amos 6.4

Psa. 132.3

Apoc. 2.22

Mat. 8.6

Mar. 2.3

Mat. 8.14

2 Miserable, and,] Miserable, and 1624(2), 1626   *Margin* 19.14 *Ed.*: 19.13 all edd.   20, 21 vented? . . . Ebony; *Ed.*: vented; . . . Ebony? all edd.   21 beds 1624(2), 1626: bebs 1624(1)   *Margin* Mar. 2.3 *Ed.*: [Mat.] 8.4 all edd.   *Margin* Mat. 8.14 *Ed.*: 8.14 all edd.

carrie mee home to thee, in their prayers in the *Congregation*; Thou must come home to me in the visitation of thy *Spirit*, and in the seale of thy *Sacrament*: But when I am cast into this bedd, my slacke sinewes are yron fetters, and those thin sheets, yron dores upon me;

5 And, *Lord, I have loved the habitation of thy house, and the place where thine honour dwelleth*: I lye here, and say, *Blessed are they, that dwell in thy house*; but I cannot say, *I will come into thy house*; I may say, *In thy feare will I worship towards thy holy Temple*, but I cannot say in thy holy *Temple*: And, *Lord, the zeale of thy House, eats me up*, as fast as

10 my fever; It is not a *Recusancie*, for I would come, but it is an *Excommunication*, I must not. But *Lord*, thou art *Lord of Hosts*, & lovest *Action*; Why callest thou me from my calling? *In the grave no man shall praise thee*; In the doore of the grave, this sicke bed, no Man shal heare mee praise thee: Thou hast not opened my lips, that my

15 mouth might shew *thee* thy praise, but that my mouth might shew *foorth* thy praise. But thine *Apostles* feare takes hold of mee, *that when I have preached to others, I my selfe should be a cast-way*; and therefore am I *cast downe*, that I might not be *cast away*; Thou couldst take mee by the head, as thou didst *Abacuc*, and carrie mee so; By a

20 *Chariot*, as thou didst *Eliah*, & carrie me so; but thou carriest me thine own private way, the way by which thou carryedst thy *Sonne*, who first lay upon the *earth*, & praid, and then had his *Exaltation*, as himselfe calls his *Crucifying*, and first *descended into hell*, and then had his *Ascension*. There is another *Station* (indeed neither are

25 *stations* but *prostrations*) lower then this bed; To morrow I may be laid one Story lower, upon the *Floore*, the face of the earth, and next day another Story, in the *grave*, the wombe of the Earth: As yet God suspends mee betweene *Heaven* and *Earth*, as a *Meteor*; and I am not in Heaven, because an earthly bodie clogges me, and I am not in

30 the Earth, because a heavenly *Soule* sustaines mee. And it is thine owne Law, O God, that *if a man bee smitten so by another, as that hee keepe his bed, though he dye not, hee that hurt him, must take care of his healing, and recompence him*. Thy hand strikes mee into this bed; and therefore if I rise againe, thou wilt bee my recompence, all the dayes

35 of my life, in making the memory of this sicknes beneficiall to me;

Margin (right column):
Psa. 26.8
84.4
5.7
69.9
1 Cor. 9.27
2 Reg. 2.11
Exod. 21.
18, 19

5 And,] And; 1626   *Margin* 5.7 *Ed.*: 5.8 all edd.   *Margin* 69.9 *S*: 69.10 all edd.   10 fever;] fever, 1626   14 opened 1624(2), 1626: opned 1624(1)   *Margin* 18, 19 *Ed.*: 18 all edd.   35 me; *A*: me, 1624(1&2), 1626

and if my body fall yet lower, thou wilt take my *soule* out of this bath, & present it to thy Father, washed againe, and againe, and again, in thine own *teares*, in thine owne *sweat*, in thine owne blood.

3. PRAYER

O most mightie and most merciful *God*, who though thou have 5
taken me off my feet, hast not taken me off of my foundation, which is *thy selfe*, who though thou have removed me from that upright forme, in which I could stand, and see thy throne, the *Heavens*, yet hast not removed from mee that light, by which I can lie and see thy selfe, who, though thou have weakened my bodily 10
knees, that they cannot bow to thee, hast yet left mee the knees of my heart, which are bowed unto thee evermore; As thou hast made this *bed*, thine *Altar*, make me thy *Sacrifice*; and as thou makest thy *Sonne Christ Jesus* the *Priest*, so make me his *Deacon*, to minister to him in a cherefull surrender of my body, & soule to thy pleasure, by 15
his hands. I come unto thee, *O God, my God*, I come unto thee, (so as I can come, I come to thee, by imbracing thy comming to me) I come in the confidence, & in the application of thy servant *Davids* promise, *That thou wilt make all my bed in my sicknesse; All my bedd;* That which way soever I turne, I may turne to thee; And as I feele 20
thy hand upon all my body, so I may find it upon all my bedde, and see all my *corrections*, and all my *refreshings* to flow from one, and the same, and all, from thy hand. As thou hast made these *feathers, thornes,* in the sharpnes of this sicknes, so, *Lord,* make these *thornes, feathers,* againe, *feathers* of thy *Dove,* in the peace of Conscience, and 25
in a holy recourse to thine *Arke,* to the Instruments of true comfort, in thy Institutions, and in the Ordinances of thy *Church.* Forget my bed, *O Lord,* as it hath beene a bedde of sloth, and worse then sloth; Take mee not, *O Lord,* at this advantage, to terrifie my soule, with saying, now I have met thee there, where thou hast so often departed 30
from me; but having burnt up that bed, by these vehement heates, and washed that bed in these abundant sweats, make my bed againe,

Psa. 41.3

10 who,] who 1624(2), 1626   16,17 thee, (so . . . me)] thee, so . . . me, 1624(2), 1626

18

O *Lord* and enable me according to thy command, *to commune with* Psa. 4.4
mine owne heart upon my bed, and be still. To provide a bed for all my
former sinnes, whilest I lie upon this bed, and a grave for my sins,
before I come to my grave; and when I have deposed them in the
5 wounds of thy Sonn, to rest in that assurance, that my Conscience is
discharged from further *anxietie*, and my soule from farther *danger*,
and my Memory from further *calumny.* Doe this, *O Lord,* for his sake,
who did, and suffered so much, that thou mightest, as well in thy
Justice, as in thy Mercy, doe it for me, thy *Sonne,* our *Saviour,*
10 *Christ Jesus.*

4. Medicusque vocatur.

The Physician is sent for.

4. MEDITATION

It is too little to call *Man* a *little World*; Except *God,* Man is a *diminu-*
15 *tive* to nothing. Man consistes of more pieces, more parts, then the
world; then the world doeth, nay then the world is. And if those
pieces were extended, and stretched out in Man, as they are in the
world, Man would bee the *Gyant,* and the world the *Dwarfe,* the
world but the *Map,* and the Man the *World.* If all the *Veines* in our
20 bodies, were extented to *Rivers,* and all the *Sinewes,* to *vaines of*
Mines, and all the *Muscles,* that lye upon one another, to *Hilles,* and
all the *Bones* to *Quarries* of stones, and all the other pieces, to the
proportion of those which correspond to them in the *world,* the *aire*
would be too litle for this *Orbe* of Man to move in, the firmament
25 would bee but enough for this *star*; for, as the whole world hath
nothing, to which something in man doth not answere, so hath man
many pieces, of which the whol world hath no representation.
Inlarge this Meditation upon this *great world, Man,* so farr, as to
consider the immensitie of the creatures this world produces; our

14 *World*;] *world,* 1626   17 extended,] extended 1626   24 move] mone
1624(2)

creatures are our *thoughts*, *creatures* that are borne *Gyants*: that reach from *East* to *West*, from *earth* to *Heaven*, that doe not onely bestride all the *Sea*, and *Land*, but span the *Sunn* and *Firmament* at once; My thoughts reach all, comprehend all. Inexplicable mistery; I their *Creator* am in a close prison, in a sicke bed, any where, and any one of 5 my *Creatures*, my *thoughts*, is with the *Sunne*, and beyond the *Sunne*, overtakes the *Sunne*, and overgoes the *Sunne* in one pace, one steppe, every where. And then as the other *world* produces *Serpents*, and *Vipers*, malignant, & venimous creatures, and *Wormes*, and *Cater-pillars*, that endeavour to devoure that world which produces them, 10 and *Monsters* compiled and complicated of divers parents, & kinds, so this world, our selves, produces all these in us, in producing *diseases*, & *sicknesses*, of all those sorts; venimous, and infectious diseases, feeding & consuming diseases, and manifold, and entangled diseases, made up of many several ones. And can the other world 15 name so many *venimous*, so many consuming, so many monstrous creatures, as we can diseases, of all these kindes? O miserable abun-dance, O beggarly riches! how much doe wee lacke of having *remedies* for everie disease, when as yet we have not *names* for them? But wee have a *Hercules* against these *Gyants*, these *Monsters*; that is, 20 the *Phisician*; hee musters up al the forces of the other world, to succour this; all Nature to relieve Man. We *have* the Phisician, but we *are not* the Phisician. Heere we shrinke in our proportion, sink in our dignitie, in respect of verie meane creatures, who are *Phisicians* to themselves. The *Hart* that is pursued and wounded, they say, 25 knowes an Herbe, which being eaten, throwes off the arrow: A strange kind of *vomit*. The *dog* that pursues it, though hee bee subject to sicknes, even *proverbially*, knowes his *grasse* that recovers him. And it may be true, that the *Drugger* is as neere to *Man*, as to other *creatures*, it may be that obvious and present *Simples*, easie to bee had, 30 would cure him; but the *Apothecary* is not so neere him, nor the *Phisician* so neere him, as they two are to other creatures; Man hath not that *innate instinct*, to apply those naturall medicines to his present danger, as those inferiour creatures have; he is not his owne *Apothecary*, his owne *Phisician*, as they are. Call back therefore thy 35

12 selves,] selves 1626

Meditations again, and bring it downe; whats become of mans great extent & proportion, when himselfe shrinkes himselfe, and consumes himselfe to a handfull of dust; whats become of his soaring thoughts, his compassing thoughts, when himselfe brings himselfe to the
5 ignorance, to the thoughtlesnesse of the *Grave*? His *diseases* are his owne, but the *Phisician* is not; hee hath them at home, but hee must send for the Phisician.

4. EXPOSTULATION

I have not the *righteousnesse* of *Job*, but I have the desire of *Job, I*   Job 13.3
10 *would speake to the Almighty, and I would reason with God.* My God, my God, how soone wouldest thou have me goe to the *Phisician*, & how far wouldest thou have me go with the *Phisician*? I know thou hast made the *Matter*, and the *Man*, and the *Art*, and I goe not from *thee* when I go to the *Phisician*. Thou didst not make *clothes* before
15 there was a shame of the nakednes of the body; but thou didst make *Phisick* before there was any grudging of any *sicknes*; for thou didst imprint a *medicinall* vertue in many *Simples*, even from the beginning; didst thou meane that wee should be *sicke*, when thou didst so? when thou madest them? No more then thou didst meane, that we
20 should *sinne*, when thou madest us: thou fore-sawest both, but *causedst* neither. Thou, *Lord*, promisest heere trees, *whose fruit shall*   Ezec. 47.12
bee for meat, and their leaves for Medicine. It is the voyce of thy Sonn, *Wilt thou bee made whole?* That drawes from the patient a confession   Joh. 5.6, 7
that hee was ill, and could not make himselfe wel. And it is thine
25 owne voyce, *Is there no Phisician?* That inclines us, disposes us to   Jer. 8.22
accept thine *Ordinance.* And it is the voyce of the Wise man, both for the *matter, phisicke* it selfe, *The Lorde hath created Medicines out of*   Ecclus. 38.4
the Earth, and hee that is wise, shall not abhorre them, And for the *Arte*, and the *Person, The Phisician cutteth off a long disease.* In all these
30 voyces, thou sendest us to those helpes, which thou hast afforded us in that. But wilt not thou avowe that voyce too, *Hee that hath sinned*   Ecclus. 38.15
against his Maker, let him fall into the hands of the Phisician; and wilt

15 there 1624(2), 1626: ther 1624(1)   21 Thou, *S*: Thou all edd.   *Margin*
5.6,7 *Ed.*: 5.6 all edd.

not thou affoord me an understanding of those wordes? Thou who sendest us for a blessing to the *Phisician*, doest not make it a curse to us, to go, when thou sendest. Is not the curse rather in this, that onely hee falls into the hands of the *Phisician*, that casts himself wholy, intirely upon the *Phisician*, confides in him, relies upon him, attends 5 all from him, and neglects that *spirituall phisicke*, which thou also hast instituted in thy *Church*: so *to fall into the hands of the Phisician, is a sinne*, and a *punishment* of former sinnes; so, as *Asa fell*, who in his disease, *sought not to the Lord, but to the Phisician*. Reveale therefore to me thy *method, O Lord*, & see, whether I have followed it; that 10 thou mayest have glory, if I have, and I, pardon, if I have not, & helpe that I may. Thy *Method* is, *In time of thy sicknesse, be not negligent*: Wherein wilt thou have my diligence expressed? *Pray unto the Lord, and hee will make thee whole*. O Lord, I doe; I pray, and pray thy Servaunt *Davids* prayer, *Have mercy upon mee, O Lord, for I am weake;* 15 *Heale mee, O Lord, for my bones are vexed*: I knowe, that even my weaknesse is a reason, a motive, to induce thy mercie, and my sicknes an occasion of thy sending health. When art thou so readie, when is it so seasonable to thee, to commiserate, as in miserie? But is Prayer for health in season, as soone as I am sicke? Thy *Method* goes 20 further; *Leave off from sinne, and order thy handes aright, and cleanse thy heart from all wickednesse*; Have I, O Lord, done so? O Lord, I have; by thy grace, I am come to a holy detestation of my former sin; Is there any more? In thy *Methode* there is more; *Give a sweet savor and a memoriall of fine flower, and make a fat offering, as not being*. And, Lord, 25 by thy grace, I have done that, sacrificed a little, of that litle which thou lentst me, to them, for whom thou lentst it: and now in thy method, and by thy steps, I am come to that, *Then give place to the Phisician, for the Lord hath created him, let him not goe from thee, for thou hast need of him*, I send for the *Phisician*. but I will heare him 30 enter with those wordes of *Peter, Jesus Christ maketh thee whole*; I long for his presence, but I look, *that the power of the Lord, should bee present to heale mee*.

2 Chro. 16.12

Ecclus. 38.9

Psa. 6.2

Ecclus. 38.10

v. 12

Act. 9.34
Luc. 5.17

Margin 2 Chro. *S*: 1 Chro. all edd.   11 I, pardon *Ed.*: I pardon all edd.   18 readie] read, 1626   *Margin* Ecclus. 38.10 *S*: *v.* 10 all edd.   25 Lord,] *Lord* 1626   *Margin v.* 12 1624(2), 1626: *v.,* 12 1624(1)   32 look,] look 1624(2), 1626   32 Lord,] *Lord* 1626

4. PRAYER

O most mightie, and most merciful *God*, who art so the *God* of *health*, & *strength*, as that without thee, all health is but the fuell, and all strength, but the bellows of sinne; Behold mee under the vehem-
5 ence of two diseases, and under the necessity of two *Phisicians*, authorized by thee, the *bodily*, and the *spiritual Phisician*. I come to both, as to thine *Ordinance*, & blesse, and glorifie thy Name, that in both cases, thou hast afforded help to Man by the Ministery of man. Even in the new *Jerusalem*, in *Heaven* it selfe, it hath pleased thee to
10 discover a *Tree*, which *is a Tree of life there, but the leaves thereof are for the healing of the Nations*; *Life* it selfe is with thee there, for thou art *life*; and all kinds of *Health*, wrought upon us here, by thine *Instruments*, descend from thence. *Thou wouldest have healed* Babylon, *but she is not healed*; Take from mee, O *Lord*, her perversenesse, her
15 wilfulnesse, her refractarinesse, and heare thy *Spirit* saying in my *Soule*, Heale mee, O *Lord*, for I would bee healed. *Ephraim saw his sicknesse, and Judah his wound; then went Ephraim to the Assyrian, and sent to King Jareb, yet could not hee heale you, nor cure you of your wound.* Keepe me back O *Lord*, from them who misprofesse artes of healing
20 the *Soule*, or of the *Body*, by meanes not imprinted by thee in the *Church*, for the *soule*, or not in *nature* for the *body*; There is no *spirituall health* to be had by *superstition*, nor *bodily* by *witchcraft*; thou *Lord*, and onely thou art *Lord* of both. Thou in thy selfe art *Lord* of both, and thou in thy *Son* art the *Phisician*, the *applyer* of both. *With*
25 *his stripes wee are healed*, sayes the *Prophet* there; there, *before* hee was scourged, wee were healed with his stripes; how much more shall I bee healed now, now, when that which he hath already suffred actually, is actually, and effectually applied to me? Is there any thing incurable, upon which that *Balme* dropps? Any vaine so
30 emptie, as that that *blood* cannot fil it? Thou promisest to *heale the earth*; but it is when the inhabitants of the earth *pray that thou wouldest heale it*. Thou promisest to heale their *Waters*, but *their miery places, and standing waters*, thou sayest there, *Thou wilt not heale*: My

Apo. 22.2

Jer. 51.9

Ose. 5.13

Esa. 53.5

2 Chro. 7.14

Ezech. 47.11

17 *Assyrian*,] *Assyrian* 1626   19 back] back, 1624(2), 1626   *Margin* Esa. 53.5
Ed.: Esa. all edd.   25 there, *before*] there *before* 1626   29 dropps?] drops;
1626   30 fil it?] fill It; 1626

23

returning to any sinne, if I should returne to the abilitie of sinning over all my sins againe, thou wouldest not pardon. Heale this *earth*, O my *God*, by repentant tears, and heale these *waters*, these teares from all bitternes, from all diffidence, from all dejection, by estab-

Mat. 4.23

lishing my irremovable assurance in thee. *Thy Sonn went about healing* 5 *all manner of sickenesses.* (No disease incurable, none difficult; he

Luc. 6.19

healed them *in passing*) *Vertue went out of him, and he healed all*, all the

Jo. 7.23

multitude (no person incurable) he healed them *every whit*, (as himselfe speaks) he left no relikes of the disease; and will this universall *Phisician* passe by this *Hospitall*, and not visit mee? not 10 heale me? not heale me wholy? *Lord*, I looke not that thou shouldest

2 Reg. 20.5

say by thy Messenger to mee, as to *Ezechias, Behold, I will heale thee, and on the third day thou shalt goe up to the house of the Lord.* I looke not that thou shouldst say to me, as to *Moses* in *Miriams* behalfe, when

Num. 12.14

Moses would have had her heald presently, *If her father had but spit in* 15 *her face, should she not have been ashamed seven dayes? Let her be shut up seven daies, and then returne;* but if thou be pleased to multiply seven dayes, (and seven is infinite) by the number of my *sinnes*, (and that is more infinite) if this day must remove me, till *dayes shall bee no more*, seale to me, my spirituall health in affording me the *Seales* of thy 20 *Church*, & for my temporall health, prosper thine *ordinance*, in their hands who shall assist in this sicknes, in that manner, and in that measure, as may most glorifie thee, and most edifie those, who observe the issues of thy servants, to their owne spirituall benefit.

5. **Solus adest.**   25

The Phisician comes.

5. MEDITATION

As Sicknesse is the greatest misery, so the greatest misery of sicknes is *solitude*; when the infectiousnes of the disease deterrs them who

10 *Phisician*] *Phisician,* 1624(2), 1626   12 *Ezechias,*] *Ezechias.* 1626   16 *not have been* 1626, *A, S: not been* 1624(1&2)   20 health] health, 1624(2), 1626   23 *and most* 1624(2), 1626: *aud most* 1624(1)   28 Sicknesse] *Sickenes* 1626   28 sicknes] sicknes, 1624(2), 1626

⌐ should assist, from comming; Even the *Phisician* dares scarse come. *Solitude* is a torment, which is not threatned in *hell* it selfe. Meere *vacuitie*, the first *Agent*, *God*, the first *instrument* of *God*, *Nature*, will not admit; Nothing can be utterly *emptie*; but so neere a degree
5 towards *Vacuitie*, as *Solitude*, to bee but one, they love not. When I am dead, & my body might infect, they have a remedy, they may bury me; but when I am but sick, and might infect, they have no remedy, but their absence and my solitude. It is an *excuse* to them that are *great*, and pretend, & yet are loth to come; it is an *inhibition*
10 to those who would truly come, because they may be made instruments, and pestiducts, to the infection of others, by their comming. And it is an *Outlawry*, an *Excommunication* upon the *patient*, and seperats him from all offices not onely of *Civilitie*, but of *working Charitie*. A long sicknesse will weary friends at last, but a pestientiall
15 sicknes averts them from the beginning. *God* himself wold admit a *figure* of *Society*, as there is a plurality of persons in *God*, though there bee but one *God*; & all his externall actions testifie a love of *Societie*, and *communion*. In *Heaven* there are *Orders* of *Angels*, and *Armies of Martyrs*, & *in that house, many mansions*; in *Earth, Families, Cities,*
20 *Churches, Colleges*, all *plurall things*; and lest either of these should not be company enough alone, there is an association of both, a *Communion of Saints*, which makes the *Militant*, and *Triumphant Church*, one *Parish*; So that *Christ*, was not out of his *Dioces*, when hee was upon the *Earth*, nor out of his *Temple*, when he was in our flesh. *God*,
25 who sawe that all that hee made, was good, came not so neer seeing a *defect* in any of his works, as when he saw that it was not good, for man to bee *alone*, therefore *hee made him a helper*; and one that should helpe him so, as to increase the *number*, and give him *her owne*, and *more societie*. *Angels*, who do not propagate, nor multiply, were made
30 at first in an abundant number; and so were starres: But for the things of this world, their blessing was, *Encrease*; for I think, I need not aske leave to think, that there is no *Phenix*; nothing singular, nothing alone: Men that inhere upon *Nature* only, are so far from thinking, that there is any thing *singular* in this world, as that they
35 will scarce thinke, that this world it selfe is *singular*, but that every

4 *emptie*; *Ed.*: emptie, all edd.   13 offices] offices, 1624(2), 1626   15 beginning.] beginning 1626   19 *house*,] house 1626   24 flesh. 1624(1) *errata*, 1624(2), 1626: flesh 1624(1)

25

Planet, and every *Starre*, is another *World* like this; They finde
reason to conceive, not onely a *pluralitie* in every *Species* in the world,
but a *pluralitie of worlds*; so that the abhorrers of *Solitude*, are not
solitary; for *God*, and *Nature*, and *Reason* concurre against it. Now, a
man may counterfeyt the *Plague* in a *vowe*, and mistake a *Disease* for 5
Religion; by such a retiring, and recluding of himselfe from all men,
as to doe good to no man, to converse with no man. *God* hath two
Testaments, two *Wils*; but this is a *Scedule*, and not of his, a *Codicill*,
and not of his, not in the *body* of his *Testaments*, but *interlind*, and
postscrib'd by others, that the way to the *Communion of Saints*, should 10
be by such a *solitude*, as excludes all doing of good here. That is a
disease of the *mind*; as the height of an infectious disease of the body,
is *solitude*, to be left alone: for this makes an infectious bed, equall,
nay worse then a *grave*, that thogh in both I be equally alone, in my
bed I *know* it, and *feele* it, and shall not in my *grave*: and this too, that 15
in my bedd, my soule is still in an infectious body, and shall not in
my grave bee so.

5. EXPOSTULATION

O *God*, my *God*, thy *Son* tooke it not ill at *Marthaes* handes, that when
Jo. 11.23 he said unto her, *Thy brother Lazarus shall rise againe*, she expostulated 20
it so far with him, as to reply, *I know that he shal rise againe in the
Resurrection, at the last day*; for shee was miserable by wanting him
then. Take it not ill, *O my God*, from me, that thogh thou have
Num. 23.9 ordained it for a *blessing*, and for a *dignitie* to thy people, *That they
should dwell alone, and not bee reckoned among the Nations*, (because 25
Deu. 33.28 they should be above them) & that *they should dwell in safetie alone*,
(free from the infestation of enemies) yet I take thy leave to remem-
Eccles. 4.10 ber thee, that thou hast said to, *Two are better then one*; And *Woe be
unto him that is alone when he falleth*; and so, when he is fallen, and
Sap. 1.15 laid in the bedde of sicknesse too. *Righteousnesse is immortall*; I know 30
thy *wisdome* hath said so; but no *Man*, though covered with the
righteousnes of thy *Sonne*, is immortall so, as not to die; for he who

Margin 11.23 *S*: 13.23 all edd.   28 And] And, 1624(2), 1626   29 so,] so 1626
Margin 1.15 *Ed.*: 1.9 all edd.

was *righteousnes* it selfe, did die. I know that the *Son of righteousnes*, thy *Son*, refused not, nay affected *solitarinesse, lonenesse*, many, many times; but at all times, he was able to command *more than twelve legions of Angels* to his service; and when he did not so, he was farre
⸺5 from being alone; for, *I am not alone*, saies he, *but I, and the Father that sent me.* I cannot feare, but that I shall alwaies be with thee, and him; but whether this *disease* may not alien, & remoove my friends, so that *they stand aloofe from my sore, and my kinsmen stand afar off*, I cannot tel. I cannot feare, but that thou wilt reckon with me from
10 this minute, in which, by thy grace, I see thee; whether this *under-standing*, & this *will*, and this *memory*, may not decay, to the *dis-couragement*, and the *ill interpretation* of them, that see that heavy change in me, I cannot tell. It was for thy blessed, thy powerfull *Sonne* alone, *to tread the wine-presse alone, and none of the people with*
⸺15 *him*; I am not able to passe this agony alone; not alone without *thee*; Thou art thy spirit; not alone without *thine*; spirituall and temporall *Phisicians*, are *thine*; not alone without *mine*; Those whom the bands of *blood*, or *friendship*, hath made *mine*, are *mine*; And if *thou*, or *thine*, or *mine*, abandon me, I am *alone*; and wo unto me if I bee
20 alone. *Elias* himselfe fainted under that apprehension, *Loe, I am left alone*; and *Martha* murmured at that, and said to *Christ, Lord doest not thou care, that my sister hath left me to serve alone*? Neither could *Jeremiah* enter into his *Lamentations*, from a higher ground, then to say, *How doth the citie sit solitary, that was full of people.* O my God, it is
25 the *Leper*, that thou hast condemned *to live alone*; Have I such a *Leprosie* in my *Soule*, that I must die alone; alone without thee? Shall this come to such a *Leprosie* in my *body*, that I must die alone? Alone without them that should assist, that shold comfort me? But comes not this *Expostulation* too neere a *murmuring*? Must I bee
30 concluded with that, that *Moses was commaunded to come neere the Lord alone*? That solitarines, & dereliction, and abandoning of others, disposes us best for *God*, who accompanies us most alone? May I not remember, & apply to; that though *God* came not to *Jacob*, till he found him *alone*, yet when he found him alone, *hee wrestled with him*,
35 *and lamed him*? That when in the dereliction and forsaking of friends

	Mat. 14.23
	Mat. 26.53
	Jo. 8.16
	Psa. 38.11
	Esa. 63.3
	1 Reg. 19.14
	Luc. 10.40
	Lam. 1.1
	Lev. 13.46
	Exo. 24.2
	Gen. 32.24

Margin 26.53 Ed.: 26.13 all edd.   10 thee;] thee, 1624(2), 1626   16 without 1624(2), 1626: with out 1624(1)   19 me] mee, 1624(2), 1626   *Margin* 1 Reg. 19.14 *Ed.*: 1. reg. 14.14 all edd.   *Margin* Lam. 1.1 *S*: Jer. 1.1 all edd.   *Margin* 13.46] 13.49 1626   *Margin* 24.2 *Ed.*: 14.2 all edd.   33 came *S*: come all edd. 34 *with him*,] *with him* 1626

and *Phisicians*, a man is left alone to *God, God* may so wrestle with this *Jacob*, with this *Conscience*, as to put it out of *joynt*, & so appeare to him, as that he dares not looke upon him face to face, when as by way of *reflection*, in the consolation of his temporall or spirituall servants, and ordinances hee durst, if they were there? But a *faithfull* 5 *friend is the phisicke of life, and they that feare the Lord, shall finde him.* Therefore hath the *Lord* afforded me both in one person, that —— *Phisician*, who is my faithfull *friend.*

Ecclus. 6.16

5. PRAYER

O *Eternall*, and most *gracious God*, who calledst down fire from 10 *Heaven* upon the sinfull *Cities*, but *once*, and openedst the *Earth* to swallow the *Murmurers*, but *once*, and threwst down the *Tower of Siloe* upon sinners, but *once*, but for thy workes of mercie repeatest them often, & still workest by thine owne paternes, as thou broghtest *Man* into this world, by giving him a *helper* fit for him 15 here, so whether it bee thy will to continue mee long thus, or to dismisse me by death, be pleased to afford me the helpes fit for both conditions, either for my weak stay here, or my finall trans-migration from hence. And if thou mayest receive glory by that way (and, by all wayes thou maist receive glory) glorifie thy selfe in 20 preserving this *body* from such infections, as might withhold those, who would come, or indanger them who doe come; and preserve this *soule* in the faculties thereof, from all such distempers, as might shake the assurance which my selfe & others have had, that because thou hast loved me, thou wouldst love me to my *end*, and at my *end*. 25 Open none of my *dores*, not of my *hart*, not of mine *eares*, not of my *house*, to any *supplanter* that would enter to undermine me in my *Religion* to thee, in the time of my weaknesse, or to defame me, & magnifie himselfe, with false rumors of such a victory, & surprisall of me, after I am dead; *Be* my salvation, and *plead* my salvation; 30 *work* it, and *declare* it; and as thy *triumphant* shall be, so let the *Militant Church* bee assured, that thou wast my *God*, and I thy servant,

15 *helper* fit 1624(1) *corrected:* Helprſiet 1624(1) O, *originally*   15,16 him here, so] him, so 1626

to, and *in* my consummation. Blesse thou the learning, and the labours of this Man, whom thou sendest to assist me; and since thou takest mee by the hand, & puttest me into his hands (for I come to him in thy name, who, in thy name comes to me) since I clog not my
5 hopes in him, no nor my *prayers* to thee, with any limited conditions, but inwrap all in those two petitions, *Thy kingdome come, thy will be done*, prosper him, and relieve me, in thy way, in thy time, and in thy measure. *Amen.*

6. Metuit.

10 *The Phisician is afraid.*

6. MEDITATION

I observe the *Phisician*, with the same diligence, as hee the *disease*; I see hee *feares*, and I feare with him: I overtake him, I overrun him in his feare, and I go the faster, because he makes his pace slow; I feare
15 the more, because he disguises his fear, and I see it with the more sharpnesse, because hee would not have me see it. He knowes that his *feare* shall not disorder the practise, and exercise of his Art, but he knows that my *fear* may disorder the effect, and working of his practise. As the ill affections of the *spleene*, complicate, and mingle
20 themselves with every infirmitie of the body, so doth *feare* insinuat it self in every *action*, or *passion* of the *mind*; and as *wind* in the body will counterfet any disease, and seem the *Stone*, & seem the *Gout*, so *feare* will counterfet any disease of the *Mind*; it shall seeme *love*, a love of having, and it is but a *fear*, a jealous, and suspitious feare of
25 loosing; It shall seem *valor* in despising, and undervaluing danger, and it is but *feare*, in an overvaluing of *opinion*, and *estimation*, and a feare of loosing that. A man that is not afraid of a *Lion*, is afraid of a *Cat*; not afraid of *starving*, & yet is afraid of some *joynt of meat* at the table, presented to feed him; not afraid of the sound of *Drummes*,
30 and *Trumpets*, and *Shot*, and those, which they seeke to drowne, the last cries of men, and is afraid of some particular *harmonious instru-*

13 overtake] overtooke 1626   16 it.] it, 1626   20 themselves 1624(2): them-
selvs 1624(1), themselves, 1626

ment; so much afraid, as that with any of these the *enemy* might drive this man, otherwise valiant enough, out of the field. I know not, what fear is, nor I know not what it is that I fear now; I feare not the hastening of my *death*, and yet I do fear the increase of the *disease*; I should belie *Nature*, if I should deny that I feard this, & if I 5 should say that I feared *death*, I should belye *God;* My weaknesse is from *Nature*, who hath put her *Measure*, my strength is from *God*, who possesses, & distributes infinitely. As then every cold ayre, is not a *dampe*, every *shivering* is not a *stupefaction*, so every *feare*, is not a *fearefulnes*, every declination is not a running away, every debating 10 is not a resolving, every wish, that it were not thus, is not a murmuring, nor a dejection though it bee thus; but as my *Phisicians* fear puts not him from his *practise*, neither doth mine put me, from receiving from *God*, and *Man*, and *my selfe*, *spirituall*, and *civill*, and *morall* assistances, and consolations. 15

6. EXPOSTULATION

My God, my God, I find in thy *Booke*, that *feare* is a stifling spirit, a spirit of *suffocation;* That *Ishbosheth could not speak, not reply in his*

2 Sam. 3.11

own defence to Abner, because hee was afraid. It was thy servant *Jobs*

Job 9.34

case too, who before hee could say any thing *to thee*, saies *of thee, Let* 20

v. 35

him take his rod away from me, and let not his feare terrifie mee, then would I speake with him, and not feare him; but it is not so with mee. Shall a feare *of thee*, take away my devotion *to thee?* Dost thou command me to *speake* to thee, and commaund me to feare thee, and do these destroy one another? There is no perplexity in thee, *my* 25 *God;* no inextricablenes in thee, my *light*, & my *clearnes*, my *Sun*, and my *Moone*, that directest me as wel in the night of adversity and fear, as in my day of prosperity & confidence. I must then *speak* to thee, at all times, but when must I *feare* thee? At all times to. When didst thou rebuke any petitioner, with the name of *Importunate?* 30 Thou hast proposd to us a *parable* of a *Judge* that did Justice at last,

Luc. 18.5

because the client was importunate, and troubled him; But thou hast told

12 thus;] thus, 1626   18 *not*] *nor* 1626   *Margin* Job 9.34 *S*: 9.34 all edd.
Margin v. 35 *Ed*.: Job 9.34 all edd.   *Margin* 18.5 *Ed*.: 18.1 all edd.
PAGE 31   *Margin* 18.1 *Ed*.: 11.5 all edd.   6 thou 1624(2), 1626; thon 1624(1)
8 to morrow 1624(2), 1626: to row 1624(1)   11 asleep] asleepe, 1626   19

us plainely, that thy use in that *parable*, was not, that thou wast troubled with our importunities, but (as thou sayest there) *That wee should alwayes pray.* And to the same purpose thou proposest another, that *If I presse my friend, when hee is in bed, at midnight, to lend*
5 *mee bread, though hee will not rise because I am his friend, yet because of mine importunitie, he will. God* will do this, whensoever thou askest, and never call it *importunitie.* Pray in thy bed at midnight, and God wil not say, I will heare thee to morrow upon thy knees, at thy bed side; pray upon thy knees there, then, & God will not say, I will
10 heare thee on *Sunday*, at *Church*; *God* is no *dilatory God*, no froward *God*; *Praier* is never *unseasonable*, *God* is never asleep nor absent. But, *O my God*, can I doe this, and *feare* thee; come to thee, and speak to thee, in all places, at all houres, and *feare* thee? Dare I aske this question? There is more boldnesse in the *question*, then in the *com-*
15 *ming*: I may doe it, though I *feare* thee; I cannot doe it, except I feare thee. So well hast thou provided, that we should alwayes feare thee, as that thou hast provided, that we shold fear no person but thee, nothing but thee; no men? No. Whom? *The Lord is my helpe, and my salvation, whome shall I feare? Great enemies?* not *great enemies*; for
20 no enemies are great to them that feare thee; *Feare not the people of this land, for they are Bread to you;* They shall not only not *eat* us, not *eat* our *bread*, but they shall bee our *Bread;* Why should we feare them? But for all this *Metaphoricall Bread*, victory over enemies, that thought to devoure us, may we not feare, that we may lack
25 bread literally? And feare famine, though we feare not enemies? *Young Lyons do lacke, and suffer Hunger, but they that seeke the Lord, shall not want any good thing.* Never? Though it bee well with them at one time, may they not fear, that it may be worse? *Wherfore should I feare in the dayes of evill,* saies thy servant *David?* Though his
30 own sins had made them evill, he feared them not. No? not if this evill determin in death? Not though in a death; not, though in a death inflicted by violence, by malice, by our own desert; *feare not the sentence of death,* if thou feare *God.* Thou art, *O my God*, so far from admitting us, that feare thee, to feare others, as that thou
35 makest others to feare us; As *Herod feared John, because hee was a holy,*

Luc. 18.1

Luc. 11.5

Psa. 27.1

Num. 14.9

Psa. 34.10

49.5

Ecclus. 41.3

Mar. 6.20

salvation,] salvation: 1626   19 *Great enemies?* S: Great enemies: all edd.   22
should 1624(2), 1626: should, 1624(1)   23 them?] them; 1626   *Margin* 34.10
S: 35.70 all edd.   27 *thing.*] thing, 1626   *Margin* 49.5 S: 46.5 all edd.   30
sins] sin 1624(2), 1626   30 not.] not 1626   32 malice,] malice 1626   32
desert; *Ed.:* desert, all edd.   33 *God.* 1624(2), 1626: God 1624(1)   35 *holy,*]
holy 1626

and a just man, & observed him. How *fully* then *O my abundant God,* how *gently, O my sweet,* my *easie God,* doest thou unentangle mee, in any scruple arising out of the consideration of this thy feare? Is not

Psa. 25.14   this that which thou intendest, when thou sayst, *The secret of the Lord is with them, that feare him;* The secret, the mistery of the right use of 5

Pro. 2.5   feare. Dost thou not meane this, when thou sayest, *Wee shall understand the feare of the Lord? Have* it, and *have benefit by it;* have it, and stand under it; be directed by it, and not bee dejected with it. And doest thou not propose that *Church* for our example, when thou

Acts 9.31   sayest, *The Church of Judea, walked in the feare of God;* they had it, but 10 did not sit down lazily, nor fall downe weakly, nor sinke under it.

Gen. 3.10   There is a feare which weakens men in the service of God: *Adam was afrayde, because hee was naked.* They who have put off *thee,* are a prey

Pro. 1.26:   to all. They may feare, *for thou wilt laugh, when their feare comes upon*
10.24
Psa. 53.5   *them,* as thou hast tolde them, *more then once;* And *thou wilt make them* 15
14.5   *feare, where no cause of feare is,* as thou hast told them *more then once too.* There is a feare that is a punishment of *former* wickednesses, &

Jo. 7.12, 13   induces *more: Though some said of thy Sonne, Christ Jesus, that hee was*
19.38   *a good Man, yet no Man spake openly, for feare of the Jewes: Joseph was his Disciple; but secretly, for feare of the Jewes:* The *Disciples* kept some 20

20.19   meetings, but with dores shut, *for feare of the Jewes.* O my God, thou givest us *feare* for ballast to cary us stedily in all weathers. But thou wouldst *ballast* us, with such sand, as should have *gold* in it, with that

Esai. 33.6   feare which is *thy feare;* for *the feare of the Lord is his treasure.* Hee that hath that, lacks nothing that Man can have, nothing that *God* does 25

Mat. 8.26   give. Timorous men thou rebukest; *Why are yee fearfull, O yee of little faith?* Such thou dismissest from thy Service, with scorne,

Jud. 7.3   though of them there went from *Gideons* Army, 22000. and remained but 10000. Such thou sendest farther then so; thither from whence

Apo. 21.8   they never returne, *The fearefull and the unbeleeving, into that burning* 30 *lake, which is the second death.* There is a *feare,* & there is a *hope,*

Job 6.20   which are equall abominations to thee: for, *they were confounded, because they hoped,* saies thy servant *Job:* because they had *mis-placed, mis-centred* their *hopes;* they hoped, and not in *thee,* and such shall *feare,* and not feare *thee.* But in *thy feare, my God,* and my feare, my 35

1 *God,*] *God?* 1626   5 right 1624(2), 1626: righr 1624(1)   10 *Judea,*] *Judea* 1626   12 weakens] weaknes 1626   *Margin* 53.5 *S:* 14.5 all edd.   *Margin* 14.5 *S:* 53.6 all edd.   17 wickednesses,] wickednesse; 1626   *Margin* 7.12,13 *Ed.:* 7.13 all edd   18 *Sonne,*] *Son* 1626   21 for feare 1624(1) *corrected,* 1624(2), 1626: for for feare 1624(1) St. A., HN *originally*   *Margin* 20.19 *S:* 29.19 all edd.

God, and my hope, is *hope*, and *love*, & *confidence*, and *peace*, and every limbe, and ingredient of *Happinesse* enwrapped; for *Joy* includes all; and *feare*, and *joy* consist together; nay, constitute one another; *The women departed from the sepulchre*, the women who were

5 made *supernumerary Apostles, Apostles* to the *Apostles*; *Mothers* of the *Church*, and *of the Fathers, Grandfathers of the Church*, the *Apostles* themselves, the *women, Angels* of the *Resurrection*, went from the *sepulchre*, with *feare* and *joy*; they *ran*, sayes the text, and they ran upon those two legs, *feare*, & *joy*; & both was the *right legg*; they

10 *joy* in thee *O Lord*, that *feare* thee, and *feare* thee only, who feele this *joy in thee*. Nay, thy *feare* and thy *love*, are inseperable; still we are called upon, in infinite places, to *feare* God; yet the *Commandement*, which is the *roote* of all, is, *Thou shalt love the Lord thy God*; Hee doeth *neither*, that doth not *both*; hee omits *neither*, that does *one*. Ther-

15 fore when thy servant *David* had said, that *the feare of the Lord is the beginning of wisedome*, And his *Sonne* had *repeated* it againe, Hee that collects both, calls this *feare*, the *root of wisdome*; And that it may embrace all, hee calls it *wisedome it selfe*. A wise man therefore is never without it, never without the exercise of it: Therefore thou

20 sentest *Moses* to thy people, *That they might learne to feare thee all the dayes of their lives*: not in heavy, and calamitous, but in good, and cheerfull dayes too: for, *Noah*, who had assurance of his deliverance, yet *mooved with feare, prepared an Arke, for the saving of his house. A wise man wil feare in every thing*. And therefore though I pretend, to

25 no other degree of wisedome, I am abundantly rich in this, that I lie heere possest with that feare, which is *thy feare*, both that this sicknesse is thy immediate correction, and not meerely a *naturall accident*, and therefore fearefull, because *it is a fearfull thing to fall into thy hands*, and that this feare preserves me from all inordinate feare,

30 arising out of the infirmitie of Nature, because thy hand being upon me, thou wilt never let me fall out of thy hand.

Mat. 28.8

Psa. 111.10
Pro. 1.7
Ecclus. 1.20, 27

Deu. 4.10

Heb. 11.7
Ecclus. 18.27

PAGE 32   24 *the feare* 1624(1) corrected, 1624(2), 1626: *tke feare* 1624(1) HN *originally*   29 10000. 1624(2), 1626: 10. 1624(1)

3 *feare*,] *feare* 1626   5,6 *the Church*,] *the Church* 1626   7 *Angels*] *Angels*, 1626
9 *legg*;] *legge*, 1626   10 *in thee*] *in thee*, 1624(2), 1626   11 *love*,] *love* 1624(2),
1626   16 *againe*,] *againe*. 1626

6. PRAYER

O *most mightie God & mercifull God*, the *God* of all true *sorrow*, & true *joy* to, of all *feare*, & of al *hope* to, as thou hast given me a *Repentance*, not to be repented of, so give me, *O Lord*, a *feare*, of which I may not be *afraid*. Give me tender, and supple, and conformable affections, that as I *joy* with them that *joy*, and *mourne* with them, that *mourne*, 5 so I may *feare* with them that *feare*. And since thou hast vouchsafed to discover to me, in his *feare* whom thou hast admitted to be my assistance, in this sicknesse, that there is danger therein, let me not, *O Lord*, go about to overcome the sense of that fear, so far, as to pretermit the fitting, and preparing of my selfe, for the worst that may bee 10 feard, the passage out of this life. Many of thy blessed *Martyrs*, have passed out of this life, without any showe of *feare*; But thy *most blessed Sonne* himselfe did not so. Thy *Martyrs* were known to be but *men*, and therfore it pleased thee, to fill them with thy *Spirit*, and thy *power*, in that they did *more* then *Men*; Thy *Son* was declared by thee, 15 & by himselfe to be *God*; and it was requisite, that he should declare himselfe to be *Man* also, in the weaknesses of man. Let mee not therefore, *O my God*, bee ashamed of these *feares*, but let me feel them to determine, where his feare did, in a present submitting of all to thy will. And when thou shalt have inflamd, & thawd my former 20 coldnesses, and indevotions, with these heats, and quenched my former heates, with these sweats, and inundations, and rectified my former presumptions, and negligences with these fears, bee pleased, *O Lord*, as one, made so by thee, to thinke me fit for thee; And whether it be thy pleasure, to dispose of this body, this garment so, 25 as to put it to a farther wearing in this world, or to lay it up in the *common wardrope*, the grave, for the next, glorifie thy selfe in thy choyce now, & glorifie it then, with that glory, which thy *Son*, our *Saviour Christ Jesus* hath purchased for them, whome thou makest partakers of his *Resurrection. Amen.* 30

2 *God &*] *God, &* 1626   13 *Martyrs* 1624(2), 1626: *Martys* 1624(1)

7. Socios sibi iungier instat.

The Phisician desires to have others joyned with him.

7. MEDITATION

There is *more feare*, therefore *more cause*. If the *Phisician* desire help,
5 the burden grows great: There is a grouth of the *Disease* then; But
there must bee an *Autumne* to; But whether an *Autumne* of the *disease*
or *mee*, it is not my part to choose: but if it bee of *me*, it is of *both*;
My disease cannot *survive mee*, I may *overlive it*. Howsoever, his
desiring of others, argues his *candor*, and his *ingenuitie*; If the danger
10 be *great*, hee *justifies* his proceedings, & he *disguises* nothing, that
calls in *witnesses*; And if the danger bee not *great*, hee is not *ambitious*,
that is so readie to divide the thankes, and the honour of that work,
which he begun alone, with others. It diminishes not the dignitie of
a *Monarch*, that hee derive part of his care upon others; *God* hath not
15 made many *Suns*, but he hath made many *bodies*, that *receive*, and
give light. The *Romanes* began with *one King*; they came to two
Consuls; they returned in extremities, to *one Dictator*: whether in
one, or many, the *soveraigntie* is the same, in all *States*, and the danger
is not the more, and the providence is the more, wher there are more
20 *Phisicians*; as the State is the happier, where businesses are carried by
more counsels, then can be in one breast, how large soever. *Diseases*
themselves hold *Consultations*, and conspire how they may multiply,
and joyn with one another, & *exalt* one anothers force, so; and shal
we not call *Phisicians*, to *consultations*? *Death* is in an olde mans dore,
25 he appeares, and tels him so, & *death* is at a yong man's *backe*, and
saies nothing; *Age* is a *sicknesse*, and *Youth* is an *ambush*; and we need
so many *Phisicians*, as may make up a *Watch*, and spie every incon-
venience. There is scarce any thing, that hath not killed some body;
a *haire*, a *feather* hath done it; Nay, that which is our best *Antidote*
30 against it, hath donn it; the best *Cordiall* hath bene *deadly poyson*;
Men have dyed of *Joy*, and allmost forbidden their friends to weep

for them, when they have seen them dye laughing. Even that *Tiran Dyonisius* (I thinke the same, that suffered so much after) who could not die of that sorrow, of that high fal, from a *King* to a *wretched private man*, dyed of so poore a *Joy*, as to be declard by the *people* at a *Theater*, that hee was a good *Poet*. We say often that a *Man may* 5 *live of a litle*, but, alas, of how much lesse may a Man *dye*? And therfore the more assistants, the better; who comes to a day of hearing, in a caus of any importance, with one *Advocate*? In our *Funerals*, we our selves have no interest; there wee cannot *advise*, we cannot *direct*: And though some *Nations*, (the *Egiptians* in particular) built 10 themselves better *Tombs*, then *houses*, because they were to dwell *longer* in them; yet, amongst our selves, the greatest *Man of Stile*, whom we have had, *The Conqueror*, was left, as soone as his soule left him, not only without persons to assist at his *grave*, but without a *grave*. Who will keepe us then, we know not; As long as we can, let 15 us admit as much helpe as wee can; Another, and another *Phisician*, is not another, and another *Indication*, and *Symptom* of death, but another, and another *Assistant*, and *Proctor* of *life*: Nor doe they so much feed the imagination with apprehension of *danger*, as the understanding with *comfort*; Let not one bring *Learning*, another 20 *Diligence*, another *Religion*, but every one bring all, and, as many Ingredients enter into a Receit, so may many men make the Receit. But why doe I exercise my Meditation so long upon this, of having plentifull helpe in time of need? Is not my Meditation rather to be enclined another way, to condole, and commiserate their distresse, 25 who have *none*? How many are sicker (perchance) then I, and laid in their wofull straw at home (if that corner be a home) and have no more hope of helpe, though they die, then of preferment, though they live? Nor doe no more expect to see a *Phisician* then, then to bee an *Officer* after; of whome, the first that takes knowledge, is the 30 *Sexten* that buries them; who buries them in *oblivion* too? For they doe but fill up the number of the dead in the Bill, but we shall never heare their *Names*, till wee reade them in the Booke of life, with our owne. How many are sicker (perchance) then I, and thrown into *Hospitals*, where, (as a fish left upon the Sand, must stay the tide) 35

4 *Joy*, 1624(2), 1626: *Joy* 1624(1)   5 often] often, 1624(2), 1626   9 selves 1624(2), 1626: selfs 1624(1)   17 *Symptom*] *Symptone* 1626

they must stay the *Phisicians* houre of visiting, and then can bee but *visited*? How many are sicker (perchaunce) then all we, and have not this *Hospitall* to cover them, not this straw, to lie in, to die in, but have their *Grave-stone* under them, and breathe out their soules in
5 the eares, and in the eies of passengers, harder then their bed, the flint of the street? That taste of no part of our *Phisick*, but a *sparing dyet*; to whom ordinary porridge would bee *Julip* enough, the refuse of our servants, *Bezar* enough, and the off-scouring of our Kitchin tables, *Cordiall* enough. O my *soule*, when thou art not
10 enough awake, to blesse thy *God* enough for his plentifull mercy, in affoording thee many *Helpers*, remember how many lacke them, and helpe them to them, or to those other things, which they lacke as much as them.

7. EXPOSTULATION

15 *My God, my God*, thy blessed *Servant Augustine* begg'd of thee, that *Moses* might come, and tell him what hee meant by some places of *Genesis*: May I have leave to aske of that *Spirit*, that writ that Booke, why when *David* expected newes from *Joabs* armie, and that the Watchman tolde him, that *hee sawe a man running alone, David*   2 Sam. 18.25
20 concluded out of that circumstance, *That if hee came alone, hee brought good newes*? I see the *Grammar*, the word signifies so, and is so   *So al,* ever accepted, *Good newes*; but I see not the *Logique*, nor the   *but our*   *Translation* *Rhetorique*, how *David* would proove, or perswade that his newes   *take it.* was *good*, because hee was *alone*, except a greater company might   *Even Buxdor*
   & Schindler.
25 have made great impressions of danger, by imploring, and importuning present supplies. Howsoever that bee, I am sure, that that which thy *Apostle* sayes to *Timothy, Onely Luke is with me, Luke*, and   2.4.11 no body but *Luke*, hath a taste of complaint, & sorrow in it: Though *Luke* want no testimony of *abilitie*, of *forwardnes*, of *cons-*
30 *tancie, & perseverance*, in assisting that great building, which *S. Paul* laboured in, yet *S. Paul* is affected with that, that ther was none but *Luke*, to assist. We take *S. Luke* to have bin a *Phisician*, & it admits

7 *dyet*;] diet, 1624(2), 1626   *Margin* take S: takes all edd.   *Margin Buxdor* errata 1624(1), 1624(2), 1626: *Burcdorf* 1624(1)   27 *me*,] mee; 1626

37

the application the better, that in the presence of one good *Phisician*, we may bee glad of more. It was not only a civill spirit of policy, or order that moved *Moses* father in law, to perswade him to divide the burden of Government, & Judicature, with others, & take others to his assistance, but it was also thy immediat spirit *O my God*, that 5 mov'd *Moses* to present unto thee 70 *of the Elders of Israel*, to receive of that spirit, which was upon *Moses* onely before, such a portion as might ease him in the government of that people; though *Moses* alone had indowments above all, thou gavest him other assistants. I consider thy plentifull goodnesse, *O my God*, in employing *Angels*, 10 more then one, in so many of thy remarkable workes. Of thy *Sonne*, thou saist, *Let all the Angels of God worship him*; If that bee in *Heaven*, upon *Earth*, hee sayes *that hee could commaund twelve legions of Angels*; And when *Heaven*, and *Earth* shall bee all one, at the last day, *Thy Sonne, O God, the Son of Man, shall come in his glory, and all the* 15 *holy Angels with him*. The *Angels* that celebrated his birth to the *Shepheards*, the *Angels* that celebrated his second birth, his *Resurrection* to the *Maries*, were in the *plurall, Angells* associated with *Angels*. In *Jacobs* ladder, they which *ascended and descended*, & maintain'd the trade between *Heaven* and *Earth*, between thee and us, they who have 20 the Commission, and charge *to guide us in all our wayes*, they who hastned *Lot*, and in him, us, from places of danger, and tentation, they who are *appoynted to instruct & governe us in the Church heere*, they who are sent to *punish the disobedient and refractarie*, they that are to be the *Mowers*, and *harvest men*, after we are growne up in one 25 field, *the church*, at the day of *Judgment*, they that are to carrie our *soules* whither they caried *Lazarus*, they who attend at the several gates of the new *Jerusalem*, to admit us there; all these, who administer to thy servants, from the first, to their last, are *Angels, Angels* in the plurall, in every service, *Angels* associated with *Angells*. The 30 power of a single *Angell* wee see in that one, who in one night destroyed almost 200. thousand in *Sennacheribs* army, yet thou often imployest many; as we know the power of salvation is abundantly in any one *Evangelist*, and yet thou hast afforded us *foure*. Thy *Sonne* proclaimes of himselfe, *that thy Spirit, hath annoynted him to preach the* 35

Margin notes (left):
Exod. 18.14, 21, 22
Num. 11.16
Heb. 1.6
Mat. 26.53
Mat. 25.31
Luc. 2.11
Jo. 20.12
Gen. 28.12
Psa. 91.11
Gen. 19.15
Apo. 1.20
Apo. 8.2
Mat. 13.39
Luc. 16.22
Apoc. 21.12
2 Reg. 19.35
Luc. 4.18

Margin 18.14,21,22 *Ed.*: 18.13 all edd.   4 with others,] with others 1626   12
saist,] saist; 1626   *Margin* Mat. 25.31] Maa 25 31, 1624(2); Mar. 25 31. 1626
Margin 2.11 *Ed.*: 21.15 all edd.   *Margin* 91.11 *S*: 91.13 all edd.   22 danger,]
danger 1624(2), 1626   *Margin* Apoc. 21.12] Apo. 21.21 1626   *Margin* 2 Reg.
S: 1 Reg. all edd.   32 200. thousand] 200000. 1624(2), 1626

Gospell, yet he hath given others *for the perfiting of the Sts in the*   Eph. 4.12
worke of the Ministery. Thou hast made him *Bishop of our soules*, but   1 Pet. 2.25
there are other *Bishops* too. Hee gave the *holy Ghost*, & others gave   Jo. 20.22
it also. Thy way, *O my God*, (and, *O my God*, thou lovest to walk in
5 thine own waies, for they are large) thy way from the beginning, is
multiplication of thy helps; and therfore it were a degree of *ingratitude*,
not to accept this mercy of affording me many *helpes* for my bodily
health, as a *type* and *earnest* of thy gracious purpose now, and ever,
to affoord mee the same assistances. That for thy great *Helpe*, thy
10 *Word*, I may seeke that, not from *corners*, nor *Convenventicles*, nor
schismatical singularities, but from the assotiation, & communion of
thy *Catholique Church*, and those persons, whom thou hast alwayes
furnished that *Church* withall: And that I may associate thy *Word*,
with thy *Sacrament*, thy *Seale* with thy *Patent*; and in that *Sacrament*
15 associate *the signe* with the *thing signified*, the *Bread* with the *Body* of
thy *Sonne*, so, as I may be sure to have received both, and to bee
made thereby, (as thy blessed servant *Augustine* sayes) the *Arke*, and
the *Monument*, & the *Tombe* of thy most blessed *Sonne*, that *hee*, and
all the *merits* of his death, may, by that receiving, bee buried in me,
20 to my quickning in this world, and my immortall establishing in the
next.

7. PRAYER

O *eternall*, and *most gracious God*, who gavest to thy servants in the
wildernes, thy *Manna*, bread so conditiond, qualified so, as that, to
25 every man, *Manna tasted like that, which that man liked best*, I humbly
beseech thee, to make this correction, which I acknowledg to be part
of my *daily bread*, to tast so to me, not as I would but as thou wouldest
have it taste, and to conform my tast, and make it agreeable to thy
will. Thou wouldst have thy corrections tast of *humiliation*, but thou
30 wouldest have them tast of *consolation*, too; taste of *danger*, but tast of
assurance too. As therefore thou hast imprinted in all thine *Elements*,
of which our bodies consist, two manifest qualities, so that, as thy
fire *dries*, so it *heats* too; and as thy water *moysts*, so it *cooles* too, so, O

Margin 4.12 *Ed.*: 4:11 all edd.   3 other *Bishops* 1626: others *Bishops* 1624 (1&2)
13 I] it 1626   14 *Seale*] Seale, 1626   16 *Sonne*,] Son; 1626   20 establishing
in the] establishing the 1624(2), 1626

Lord, in these corrections, which are the *elements of our regeneration*, by which our *soules* are made thine, imprint thy two qualities, those two operations, that as they *scourge* us, they may scourge us into the way to thee: that when thy have shewed us, that we are nothing in our selves, they may also shew us, that thou art all things unto us. 5
When therfore in this particular circumstance, *O Lord* (but none of thy judgements are *circumstances*; they are all of the *substance* of thy good purpose upon us) when in this particular, that he, whom thou hast sent to assist me, desires *assistants* to him, thou hast let mee see, in how few houres thou canst throw me beyond the helpe of man, 10
let me by the same light see, that no vehemence of sicknes, no tentation of Satan, no guiltines of sin, no prison of death, not this first, this *sicke bed*, not the other prison, the close and dark *grave*, can remoove me from the determined, and good purpose, which thou hast sealed concerning mee. Let me think no degree of this thy 15
correction, *casuall*, or without *signification*; but yet when I have read it in that language, as it is a *correction*, let me translate it into another, and read it as a *mercy*; and which of these is the *Originall*, and which is the *Translation*, whether thy *Mercy*, or thy *Correction*, were thy primary, and original intention in this sicknes, I cannot conclude, 20
though death conclude me; for as it must necessarily appeare to bee a *correction*, so I can have no greater argument of thy *mercy*, then to die in *thee*, and by that death, to bee united to him, who died for me.

8. Et Rex ipse suum mittit.

The King sends his owne Phisician. 25

8. MEDITATION

Stil when we return to that Meditation, that *Man is a World*, we find new *discoveries*. Let him be a *world*, and him self will be the *land*, and *misery* the *sea*. His misery, (for misery is his, his own; of the happi-

7 of the *substance*] of all *substance* 1624(2), 1626   11 see,] see 1624(2), 1626   11
vehemence 1624(2), 1626: vehimence 1624(1)   14, 15 thou hast 1624(1) *errata*,
1624(2), 1626: thou 1624(1)   19 *Translation*,] *Translation*; 1624(2), 1626

nesses even of this world, hee is but *tenant*, but of misery the *free-holder*; of happines hee is but the *farmer*, but the *usufructuary*; but of misery, the *Lord*, the *proprietary*) his misery, as the *sea*, swells above all the hilles, and reaches to the remotest parts of this earth, *Man*;

5 who of himselfe is but *dust*, and coagulated and kneaded into earth, by *teares*; his *matter* is *earth*, his *forme*, *misery*. In this *world*, that is *Mankinde*, the highest ground, the eminentest *hils*, are *kings*; and have they line, and lead enough to fadome this *sea*, and say, My misery is but this deepe? Scarce any misery equals to *sicknesse*; and

10 they are subject to that equally, with their lowest subject. A glasse is not the lesse brittle, because a *Kings* face is represented in it; nor a King the lesse brittle, because *God* is represented in him. They have *Phisicians* continually about them, & therfore *sicknesses*, or the worst of sicknesses, continuall feare of it. Are they *gods*? He that

15 calld them so, cannot flatter. They are *Gods*, but *sicke gods*; and *God* is presented to us under many human affections, as far as *infirmities*; *God* is called *angry*, and *sorry*, and *weary*, and *heavy*; but never a *sicke God*: for then hee might *die* like men, as our *gods* do. The worst that they could say in reproch, & scorne of the *gods* of the *Heathen*,

20 was, that perchance they were *asleepe*; but *Gods* that are so sicke, as that they cannot sleepe, are in an infirmer condition. A *God*, and need a *Phisician*? A *Jupiter* & need an *Æsculapius*? that must have *Rheubarbe* to purge his *Choller*, lest he be too angry, and *Agarick* to purge his *flegme*, lest he be too drowsie; that as *Tertullian* saies of the

25 *Ægyptian gods*, *plants* and *herbes*, *That God was beholden to Man*, *for growing in his garden*, so wee must say of these *gods*, *Their eternity*, (an *eternity* of threescore & ten yeares) is in the *Apothecaryes* shop, and not in the *Metaphoricall Deity*. But their *Deitye* is better expressed in their *humility*, then in their *heighth*; when abounding and overflow-

30 ing, as *God*, in means of doing good, they descend, as *God*, to a communication of their abundances with men, according to their necessities, then they are *Gods*. No man is well, that understands not, that values not his being well; that hath not a cheerefulnesse, and a joy in it; and whosoever hath this *Joy*, hath a desire to communicate,

35 to propagate that, which occasions his happinesse, and his *Joy*, to

2 *usufructuary*; *A*: *usufructuary* 1624(1); *usufructuary*, 1624(2), 1626   5,6 earth, by *teares*; *S*: earth, by *teares*, 1624(1); earth; by teares, 1624(2), 1626   9 equals *Ed.*: equal all edd.   22 *Aesculapius S*, 1624(2), 1626: *Aesulapius* 1624(1)

others; for every man loves witnesses of his happinesse; and the best witnesses, are experimentall witnesses; they who have tasted of that in themselves, which makes us happie; It consummates therefore, it perfits the happinesse of *Kings*, to confer, to transfer, honor, and riches, and (as they can) health, upon those that need them.   5

8. EXPOSTULATION

Ecclus. 13.23

My God, my God, I have a warning from the *Wiseman, that when a rich man speaketh, every man holdeth his tongue, and looke what hee saith, they extoll it to the clouds; but if a poore man speake, they say, what fellowe is this? And if hee stumble, they will help to overthrow him.* 10 Therefore may my words be undervalued, and my errors aggravated, if I offer to speak of *Kings*; but not by thee, *O my God,* because I speak of them as they are in *thee,* & of *thee,* as thou art *in them.* Certainly those men prepare a way of speaking negligently, or irreverently of *thee,* that give themselves that liberty, in speaking of 15 thy *Vice-gerents, Kings*: for thou who gavest *Augustus* the *Empire,* gavest it to *Nero* to, and as *Vespasian* had it from thee, so had *Julian*; Though *Kings* deface in themselves thy first *image,* in their owne *soule,* thou givest no man leave to deface thy second *Image,* imprinted indelibly in their *power.* But thou knowest, *O God,* that if I should be 20 slacke in celebrating thy mercies to mee exhibited by that royall Instrument, my *Soveraigne,* to many other faults, that touch upon *Allegiance,* I should add the worst of all, *Ingratitude*; which constitutes an il man; & faults which are defects in any particular function, are not so great, as those that destroy our *humanitie*; It is not so ill, to bee 25 an ill *subject,* as to be an ill *man*; for he hath an universall illnesse, ready to flow, and powre out it selfe into any mold, any form, and to spend it selfe in any function. As therfore thy *Son* did upon the *Coyne,* I look upon the *King,* and I aske whose *image,* & whose *inscription* hee hath; and he hath *thine*; And I give unto thee, that 30 which is *thine,* I recommend his happines to thee, in all my sacrifices of thanks, for that which hee enjoyes, and in al my praiers, for the

Augustin

1 witnesses] witnesses; 1626   6 8. 1624(2), 1626: .8 1624(1)   8 *tongue,* 1624(2), 1626, *A: tong*; 1624(1)   13 them] them, 1624(2), 1626   *Margin* Augustin 1624(1) *errata:* Augustus, 1624(1); August. 1624(2), 1626   25 great,] great 1624(2), 1626   27 flow 1624(1) *errata,* 1624(2), 1626: blow 1624(1)

continuance and inlargement of them. But let me stop, *my God*, and consider; will not this look like a piece of art, & cunning, to convey into the world an opinion, that I were more particularly in his care, then other men? And that heerein, in a shew of *humilitie*, and
5 *thankefulnesse*, I magnifie my selfe more then there is cause? But let not that *jealousie* stopp mee, O God, but let me go forward in celebrating thy *mercy* exhibited by *him*. This which hee doth now, in assisting so my bodily health, I know is common to me with many; Many, many, have tasted of that expression of his graciousnes.
10 Where hee can give health by his owne hands, hee doth; and to more then any of his predecessors have done: Therefore hath *God* reserved one disease for him, that hee onely might cure it, though perchance not onely by one *Title*, and *Interest*, nor only as *one king*. To those that need it not, in that kind, and so cannot have it by his owne
15 hand, he sends a *donative* of *health*, in sending his *Phisician*. The holy *King S. Lewis in France*, & our *Maud* is celebrated for that, that personally they visited *Hospitals*, & assisted in the Cure, even of loathsome *Diseases*. And when that religious *Empress Placilla*, the wife of *Theodosius* was told, that she diminished her selfe to much in
20 those personal assistances, & might doe enough in sending reliefe, shee said, *Shee would send in that capacitie, as Empresse, but shee would go to, in that capacitie, as a Christian, as a fellow member of the body of thy Son, with them.* So thy servant *David* applies him selfe to his people, so he incorporates himselfe in his people, by calling them *his* | 2 Sam. 19.12
25 *brethern, his bones, his flesh*; and when they fel under thy hand, even to the pretermitting of himselfe, he presses upon thee, by prayer for them; *I have sinned, but these sheepe what have they donne? let thine* | 2 Sam. 24.17
hand I pray thee be against me and against my fathers house. It is kingly to *give*; when *Araunah* gave that great, & free present to *David*, that
30 place, those instruments for sacrifice, and *sacrifices* themselves, it is said there, by thy *Spirit, Al these things did Araunah give, as a King, to* | v. 23
the King. To *give* is an approaching to the Condition of *Kings*, but to give *health*, an approching to the *King*, of *Kings*, to *thee*. But this his assisting to my bodily health, thou knowest O God, and so doe
35 some others of thine *Honorable servants* know, is but the twi-light, of

8 many; *A*: many? all edd.   9 many,] many 1624(2), 1626   9 graciousnes 1624(2), 1626: gracionsnes 1624(1)   *Margin* 24.17 *S*: 24.14 all edd.   29 and 31 *Araunah A, S: Araumah* all edd.   *Margin v.* 23 : *Ed.: v.* 17 all edd.   34 knowest] knowest, 1624(2), 1626

that day, wherein thou, thorow him, hast shind upon mee before;
but the *Eccho* of that voice, whereby thou, through him, hast spoke
to mee before; Then, when he, first of any man conceiv'd a hope,
that I might be of some use in thy *Church*, and descended to an
intimation, to a perswasion, almost to a solicitation, that I would 5
embrace that calling. And thou who hadst put that desire into his
heart, didst also put into mine, an obedience to it; and I who was
sicke before, of a vertiginous giddines, and irresolution, and almost
spent all my time in consulting how I should spend it, was by this
man of God, and *God of men*, put into the poole, and recoverd: when 10
I asked, perchance, a *stone*, he gave me *bread*, when I asked, perchance, a *Scorpion*, he gave me a *fish*; when I asked a temporall
office, hee denied not, refused not that, but let mee see, that hee had
rather I took this. These things, thou O *God*, who forgettest nothing,
hast not forgot, though perchance, he, because they were benefits, 15
2 Chro. 19.8   hath; but I am not only a *witnesse*, but an *instance*, that our *Jehosophat*
hath a care to ordaine *Priests*, as well as *Judges*: and not only to send
Phisicians for *temporall*, but to bee the *Phisician* for *spirituall* health.

8. PRAYER

O eternall and most gracious *God*, who though thou have reserved 20
thy tresure of perfit joy, and perfit glory, to be given by thine own
hands then, when by seeing thee, as thou art in thy selfe, and knowing
thee, as we are known, wee shall possesse in an instant, and possesse
for ever, all that can any way conduce to our happinesses, yet here
also in this world, givest us such *earnests* of that full payment, as by 25
the value of the *earnest*, we may give some estimat of the tresure,
humbly, and thankfully I acknowledge, that thy blessed *spirit* instructs mee, to make a difference of thy blessings in this world, by that
difference of the *Instruments*, by which it hath pleased thee to derive
them unto me. As we see thee heere in a *glasse*, so we receive from 30
thee here by *reflexion*, & by *instruments*. Even *causal things* come from
thee; and that which we call *Fortune* here, hath another *name* above.

1 thou,] thou 1626   2 thou,] thou 1626   *Margin* 2 Chro. 19.8 *S*: 2 Chro.
14.8 1624(1); 2 Chor. 14.8 1624(2), 1626

Nature reaches out her hand, and gives us corne, and wine, and oyle, and milk, but thou fillest her hand before, and thou openest her hand, that she may rain down her showres upon us. *Industry* reaches out her hand to us, and gives us fruits of our labor, for our selves, &
5 our posteritie; but thy hand guides that hand, when it *sowes*, and when it *waters*, and the *increase* is from thee. *Friends* reach out their hands, & prefer us, but thy hand supports that hand, that supports us. Of all these thy *instruments* have I received thy blessing, *O God*, but bless thy name most for the greatest; that as a member of the
10 publike, and as a partaker of private favours too, by thy right hand, thy powerfull hand set over us, I have had my portion, not only in the hearing, but in the *preaching of thy Gospel.* Humbly beseeching thee, that as thou continuest thy wonted goodnes upon the whol world, by the wonted meanes, & instruments, the same *Sun*, and
15 *Moon*, the same *Nature*, and *Industry*, so to continue the same blessings upon this *State*, and this *Church* by the same hand, so long, as that thy *Son* when he comes in the *clouds*, may find *him*, or his *Son*, or his *sonnes sonnes* ready to give an account, & able to stand in that *judgment*, for their faithfull *Stewardship*, and *dispensation* of thy *talents*
20 so abundantly committed to them; & be to him, *O God*, in all distempers of his body, in all anxieties of *spirit*, in all holy *sadnesses of soule*, such a *Phisician* in thy proportion, who art the greatest in *heaven*, as hee hath bin in *soule*, & *body* to me, in his proportion, who is the greatst upon earth.

25

9. Medicamina scribunt.

Upon their Consultation, they prescribe.

9. MEDITATION

They have seene me, and heard mee, arraign'd mee in these fetters, and receiv'd the *evidence*; I have cut up mine own *Anatomy*, dissected

---

4 labor,] labour 1624(2), 1626   20 them;] them, 1624(2), 1626   23 proportion,] proportion 1624(2), 1626

myselfe, and they are gon to *read* upon me. O how manifold, and perplexed a thin, nay, how wanton and various a thing is *ruine* and *destruction*? *God* presented to *David* three kinds, *War*, *Famine*, and *Pestilence*; *Satan* left out these, and brought in, *fires from heaven*, and *windes from the wildernes*. If there were no *ruine* but *sicknes*, wee see, 5 the Masters of that *Art* can scarce *number*, nor *name* all sicknesses; every thing that *disorders* a faculty, & the function of that is a sicknesse: The names wil not serve them which are given from the *place affected*, the *Plurisie* is so; nor from the *effect* which it works, the *falling sicknes* is so; they cannot have names ynow, from *what it does*, 10 nor *where it is*, but they must extort names from what *it is like*, what it *resembles*, & but in some one thing, or els they would lack names; for the *Wolf*, and the *Canker*, and the *Polypus* are so; and that question, *whether there be more names or things*, is as perplexed in sicknesses, as in any thing else; except it be easily resolved upon that 15 side, that there are more *sicknesses* then *names*. If *ruine* were reduc'd to that one way, that Man could perish no way but by *sicknes*, yet his danger were infinit; and if *sicknes* were reduc'd to that one way, that there were no *sicknes* but a *fever*, yet the way were infinite still; for it would overlode, & oppress any naturall, disorder and discom- 20 pose any artificiall *Memory*, to deliver the *names* of severall *Fevers*; how intricate a worke then have they, who are gone to *consult*, which of these *sicknesses* mine is, and then which of these *fevers*, and then what it would do, and then how it may be countermind. But even in *ill*, it is a degree of *good*, when the *evil* wil admit *consultation*. 25 In many *diseases*, that which is but an *accident*, but a *symptom* of the main *disease*, is so violent, that the *phisician* must attend the cure of that, though hee pretermit (so far as to intermit) the cure of the *disease* it self. Is it not so in *States* too? somtimes the insolency of those that are *great*, puts the people into *commotion*; the great 30 disease, & the greatest danger to the *Head*, is the *insolency of the great ones*; & yet they execute *Martial law*, they come to present executions upon the *people*, whose commotion was indeed but a *simptom*, but an *accident* of the maine *disease*; but this *symptom*, grown so violent, wold allow no time for a *consultation*. Is it not so in the 35

6 nor 1626, *S*: not 1624(1&2)   30 puts *S*: put all edd.   30 *commotion* Ed.: *commotions* all edd.

accidents of the *diseases* of our *mind* too? Is it not evidently so in our *affections*, in our *passions*? If a *cholerick* man be ready to strike, must I goe about to purge his *choler*, or to breake the blow? But where there is room for *consultation*, things are not desperate. They *consult*;
5 so there is nothing *rashly, inconsideratly* done; and then they *prescribe*, they *write*, so there is nothing *covertly, disguisedly, unavowedly* done. In *bodily diseases* it is not alwaies so; sometimes, assoon as the *Phisicians* foote is in the chamber, his *knife* is in the patients arme; the *disease* would not allow a *minutes* forbearing of *blood*, nor prescribing
10 of other remedies. In States & matter of government it is so too; they are somtimes surprizd with such *accidents*, as that the *Magistrat* asks not what may be done by *law*, but does that, which must necessarily be don in that case. But it is a degree of *good*, in *evill*, a degree that caries hope & comfort in it, when we may have recourse
15 to that which is *written*, and that the proceedings may bee apert, and ingenuous, and candid, and avowable, for that gives satisfaction, and acquiescence. They who have received my *Anatomy* of my selfe, *consult*, and end their *consultation* in *prescribing*, and in prescribing *Phisick*, proper and convenient remedy: for if they shold come in
20 again, and chide mee, for some disorder, that had occasion'd, and inducd, or that had hastned and exalted this *sicknes*, or if they should begin to write now rules for my *dyet*, and *exercise* when I were well, this were to *antidate*, or to *postdate* their *Consultation*, not to give *phisick*. It were rather a vexation, then a reliefe, to tell a condemnd
25 prisoner, you might have liv'd if you had done this; & if you can get your pardon, you shal do wel, to take this, or this course hereafter. I am glad they know (I have hid nothing from them) glad they consult, (they hide nothing from one another) glad they write (they hide nothing from the world) glad that they write and prescribe
30 *Phisick*, that there are *remedies* for the present case.

9. EXPOSTULATION

My *God*, my *God*, allow me a just indignation, a holy detestation of the insolency of that Man, who because he was of that high ranke,

5 done;] done: 1626   10 too;] too, 1626   15 apert,] apert 1624(2), 1626
19 *Phisick, A: Phisick*; all edd.   33 was of] was of, 1626

of whom thou hast said, *They are gods*, thought himselfe more then equall to thee; That *king of Aragon Alfonsus*, so perfit in the motions of the heavenly bodies, as that hee adventured to say, That *if he had bin of councell with thee, in the making of the heavens, the heavens should have bin disposed in a better order, then they are.* The king *Amasiah* would 5 not indure thy *prophet* to reprehend him, but asked him in anger, *Art thou made of the kings councell*? When thy Prophet *Esaias* askes that question, *who hath directed the spirit of the Lord, or being his councellor hath tought him*, It is after hee had setled and determined that office, upon thy *sonne*, and him *onely*, when he joyns with those 10 great *Titles, The mighty God*, and the *prince of peace*, this also, *the Councellor*; and after he had setled upon him, *the spirit of might, and of councell*. So that then, thou O God, thogh thou have no *councell* from Man, yet doest nothing upon man, without *councell*; In the making of Man there was a *consultation*; *let us make man*. In the 15 preserving of Man, *O thou great preserver of men*, thou proceedest by *councell*; for all thy *externall* workes, are the workes of the whole *Trinity*, and their hand is to every action. How much more must I apprehend, that al you blessed, & glorious persons of the *Trinitie* are in *Consultation* now, what you wil do with this infirm *body*, with 20 this leprous *Soule*, that attends guiltily, but yet comfortably, your determination upon it. I offer not to counsell them, who meet in *consultation* for my *body* now, but I open my infirmities, I anatomise my *body* to them. So I do my *soule* to thee, O my *God*, in an humble confession, That there is no *veine* in mee, that is not full of the bloud 25 of thy *Son*, whom I have crucified, & Crucified againe, by multi-plying many, and often repeating the same sinnes: that there is no *Artery* in me, that hath not the *spirit of error, the spirit of lust, the spirit of giddines* in it; no *bone* in me that is not hardned with the custome of *sin*, and nourished, and soupled with the *marrow of sinn*; 30 no *sinews*, no *ligaments*, that do not tie, & chain sin and sin together. Yet, *O blessed and glorious Trinity, O holy, & whole Colledge*, and yet but one *Phisician*, if you take this confession into a *consultation*, my case is not desperate, my destruction is not *decreed*; If your *consultation* determin in *writing*, if you refer mee to that which is *written*, you 35

· 2 Chro.
25.16
Esa. 40.13

9.6

11.2

Gen. 1.26
Job. 7.20

1 Tim. 4.1
Ose. 4.12
Esa. 19.14

4 *the heavens* S, 1624(1) O⁹, P *corrected*, 1624(2), 1626: *the the heavens* 1624(1) *originally*   8 question, 1624(2), 1626: question 1624(1)   *Margin* Esa. 40.13 S: 42.13 all edd.   9 *him, Ed.*: *him.* all edd.   *Margin* Job 7.20 *Ed.*: Job. all edd.; 1624(1) St.A *missing*   16 proceedest 1624(1) St.A, 1624(2), 1626: proceededst 1624(1)   24 *God,*] God 1624(2), 1626

intend my recovery: for al the way, *O my God*, (ever constant to thine owne wayes) thou hast proceeded *openly, intelligibly, manifestly, by the book.* From thy first *book*, the book of *life,* never shut to thee, but never throughly open to us; from thy second *book*, the *booke* of
5 *Nature,* wher though subobscurely, and in shadows, thou hast expressed thine own *Image*; from thy third *booke*; the *Scriptures*, where thou hadst written all in the *Old*, and then lightedst us a candle to read it by, in the *New Testament*; To these thou hadst added the *booke* of just, and usefull *Lawes*, established by them, to
10 whom thou hast committed thy people; To those, the *Manualls*, the *pocket*, the *bosome books* of our own *Consciences;* To those thy particular *books* of all our particular sins; and to those, the *Booke* with *seven seales*, which only *the Lamb which was slaine, was found worthy to open*; which, I hope, it shall not disagree with the meaning of my
15 blessed *Spirit*, to interprete, the *promulgation of their pardon, and righteousnes, who are washed in the blood of that Lambe*; And if thou refer me to these *Bookes*, to a new reading, a new triall by these *bookes*, this *fever* may be but a burning in the hand, and I may be saved, thogh not by my book, mine own *conscience*, nor by thy
20 other *books*, yet by thy *first*, the book of *life*, thy *decree for my election*, and by thy *last*, the book of the *Lamb*, and the shedding of his blood upon me; If I be stil under *consultation*, I am not condemned yet; if I be sent to these books I shall not be condem'd at all: for, though there be somthing written in some of those *books* (particularly in the
25 *Scripturs*) which some men turne to *poyson*, yet upon these *consultations* (these *confessions*, these takings of our particular cases, into thy consideration) thou intendest all for *phisick*, & even from those *Sentences*, from which a too-late *Repenter* will sucke *desperation*, he that seeks thee early, shall receive thy *morning dew*, thy seasonable
30 *mercy*, thy forward *consolation*.

Apoc. 5.9

9. PRAYER

O eternall and most gracious *God*, who art so pure *eyes*, as that thou canst not look upon *sinn*, and we of so unpure constitutions, as that

11 *Consciences*; *S*: *Consciences*, all edd.   11,12 particular *Ed.*: partcular all edd.
12 sins;] sins, 1624(2), 1626   *Margin* 5.9 *Ed.*: 7.1 all edd.

wee can present no object but *sin*, and therfore might justly feare, that thou wouldst turn thine *eyes* for ever from us, as, though we cannot indure *afflictions* in our selves, yet in *thee* we can; so thogh thou canst not indure *sinne* in us, yet in thy *Sonn* thou canst, and he hath taken upon him selfe, and presented to thee, al those *sins*, which 5 might displease thee in us. There is an *Eye* in *Nature*, that kills, assoon as it sees, the eye of a *Serpent*, no eye in *Nature*, that *nourishes* us by looking upon us; But thine *Eye, O Lord*, does so. Looke therefore upon me, *O Lord*, in this distresse, and that will recall mee from the borders of this bodily death; Look upon me, and that wil raise 10 me again from that *spirituall death*, in which my parents buried me, when they begot mee in *sinne*, and in which I have pierced even to the lawes of *hell*, by multiplying such heaps of actuall sins, upon that foundation, that root of *originall sinn*. Yet take me again, into your *Consultation, O blessed* and *glorious Trinitie*; & thogh the *Father* 15 know, that I have defaced his *Image* received in my *Creation*; though the *Son* know, I have neglected mine interest in the *Redemption*, yet, *O blessed spirit*, as thou art to my *Conscience*, so be to them a witnes, that at this *minute*, I accept that which I have so often, so often, so rebelliously refused, thy blessed inspirations; be thou my witnes to 20 them, that at more poores then this slacke body sweates teares, this sad soule weeps blood; and more for the *displeasure* of my *God*, then for the stripes of his displeasure. Take me then, *O blessed, & glorious Trinitie*, into a *Reconsultation*, and prescribe me any *phisick*; If it bee a long, & painful holding of this *soule* in *sicknes*, it is *phisick*, if I may 25 discern thy hand to give it, & it is *phisick*, if it be a speedy departing of this *Soule*, if I may discerne thy hand to receive it.

10 bodily] dodily 1624(2)   13 sins,] sins 1624(2), 1626   18 *spirit*,] *spirit*; 1624(2), 1626   23 *blessed*,] *blessed* 1626

10. Lentè & Serpenti satagunt occurrere Morbo.

*They find the Disease to steale on insensibly, and endeavour
to meet with it so.*

10. MEDITATION

5 This is *Natures nest of Boxes*; The *Heavens* containe the *Earth*, the
Earth, Cities, Cities, Men. And all these are *Concentrique*; the common
center to them all, is *decay, ruine*; only that is *Eccentrique*, which was
never made; only that place, or garment rather, which we can
imagine, but not *demonstrate*, That light, which is the very emanation
10 of the light of *God*, in which the *Saints* shall dwell, with which the
Saints shall be appareld, only that bends not to this *Center*, to *Ruine*;
that which was not made of *Nothing*, is not threatned with this
annihilation. All other things are; even *Angels*, even our *soules*; they
move upon the same *poles*, they bend to the same *Center*; and if they
15 were not made immortall by *preservation*, their *Nature* could not
keepe them from sinking to this *center, Annihilation*. In all these (the
frame of the heavens, the *States upon earth*, & *Men in them*, comprehend
all) Those are the greatest mischifs, which are least discerned; the
most insensible in their *wayes* come to bee the most sensible in their
20 *ends*. The *Heavens* have had their *Dropsie*, they drownd the world,
and they shall have their *Fever*, and burn the world. Of the *dropsie*,
the flood, the world had a foreknowledge 120 yeares before it came;
and so some made provision against it, and were saved; the *fever*
shall break out in an instant, & consume all; The *dropsie* did no
25 harm to the *heavens*, from whence it fell, it did not put out those
lights, it did not quench those *heates*; but the *fever*, the fire shall burne
the *furnace* it selfe, annihilate those *heavens*, that breath it out; Though
the *Dog-Starre* have a pestilent breath, an infectious exhalation, yet
because we know when it wil rise, we clothe our selves, & wee diet
30 our selves, and wee shadow our selves to a sufficient prevention; but
Comets and *blazing starres*, whose effects or significations, no man can

17 *heavens*,] heavens 1624(1), 1626   31 effects or significations, *Ed.*: effects, or
significations 1624(1); effects or significations 1624(2), 1626

interrupt or frustrat, no man foresaw: no *Almanack* tells us, when a *blazing starre* will break out, the matter is carried up in secret; no *Astrologer* tels us when the effects wil be accomplished, for thats a secret of a higher spheare, then the other; and that which is most *secret*, is most *dangerous*. It is so also here in the *societies* of men, in 5 *States*, & *Commonwealths*. Twentie *rebellious drums* make not so dangerous a noise, as a few *whisperers*, and secret plotters in corners. The *Canon* doth not so much hurt against a wal, as a *Myne* under the wall; nor a thousand enemies that threaten, so much as a few that take an oath to say nothing. *God* knew many heavy sins of the people, in 10 the wildernes and after, but still he charges them with that one, with *Murmuring, murmuring* in their *hearts*, secret disobediences, secret repugnances against his declar'd wil; and these are the most deadly, the most pernicious. And it is so to, with the *diseases* of the *body*; and that is my case. The *pulse*, the *urine*, the *sweat*, all have sworn to say 15 *nothing*, to give no *Indication* of any dangerous *sicknesse*. My forces are not enfeebled, I find no decay in my strength; my provisions are not cut off, I find no abhorring in mine appetite; my counsels are not corrupted nor infatuated, I find no false apprehensions, to work upon mine understanding; and yet they see, that invisibly, & I feele, 20 that insensibly the *disease* prevails. The *disease* hath established a *Kingdome*, an *Empire* in mee, and will have certaine *Arcana Imperii*, *secrets of State*, by which it will proceed, & not be bound to *declare* them. But yet against those secret conspiracies in the State, the *Magistrate* hath the *rack*; and against these insensible diseases, 25 *Phisicians* have their *examiners*; and those these imploy now.

10. EXPOSTULATION

My God, my God, I have bin told, and told by relation, by her own *brother*, that did it, by thy servant *Nazianzen*, that his *Sister* in the vehemency of her *prayer*, did use to *threaten thee, with holy impor-* 30 *tunitie, with a pious impudencie*. I dare not doe so, O *God*; but as thy servant *Augustin*, wisht *that Adam had not sinned, therefore that Christ*

14 pernicious.] pernicious 1626

52

might not have died, may I not to this one purpose wish, That if the
Serpent before the tentation of *Eve*, did *goe upright*, and *speake*, that   Josephus
he did so still, because I should the sooner heare him, if he *spoke*, the
sooner see him, if he *went upright*? In his curse, I am cursed too; his
5 *creeping* undoes mee: for howsoever hee begin at the *heele*, and doe
but *bruise* that, yet *he, and Death in him is come into our windowes*; into   Jere. 9.21
our *Eyes*, and *Eares*, the entrances, & inlets of our *soule*. He works
upon us in secret, & we doe not discerne him; And one great work
of his upon us, is to make us so like himselfe, as to sin in *secret*, that
10 others may not see us; But his *Master-piece* is, to make us sin in
secret so, as that we may not see our selvs sin. For the first, the hiding
of our sins from other men, hee hath induc'd that, which was his
off-spring from the beginning, *A lye*: for man, is in Nature, yet, in   Jo. 8.44
possession of some such sparkes of *ingenuitie*, & *noblenesse*, as that,
15 but to disguise *Evill*, hee would not *lye*. The *bodie*, the *sinne*, is the
Serpents, and the *garment* that covers it, *the lye*, is his too. These are
his; but the hiding of sinne from our selves, is *Hee himselfe*: when we
have the sting of the *Serpent* in us, and doe not sting our selves, the
venim of sin, and no remorse for sinn, then, as thy blessed Sonne said
20 of *Judas*, *Hee is a devill*, not that he *had* one, but *was* one, so we are   Joh. 6.70
become *devils* to our selves, and we have not only a *Serpent* in our
bosome, but we our selves, are to our selves that *Serpent*. How farre
did thy servant *David* presse upon thy pardon, in that petition,
Clense thou me from secret sinns? can any sin bee secret? for, a great   Ps. 19.12
25 part of our sinnes, though, sayes thy *Prophet*, *we conceive them in the
darke, upon our bed*, yet sayes he, *We doe them in the light*; there are
many sins, which we *glorie* in doing, and would not doe, if no body
should know them. Thy blessed servant *August.* confesses, that hee
was *ashamed of his shamefastnes, and tendernesse of Conscience*, and *that*
30 *he often belied himself with sinnes, which he never did, lest he should be
unacceptable to his sinfull companions*. But if we would conceale them,
(thy *Prophet* found such a desire, and such a practise in some, when
he said, *Thou hast trusted in thy wickednes, and thou hast sayd, None*   Esay 47.10
shall see me) yet can we conceale them? Thou O *God*, canst heare of
35 them by others; *The voice of Abels blood*, will tell thee of *Cains*   Gen. 4.10

6 that, *Ed.*: that; all edd.   17 *his*;] his, 1626   19 sin,] sin 1626   24 for,]
for 1624(2), 1626   33 *wickednes* 1624(2), 1626: *wicked-kednes* 1624(1)

murder; the *Heavens* themselves will tell thee, *Heaven shal reveale his iniquity*; a smal creature alone, shall doe it, *A bird of the ayre shall carry the voice, and tell the matter*: Thou wilt trouble no *Informer*, thou thy selfe revealedst *Adams* sin, to thy selfe; And the manifestation of sin is so ful to thee, as that *thou shalt reveale all to all, Thou shalt bring every 5 worke to Judgement, with every secret thing, and there is nothing covered, that shall not bee revealed*: But, *O my God*, there is another way of knowing my sins, which thou lovest better then any of these; To know them by my *Confession*. As *Phisicke* works so, it drawes the *peccant humour* to it selfe, that when it is gathered together, the 10 weight of it selfe may carry that humour away, so thy *Spirit* returns to my *Memory* my former sinnes, that being so recollected, they may powre out themselves by *Confession*. *When I kept silence*, sayes thy servant *David, day, and night, thy hand was heavy upon mee*, But when I said, *I wil confesse my transgressions unto the Lord, thou forgavest the* 15 *iniquitie of my sinne*. Thou interpretest the very *purpose* of *Confession* so well, as that thou scarce leavest any *new Mercy* for the *action* it selfe. This *Mercy* thou leavest, that thou armest us thereupon, against *relapses* into the sinnes which wee have confessed. And that *mercy*, which thy servant *Augustine* apprehends, when he sayes to 20 thee, *Thou hast forgiven me those sinnes which I have done, and those sinnes which only by thy grace I have not done*: they were done in our *inclination* to them, and even that *inclination* needs thy *mercy*, and that *Mercy* he calls a *Pardon*. And these are most truly *secret* sinnes, because they were never done, and because no other man, nor I my selfe, but 25 onely thou knowest, how many and how great sinnes I have scaped by thy grace, which without that, I should have multiplied against thee.

Marginalia:
Job. 20.27
Eccle. 10.20
Gen. 3.8
Eccles. 12.14
Mat. 10.26
Psa. 32.3, 4
v. 5

10. PRAYER

O eternall, and most gracious *God*, who as thy *Sonne Christ Jesus*, though hee knew all things, yet said *hee knew not the day of Judgement*, 30 because he knew it not so, as that he might tell it us; so though thou knowest all my sins, yet thou knowest them not to my *comfort*,

1 thee, 1624(2), 1626: thee 1624(1)   *Margin* Job. *S*: Jer. all edd.   *Margin* 32.3,4 *S*: 32.34 all edd.   14 *night*,] *night* 1624(2), 1626   14 *mee*,] *me*; 1624(2), 1626   *Margin v.* 5 *S*: 8.5 all edd.

except thou know them by my telling them to thee; how shall I bring to thy knowledg by that way, those sinns, which I my selfe know not? If I accuse my selfe of *Originall sin*, wilt thou ask me if I know what *originall sin is*? I know not enough of it to satisfie others, 5 but I know enough to condemne my self, & to solicit thee. If I confesse to thee the *sinnes* of my *youth*, wilt thou aske me, if I know what those sins were? I know them not so well, as to name them all, nor am sure to live houres enough to name them al, (for I did them then, faster then I can speak them now, when every thing that I did, 10 conduc'd to some sinne) but I know them so well, as to know, that nothing but thy mercy is so *infinite* as they. If the naming of Sinnes, of *Thought*, *Word*, and *Deed*, of sinns of *Omission*, and of *Action*, of sins against *thee*, against my *neighbour*, and against *my self*, of sinns *unrepented*, and sinnes *relapsed* into after *Repentance*, of sinnes of 15 *Ignorance*, and sinnes against the testimonie of my *Conscience*, of sinnes against thy *Commaundements*, sinnes against thy *Sonnes Prayer*, and sinns against our owne *Creed*, of sins against the laws of that *Church*, & sinnes against the lawes of that *State*, in which thou hast given mee my station, If the naming of these *sinnes* reach not home 20 to all mine, I know what will; *O Lord* pardon me, me, all those *sinnes*, which thy *Sonne Christ Jesus* suffered for, who suffered for all the sinnes of all the world; for there is no sinne amongst all those which had not been my sinne, if thou hadst not beene my *God*, and *antidated* me a pardon in thy *preventing grace*. And since sinne in the 25 nature of it, retaines still so much of the author of it, that it is a *Serpent*, insensibly insinuating it selfe, into my *Soule*, let thy *brazen Serpent*, (the contemplation of thy *Sonne* crucified for me) be evermore present to me, for my recovery against the sting of the first *Serpent*; That so, as I have a *Lyon* against a *Lyon*, *The Lyon of the* 30 *Tribe of Judah*, against that *Lyon, that seekes whom hee may devoure*, so I may have a *Serpent* against a *Serpent*, the *Wisedome of the Serpent*, against the *Malice of the Serpent*, And, both against that *Lyon*, and *Serpent*, forcible, and subtill tentations, Thy *Dove* with thy *Olive*, in thy *Arke*, *Humilitie*, and *Peace*, and *Reconciliation* to thee, by the 35 ordinances of thy *Church*. *Amen*.

1 thee; *Ed.*: thee, all edd.   19 station,] station. 1626   26 selfe,] self 1624(2), 1626   27 *Serpent*,] Serpent 1624(2), 1626

11. Nobilibusque trahunt, a cincto Corde, venenum, Succis & Gemmis, & quae generosa, Ministrant, Ars, et Natura, instillant.

They use Cordials, to keep the venim and
Malignitie of the disease from the Heart.   5

11. MEDITATION

Whence can wee take a better argument, a clearer demonstration, that all the *Greatnes* of this world, is built upon *opinion* of others, and hath in it self no *reall being*, nor power of subsistence, then from the *heart of man*? It is alwayes in *Action*, and *motion*, still busie, still 10 pretending to doe all, to furnish all the powers, and faculties with all that they have; But if an enemy dare rise up against it, it is the soonest endangered, the soonest defeated of any part. The *Braine* will hold out longer then it, and the *Liver* longer then that; They will endure a *Siege*; but an unnatural heat, a rebellious heat, will blow up the 15 *heart*, like a *Myne*, in a *minute*. But howsoever, since the *Heart* hath the *birth-right*, and *Primogeniture*, and that it is *Natures eldest Sonne* in us, the part which is first borne to life in man, and that the other parts, as *younger brethren*, and servants in this family, have a dependance upon it, it is reason that the principall care bee had of it, though 20 it bee not the strongest part; as the *eldest* is oftentimes not the strongest of the family. And since the *Braine*, and *Liver*, and *Heart*, hold not a *Triumvirate in Man*, a *Soveraigntie* equally shed upon them all, for his *well-being*, as the foure *Elements* doe, for his very *being*, but the *Heart* alone is in the *Principalitie*, and in the *Throne*, as *King*, the 25 rest as *Subjects*, though in eminent *Place*, and *Office*, must contribute to that, as *Children* to their *Parents*, as all persons to all kindes of *Superiours*, though oftentimes, those *Parents*, or those *Superiours*, bee not of stronger parts, then themselves, that serve and obey them that are weaker; Neither doth this Obligation fall upon us, by second 30 *Dictates* of *Nature*, by *Consequences*, and *Conclusions* arising out of

2 Ministrant, 1624(1) O, L³, O¹², C, GK(1): Ministrant 1624(1 & 2), 1626   8
others,] others; 1626   19 this] his 1624(2), 1626   24 doe,] do 1624(2), 1626
26 *Office,*] *Office*; 1626

Nature, or deriv'd from Nature, by *Discourse*, (as many things binde us, even by the Law of *Nature*, and yet not by the *primarie* Law of *Nature*; as all Lawes of *Proprietie* in that which we possesse, are of the Law of *Nature*, which law is, *To give every one his owne*, and yet in
5 the *primarie* law of Nature, there was no *Proprietie*, no *Meum & Tuum*, but an universall *Communitie* over all; So the obedience of *Superiours*, is of the law of *Nature*, and yet in the *primarie* law of *Nature*, there was no *Superioritie*, no *Magistracie*;) but this contribution of assistance of all to the *Soveraigne*, of all parts to the *Heart*, is
10 from the very *first dictates of Nature*; which is in the first place, to have care of our owne *Preservation*, to looke first to our selves; for therefore doth the *Phisician* intermit the present care of *Braine*, or *Liver*, because there is a possibilitie, that they may subsist, though there bee not a present and a particular care had of them, but there is
15 no possibilitie that they can subsist, if the *Heart* perish: and so, when we seeme to begin with others, in such assistances, indeed wee doe beginne with our selves, and wee our selves are principally in our contemplation; and so all these officious, and mutuall assistances, are but *complements* towards others, and our true end is *our selves*. And
20 this is the reward of the paines of *Kings*; sometimes they neede the power of law, to be obeyd; and when they seeme to be obey'd *voluntarily*, they who doe it, doe it for their owne sakes. O how little a thing is all the *greatnes of man*, and through how false glasses doth he make shift to *multiply it*, and *magnifie* it to himselfe? And yet this
25 is also another misery of this *King of man*, the *Heart*, which is also applyable to the *Kings* of this world, *great men*, that the venime & poyson of every pestilentiall disease directs it selfe to the *heart*, affects that, (pernicious affection,) and the *malignity* of ill men, is also directed upon the *greatest*, and the *best*; and not only *greatnesse*, but
30 *goodnesse* looses the vigour of beeing an *Antidote*, or *Cordiall* against it. And as the noblest, and most generous *Cordialls* that *Nature* or *Art* afford, or can prepare, if they be often taken, and made *familiar*, become no *Cordialls*, nor have any extraordinary operation, so the greatest *Cordiall* of the *Heart*, patience, if it bee much exercis'd,
35 exalts the *venim* and the *malignity* of the *Enemy*, and the more we

15 so,] so 1624(2), 1626   16 others,] others; 1626   21 law,] law 1624(2), 1626

suffer, the more wee are insulted upon. When *God* had made this *Earth* of *nothing*, it was but a little helpe, that he had, to make other things of this *Earth*: nothing can be neerer nothing, then this *Earth*; and yet how little of this *Earth*, is the *greatest Man*? Hee thinkes he treads upon the *Earth*, that all is under his feete, and the *Braine* that 5 thinkes so, is but *Earth*; his highest Region, the flesh that covers that, is but *earth*; and even the toppe of that, that, wherein so many *Absolons* take so much pride, is but a bush growing upon that *Turfe of Earth*. How litle of the world is the *Earth*? And yet that is all, that *Man hath*, or *is*. How little of a *Man* is the *Heart*; and yet it is all, by 10 which he *is*: and this continually subject, not onely to forraine poysons, conveyed by others, but to intestine poysons bred in our selves by pestilentiall sicknesses. O who, if before hee had a beeing, he could have sense of this miserie, would buy a being here upon these conditions? 15

II. EXPOSTULATION

My *God*, my *God*, all that thou askest of mee, is my *Heart*, *My Sonne, give mee thy heart*; Am I thy *sonne*, as long as I have but *my heart*? Wilt thou give mee an *Inheritance*, a *Filiation*, any thing for *my heart*? O thou, who saydst to Satan, *Hast thou considered my servant Job, that* 20 *there is none like him upon earth*, shall my feare, shall my zeale, shall my jealousie have leave to say to thee, Hast thou considered *my Heart*, that there is not so perverse a *Heart* upon earth; and wouldest thou have *that*; and shall I be thy *Sonne*, thy eternall Sonnes *Coheire*, for giving that? *The Heart is deceitfull, above all things, and desperately* 25 *wicked; who can know it*? Hee that askes that question, makes the answere, *I the Lord search the Heart*. When didst thou search mine? Dost thou thinke to finde it, as thou madest it in *Adam*? Thou hast searched since, and found all these gradations in the ill of our *Hearts*, *That every imagination, of the thoughts of our hearts, is onely evill* 30 *continually*. Doest thou remember this, and wouldest thou have my *Heart*? O *God of all light*, I know thou knowest all; and it is *Thou*, that declarest unto man, what is his *Heart*. Without thee, O

7 *earth*;] *earth*, 1624(2), 1626   25 *deceitfull*,] *deceitfull* 1624(2), 1626   *Margin*
4.13 *S*: 4.14 all edd.

Soveraigne goodnesse, I could not know, how ill my *heart* were. Thou hast declared unto mee, in thy Word, That for all this *deluge* of evill, that hath surrunded all *Hearts,* yet thou foughtest and *foundest a man after thine owne heart,* That *thou couldest and wouldest give thy people*
5 *Pastours according to thine owne heart;* And I can gather out of thy *Word,* so good testimony of the *hearts* of men, as to finde *single hearts, docile,* and *apprehensive hearts;* Hearts that *can,* Hearts that *have* learnt; *wise hearts,* in one place, and in another, in a great degree, *wise, perfit* hearts; *straight* hearts, no perversnesse without, and *cleane*
10 hearts, no foulenesse within; such hearts I can find in thy Word; and if my *heart* were such a *heart,* I would give thee my *Heart.* But I find *stonie* hearts too, and I have made mine such: I have found *Hearts, that are* snares; and I have conversed with such; *hearts that burne like Ovens;* and the fuell of *Lust,* and *Envie,* and *Ambition,* hath inflamed
15 mine; *Hearts in which their Masters trust,* And *hee that trusteth in his owne heart, is a foole;* His confidence in his owne morall Constancie, and civill fortitude, will betray him, when thou shalt cast a spirituall dampe, a heavinesse, and dejection of spirit upon him. I have found these *Hearts,* and a worse then these, a *Heart* into which the *Devill*
20 himselfe is entred, *Judas heart.* The first kind of heart, alas, my *God,* I have not; The last are not *Hearts* to bee given to thee; What shall I do? Without that present I cannot bee thy *Sonne,* and I have it not. To those of the first kinde, thou givest *joyfulnes of heart,* and I have not that; To those of the other kinde, thou givest *faintnesse of heart:*
25 And blessed bee thou, *O God,* for that forbearance, I have not that yet. There is then a middle kinde of *Hearts,* not so perfit, as to bee given, but that the very giving, mends them: Not so desperate, as not to bee accepted, but that the very accepting dignifies them. This is a *melting* heart, and a *troubled* heart; and a *wounded* heart, and a
30 *broken* heart, and a *contrite* heart; and by the powerfull working of thy piercing spirit, such a *Heart* I have; *Thy Samuel* spake unto all the house of thy *Israel,* and sayd, *If you returne to the Lord with all your hearts, prepare your hearts unto the Lord.* If my heart bee *prepared,* it is a *returning* heart; And if thou see it upon the *way,* thou wilt
35 carrie it *home;* Nay, the *preparation* is thine too; this *melting,* this

1 Sam. 13.14
Jer. 3.15

Ezech. 11.19
Eccles. 7.26

Prov. 28.26

Jo. 13.2

Ecclus. 50.23
Levit. 26.36

Jos. 2.11

1 Sam. 7.3

6 men,] men 1624(2), 1626   9 *perfit* hearts;] *perfit* hearts, 1624(2), 1626   19 into which *Ed.:* into the which all edd.   35 *home*;] *home.* 1626

wounding, this *breaking*, this *contrition*, which I have now, is thy *Way*, to thy *Ende*; And those *discomforts*, are for all that, *The earnest of thy Spirit in my heart*; and where thou givest *earnest*, thou wilt performe the *bargaine*. *Naball* was confident upon his wine, but *in the morning his heart dyed within him*; Thou, O Lord, hast given mee *Worme wood*, 5 and I have had some diffidence upon that; and thou hast cleared a *Morning* to mee againe, and my heart is alive. Davids *heart smote him, when hee cut off the skirt from* Saul; and *his heart smote him, when hee had numbred his people*: My heart hath strucke mee, when I come to number my sinnes; but that blowe is not to death, because those 10 sinnes are not to death, but my heart lives in thee. But yet as long as I remaine in this great *Hospitall*, this sicke, this diseasefull world, as long as I remaine in this leprous house, this flesh of mine, this Heart, though thus prepared *for* thee, prepared *by* thee, will still be subject to the invasion of maligne and pestilent vapours. But I have my 15 *Cordialls* in thy promise; *when I shall know the plague of my heart, and pray unto thee, in thy house*, thou wilt preserve that heart, from all mortall force, of that infection: And the *Peace of God, which passeth all understanding, shall keepe my Heart and Minde through Christ Jesus*.

Margin notes:
2 Cor. 1.22
1 Sam. 25.37
24.5
2 Sam. 24.10
1 Reg. 8.38
Phil. 4.7

11. PRAYER   20

O eternall, and most gracious *God*, who in thy *upper house*, the *Heavens*, though there bee many *Mansions*, yet art alike, and equally in every *Mansion*, but heere in thy *lower house*, though thou fillest all, yet art otherwise in some roomes thereof, then in others, otherwise in thy *Church*, then in my *Chamber*, and otherwise in thy *Sacraments*, 25 then in my *Prayers*, so though thou bee alwayes present, and alwayes working in every roome of this thy House, my body, yet I humbly beseech thee to manifest alwayes a more effectuall presence in my *heart*, then in the other Offices. Into the house of thine Annoynted, disloyall persons, Traitors will come; Into thy House, the *Church*, 30 *Hypocrites*, and *Idolatrers* will come; Into some Roomes of this thy House, my *Body*, *Tentations* will come, *Infections* will come, but bee

6 thou 1624(1) *corrected*: thon 1624(1) C², O¹², St.A, HN, L, GK(1), GK(2) *originally*   7 Davids 1624(2), 1626: Danids 1624(1)   *Margin* 2 Sam. *S*: 1 Sam. all edd.   17 *thee*,] thee 1624(2), 1626

my *Heart*, thy *Bed-chamber*, O my *God*, and thither let them not enter. *Job made a Covenant with his Eyes*, but not his making of that *Covenant*, but thy dwelling in his heart, enabled him to keepe that *Covenant*. Thy *Sonne* himselfe had a *sadnesse in his Soule to death*, and 5 hee had a *reluctation*, a *deprecation* of death, in the approaches thereof; but hee had his *Cordiall* too, *Yet not my will, but thine bee done*. And as thou hast not delivered us, thine *adopted sonnes*, from these infectious tentations, so neither hast thou delivered us over to them, nor withheld thy *Cordialls* from us. I was baptized in thy *Cordiall water*, 10 against *Originall sinne*, and I have drunke of thy *Cordiall Blood*, for my recoverie, from actuall, and habituall sinne in the other *Sacrament*. Thou, *O Lord*, who hast imprinted all medicinall vertues, which are in all creatures, and hast made even the flesh of *Vipers*, to assist in *Cordialls*, art able to make this present sicknesse, everlasting health, 15 this weaknes, everlasting strength, and this very dejection, and faintnesse of heart, a powerfull *Cordiall*. When thy blessed *Sonne* cryed out to thee, *My God, my God, why hast thou forsaken mee*, thou diddest reach out thy hand to him; but not to deliver his *sad soule*, but to receive his *holy soule*; Neither did hee longer desire to hold it 20 of thee, but to recommend it to thee. I see thine hand upon mee now, O Lord, and I aske not why it comes, what it intends: whether thou wilt bidde it stay still in this *Body*, for some time, or bidd it meet thee this day in *Paradise*, I aske not, not in a *wish*, not in a *thought*: *Infirmitie of Nature, Curiositie of Minde*, are tentations that offer; but 25 a silent, and absolute obedience, to thy will, even before I know it, is my *Cordiall*. Preserve that to mee, O my *God*, and that will preserve mee to thee; that when thou hast *Catechised* mee with *affliction* here, I may take a greater *degree*, and serve thee in a higher place, in thy kingdome of *joy*, and *glory*. *Amen*.

12 Thou,] Thou 1626   20 thee.] thee 1626

12. Spirante Columbâ, Suppositâ pedibus, Revocantur ad ima vapores.

They apply Pidgeons, to draw the vapors from the Head.

12. MEDITATION

What will not kill a man, if a *vapor* will? how great an *Elephant*, how 5
small a *Mouse* destroyes? to dye by a *bullet* is the *Souldiers dayly
bread*; but few men dye by *haile-shot*: A man is more worth, then to
bee sold for *single money*; a *life* to be valued above a *trifle*. If this were
a violent shaking of the Ayre by *Thunder*, or by *Canon*, in that case
the *Ayre* is condensed above the thicknesse of *water*, of water baked 10
into *Ice*, almost *petrified*, almost made stone, and no wonder that that
kills; but that that which is but a *vapor*, and a *vapor* not forced, but
breathed, should kill, that our *Nourse* should overlay us, and *Ayre*, that
nourishes us, should destroy us, but that it is a *halfe Atheisme* to
murmure against *Nature*, who is *Gods immediate Commissioner*, who 15
would not think himselfe miserable to bee put into the hands of
Nature, who does not only set him up for a *marke* for others to shoote
at, but delights her selfe to blow him up like a *glasse*, till shee see him
breake, even with her owne breath? nay if this infectious *vapor* were
sought for, or travail'd to, as *Plinie* hunted after the *vapor* of *Aetna* 20
and dard, and challenged *Death* in the forme of a *vapor* to doe his
worst, and felt the worst, he dyed; or if this *vapor* were met withall
in an *ambush*, and we surprized with it, out of a long shutt *Well*, or
out of a new opened *Myne*, who wold lament, who would accuse,
when we had nothing to accuse, none to lament against, but *Fortune*, 25
who is lesse then a *vapour*? But when our selves are the *Well*, that
breaths out this exhalation, the *Oven* that spits out this fiery smoke,
the *Myne* that spues out this suffocating, and strangling *dampe*, who
can ever after this, aggravate his sorrow, by this *Circumstance*, That it
was his *Neighbor*, his *familiar friend*, his *brother* that destroyed him, 30
and destroyed him with a whispering, & calumniating breath, when

1 Columbâ, *Ed.*: Columbâ all edd.   7 man] wan 1626   11,12 that that kills]
that kils 1624(2), 1626   12 forced,] forced 1624(2), 1626   13 *Nourse* should]
Nourse would 1624(2), 1626   13 *Ayre*,] ayre 1624(2), 1626   26 *vapour*? *Ed.*:
vapour: all edd.

62

wee our selves doe it to our selves by the same meanes, kill our selves with our owne *vapors*? Or if these occasions of this selfe-destruction, had any contribution from our owne *wils*, any assistance from our owne *intentions*, nay from our owne *errors*, wee might

5 divide the rebuke, & chide our selves as much as them. *Fevers* upon wilful distempers of drinke, and surfets, *Consumptions* upon intemperances, & licentiousnes, *Madnes* upon misplacing, or over-bending our naturall faculties, proceed from our selves, and so, as that our selves are in the plot, and wee are not onely *passive*, but *active* too, to

10 our owne destruction; But what have I done, either to *breed*, or to *breath* these *vapors*? They tell me it is my *Melancholy*: Did I infuse, did I drinke in *Melancholly* into my selfe? It is my *thoughtfulnesse*; was I not made to *thinke*? It is my *study*; doth not my *Calling* call for that? I have don nothing, wilfully, perversly toward it, yet must

15 suffer in it, die by it; There are too many *Examples* of men, that have bin their own *executioners*, and that have made hard shift to bee so; some have alwayes had *poyson* about them, in a *hollow ring* upon their finger, and some in their *Pen* that they used to write with: some have beat out their *braines* at the wal of their prison, and some have eate

20 the *fire* out of their chimneys: and one is said to have come neerer our case then so, to have strangled himself, though his hands were bound, by crushing his throat between his knees; But I doe nothing upon my selfe, and yet am mine owne *Executioner*. And we have heard of *death*, upon small occasions, and by scornefull *instruments*; a *pinne*, a

25 *combe*, a *haire*, pulled, hath gangred, & killd; But when I have said, a *vapour*, if I were asked again, what is a *vapour*, I could not tell, it is so insensible a thing; so neere *nothing* is that that reduces us to *nothing*. But extend this *vapour*, rarifie it; from so narow a roome, as our *Naturall bodies*, to any *Politike body*, to a *State*. That which is *fume*

30 in us, is in a State, *Rumor*, and these *vapours* in us, which wee consider here pestilent, and infectious fumes, are in a State *infectious rumors*, detracting and dishonourable *Calumnies*, *Libels*. The *Heart* in that *body* is the *King*; and the *Braine*, his *Councell*; and the whole *Magistracie*, that ties all together, is the *Sinewes*, which proceed from

35 thence; and the *life* of all is *Honour*, and just *respect*, and due *reverence*;

Coma, latro.
in Val. Max.

13 *study*;] *studie*, 1626   14 nothing,] nothing 1624(2), 1626   28 roome] roame 1624(2), 1626

and therfore, when these *vapors*, these venimous *rumors*, are directed against these *Noble parts*, the whole body suffers. But yet for all their priviledges, they are not priviledged from our *misery*; that as the *vapours* most pernitious to us, arise in our owne bodies, so doe the most dishonorable *rumours*, and those that wound a *State* most, arise at 5 home. What ill *ayre*, that I could have met in the street, what *channell*, what *shambles*, what *dunghill*, what *vault*, could have hurt mee so much, as these home-bredd *vapours*? What *fugitive*, what *Almes-man of any forraine State*, can doe so much harme, as a *Detracter*, a *Libeller*, a scornefull *Jester* at home? For, as they that write of *Poysons*, and of 10 creatures naturally disposed to the ruine of Man, do as well mention the *Flea*, as the *Viper*, because the *Flea*, though hee kill none, hee does all the harme hee can, so even these libellous and licentious *Jesters*, utter the *venim* they have, though sometimes *vertue*, and alwaies *power*, be a good *Pigeon* to draw this *vapor* from the *Head*, and from 15 doing any deadly harme there.

Ardoinus.

12. EXPOSTULATION

My *God*, my *God*, as thy servant *James*, when he asks that question, *what is your life*, provides me my answere, *It is even a vapor, that appeareth for a little time, & then vanisheth away*, so if he did aske me 20 what is your *death*, I am provided of my answere, *It is a vapor too*; And why should it not be all one to mee, whether I live, or die, if life, and death be all one, both a *vapor*. Thou hast made *vapor* so indifferent a thing, as that thy *Blessings*, and thy *Judgements* are equally expressed by it, and is made by thee the *Hierogliphique* of both. Why should 25 not that bee alwaies good, by which thou hast declared thy plentifull goodnes to us? *A vapor went up from the Earth, and watred the whole face of the ground*, And that by which thou hast imputed a goodnes to us, and wherein thou hast accepted our service to thee, *sacrifices;* for *Sacrifices*, were *vapors*, And in them it is said, that a *thicke cloude of* 30 *incence went up to thee*. So it is of that, wherein thou comst to us, the dew of *Heaven*, And of that wherein we come to thee, both are

4.14

Gen. 2.6

Levit. 16.23
Ezech. 8.11

Margin Ardoinus S: Ardionus 1624(1&2), *Ardinus* 1626   17 12.] 11. 1626   18
James,] James 1626   21 my] this 1624(2), 1626

vapors; And hee, in whom we *have*, and *are* all that we *are* or *have*, temporally, or spiritually, thy blessed *Son*, in the person of *wisedome*, is called so to; *she is* (that is *he is*) *the vapor of the power of God, and the pure influence from the glory of the Almighty*. Hast thou, Thou, O my
5 *God*, perfumed *vapor*, with thine own breath, with so many sweet acceptations, in thine own *word*, and shall this *vapor* receive an ill, and infectious sense? It must; for, since we have displeased thee, with that which is but *vapor*, (for what is *sinne*, but a *vapor*, but a *smoke*, though such a smoke, as takes away our sight, and disables us from
10 seeing our danger) it is just, that thou punish us with *vapors* to. For so thou dost, as the *Wiseman* tels us, *Thou canst punish us by those things, wherein wee offend thee*; as he hath expressed it there, *By beasts newly created, breathing vapors*. Therefore that Commination of thine, by thy *Prophet*, *I will shew wonders in the heaven, and in the Earth, bloud*
15 *and fire, and pillars of smoke*, thine *Apostle*, who knewe thy meaning best, calls *vapors of smoke*. One *Prophet* presents thee in thy terriblenesse, so, *There went out a smoke at his Nostrils*, and another, the effect of thine anger so, *The house was filled with smoake*; And hee that continues his *Prophesie*, as long as the world can continue, describes
20 the miseries of the latter times so, *Out of the bottomlesse pit arose a smoke, that darkened the Sunne, and out of that smoke came Locusts, who had the power of Scorpions*. Now all *smokes* begin in *fire*, & all these will end so too: The smoke of *sin*, and of thy *wrath*, will end in the fire of *hell*. But hast thou afforded us no means to evaporate these
25 *smokes*, to withdraw these *vapors*? When thine *Angels* fell from heaven, thou tookst into thy care, the reparation of that place, & didst it, by assuming, by drawing us thither; when we fel from thee here, in this world, thou tookst into thy care the reparation of this place too, and didst it by assuming us another way, by descending
30 down to assume our nature, in thy *Son*. So that though our last act be an ascending to glory, (we shall ascend to the place of *Angels*) yet our first act is to goe the way of thy *Sonn*, *descending*, and the way of thy blessed *spirit* too, who *descended in the Dove*. Therefore hast thou bin pleased to afford us this remedy in *Nature*, by this application of a
35 *Dove*, to our lower parts, to make these *vapors* in our *bodies*, to

Sap. 7.25

Sap. 11.18

Joel. 2.30

Act. 2.19
Psa. 18.8
Esa. 6.4

Apo. 9.2, 3

---

2 spiritually] spirituall 1624(2), 1626   *Margin* 7.25 *S*: 7.24 all edd.   3 to;] to, 1624(2)   15 *smoke, Ed.*: smoke; all edd.   *Margin* 18.8 *S*: 78.8 all edd.   *Margin* 9.2,3 *Ed.*: 9.2 all edd.

descend, and to make that a *type* to us, that by the visitation of thy *Spirit*, the *vapors* of sin shall descend, & we tread them under our feet. At the baptisme of thy *Son*, the *Dove* descended, & at the exalting of thine *Apostles* to preach, the same spirit descended. Let us draw down the *vapors* of our own *pride*, our own *wits*, our own *wils*, 5 our own *inventions*, to the *simplicitie* of thy *Sacraments*, & the obedience of thy word, and these *Doves*, thus applied, shall make us live.

12. PRAYER

O eternall and most gracious *God*, who though thou have suffred 10 us to destroy our selves, & hast not given us the power of reparation in our selves, hast yet afforded us such meanes of reparation, as may easily, and familiarly be compassed by us, prosper I humbly beseech thee, this means of bodily assistance in this thy ordinary *creature*, and prosper thy meanes of spirituall assistance in thy holy *ordinances*. And 15 as thou hast caried this thy *creature* the *Dove*, through all thy wayes, through *Nature*, and made it naturally proper to conduce medicinally to our *bodily health*, Through the *law*, and made it a *sacrifice* for *sinne* there, and through the *Gospel*, and made it, & thy spirit in it, a witnes of thy *sonnes baptisme* there, so carry it, and the qualities of it 20 home to my *soule*, and imprint there that *simplicity*, that *mildnesse*, that *harmelesnesse*, which thou hast imprinted by *Nature* in this *Creature*. That so all *vapours* of all disobedience to thee, being sub-dued under my feete, I may in the power, and triumphe of thy *sonne*, treade victoriously upon my *grave*, and trample upon the 25 *Lyon*, and *Dragon*, that lye under it, to devoure me. Thou O *Lord*, by the *Prophet* callest the *Dove*, the *Dove of the Valleys*, but promisest that *the Dove of the Valleyes shall bee upon the Mountaine*: As thou hast layed mee low, in this *Valley* of sickenesse, so low, as that I am made fit for that question, asked in the field of bones, *Sonne of Man*, 30 *can these bones live*, so, in thy good time, carry me up to these *Mountaynes*, of which, even in this *Valley*, thou affordest mee a

Eze. 7.16

37.3

10 eternall] eternall, 1624(2), 1626   14 thee, 1624(2), 1626, S: thee 1624(1)
15 ordinances] Or, dinances 1624(2)   26 Lord, 1624(2), 1626: Lord 1624(1)   31
so,] so 1624(2), 1626   32 which,] which 1624(2), 1626

prospect, the Mountain where thou dwellest, the holy Hill, unto which none can ascend but *hee that hath cleane hands,* which none can have, but by that one and that strong way, of making them cleane, in the blood of thy Sonne *Christ Jesus. Amen.*

5 **13. Ingeniumque malum, numeroso stigmate, fassus, Pellitur ad pectus, Morbique Suburbia, Morbus.**

The Sicknes declares the infection and malignity thereof by spots.

13. MEDITATION

10 Wee say, that the world is made of *sea,* & *land,* as though they were equal; but we know that ther is more *sea* in the *Western,* then in the *Eastern Hemisphere*: We say that the *Firmament* is full of *starres*; as though it were equally full; but we know, that there are more *stars* under the *Northerne,* then under the *Southern Pole.* Wee say, the
15 *Elements* of man are *misery,* and *happinesse,* as though he had an equal proportion of both, and the dayes of man vicissitudinary, as though he had as many *good* daies, as *ill,* and that he livd under a perpetuall *Equinoctial, night* and *day* equall, good and ill fortune in the same measure. But it is far from that; hee *drinkes misery,* & he
20 *tastes happinesse*; he *mowes misery,* and hee *gleanes happinesse*; hee *journies in misery,* he does but *walke in happinesse*; and which is worst, his misery is *positive,* and *dogmaticall,* his happinesse is but *disputable,* and *problematicall*; All men call *Misery, Misery,* but *Happinesse* changes the name, by the taste of man. In this *accident* that befalls mee
25 now, that this sicknesse declares it selfe by *Spots,* to be a malignant, and pestilentiall disease, if there be a *comfort* in the declaration, that therby the *Phisicians* see more cleerely what to doe, there may bee as much *discomfort* in this, That the malignitie may bee so great, as that all that they can doe, shall doe *nothing*; That an enemy *declares*

5 malum,] malum 1626   5 fassus, *Ed.*: fassus all edd.   18 *night A*: *night,* all edd.

himselfe, then, when he is able to subsist, and to pursue, and to atchive his ends, is no great comfort. In intestine Conspiracies, *voluntary Confessions* doe more good, then confessions upon the *Rack*; In these Infections, when *Nature* her selfe confesses, and cries out by these outward declarations, which she is able to put forth of 5 her selfe, they minister *comfort*; but when all is by the strength of *Cordials*, it is but a *Confession upon the Racke*, by which though wee come to knowe the malice of that man, yet wee doe not knowe, whether there bee not as much malice in his heart then, as before his confession; we are sure of his *Treason*, but not of his *Repentance*; sure 10 of *him*, but not of his *Complices*. It is a faint comfort to know the worst, when the worst is *remedilesse*; and a weaker then that, to know *much ill*, & not to know, that that is the worst. A woman is comforted with the birth of her *Son*, her body is eased of a burthen; but if shee could *prophetically* read his *History*, how *ill a man*, perchance 15 *how ill a sonne*, he would prove, shee should receive a greater burthen into her *Mind*. Scarce any purchase that is not cloggd with secret *encumbrances*; scarce any *happines*, that hath not in it so much of the *nature* of false and base money, as that the *Allay* is more then the *Mettall*. Nay is it not so, (at least much towards it) even in the 20 exercise of *Vertues*? I must bee poore, and want, before I can exercise the vertue of *Gratitude*; miserable, and in torment, before I can exercise the vertue of *patience*; How deepe do we dig, and for how course gold? And what other *Touch-stone* have we of our *gold*, but *comparison*? Whether we be as happy, as others, or as our selvs at 25 other times; O poore stepp toward being well, when these *spots* do only tell us, that we are worse, then we were sure of before.

13. EXPOSTULATION

My God, my God, thou hast made this sick bed thine *Altar*, and I have no other *Sacrifice* to offer, but my self; and wilt thou accept *no* 30 *spotted sacrifice*? Doeth thy *Son* dwel bodily in this flesh, that thou shouldst looke for an unspottednes here? Or is the *Holy Ghost*, the

soule of this *body*, as he is of thy *Spouse*, who is therfore *all faire, and*   Can. 4.7
no spot in her? or hath thy *Son* himself no *spots*, who hath al our stains,
& deformities in him? Or hath thy *Spouse*, thy *Church*, no *spots*,
when every particular limbe of that faire, & spotles body, every
5 particular *soule* in that *Church* is full of staines, and spots? Thou bidst
us *hate the garment that is spotted with the flesh*. The *flesh* it selfe is the   Jud. 23
garment, and it spotteth it selfe, with it self. And *if I wash my selfe*   Job 9.30, 31
with snow water; mine own clothes shall make me abominable; and yet *no*   Ephes. 5.29
man yet ever hated his owne flesh: Lord, if thou looke for a *spotlesnesse*,
10 whom wilt thou looke upon? Thy mercy may goe a great way in
my *soule*, & yet not leave me without *spots*; Thy corrections may go
far, & burn deepe, and yet not leave me spotles: thy *children*
apprehended that, when they said, *From our former inquitie wee are not*   Josua 22.17
cleansed, untill this day, though there was a plague in the Congregation of
15 *the Lord*; Thou rainest upon us, and yet doest not alwaies mollifie all
our hardnesse; Thou kindlest thy fires in us, and yet doest not
always burne up all our drosse; Thou healst our *wounds*, and yet
leavest *scarres*; Thou purgest the *blood*, and yet leavest *spots*. But the
spots that thou hatest, are the *spotts* that we hide. *The Carvers of*   Sap. 13.14
20 *Images cover spotts*, sayes the *Wiseman*; When we hide our *spotts*, wee
become *Idolatrers* of our owne staines, of our own *foulenesses*. But if
my *spots* come forth, by what meanes soever, whether by the
strength of *Nature*, by *voluntary confession*, (for *Grace* is the *Nature* of a
Regenerate man, and the power of *Grace* is the strength of *Nature*) or
25 by the vertue of *Cordialls*, (for even thy *Corrections* are *Cordials*) if
they come forth either way, thou receivest that *Confession* with a
gracious Interpretation. When thy servant *Jacob* practised an *Inven-*   Gen. 30.37
tion to procure *spotts* in his sheepe, thou diddest prosper his *Rodds*;
and thou dost prosper thine owne *Rodds*, when *corrections* procure the
30 discovery or our *spotts*, the humble manifestation of our sinns to
thee; Till then thou maist justly say, *The whole need not the Phisician*;   Mat. 9.12
Till wee tell thee in our sicknes, wee think our selves whole, till we
shew our *spotts*, thou appliest no *medicine*. But since I do that, shall I
not, *Lord, lift up my face without spot, and be stedfast, and not feare*. Even   Job 11.15
35 my *spotts* belong to thy *Sonnes* body, and are part of that, which he

4 faire,] faire 1626   *Margin* 9.30,31 *Ed.*: 9.30 all edd.   18 *scarres*;] *scarres.*
1626   *Margin* 30.37 *Ed.*: 30.33 all edd.

came downe to this earth, to fetch, and challenge, and assume to himselfe. When I open my *spotts*, I doe but present him with that which is *His*, and till I do so, I detaine, & withhold *his right*. When therfore thou seest them upon me, as *His*, and seest them by this way of *Confession*, they shall not appear to me, as the *pinches of death*, to 5 decline my feare to *Hell*; (for *thou hast not left thy holy one in Hell*, thy *Sonne* is not there) but these *spotts* upon my *Breast*, and upon my *Soule*, shal appeare to mee as the *Constellations* of the *Firmament*, to direct my *Contemplation* to that place, where thy *Son* is, thy *right hand*. 10

13. PRAYER

O eternall, and most gratious *God*, who as thou givest all for *nothing*, if we consider any precedent Merit in us, so giv'st *Nothing*, for *Nothing*, if we consider the *acknowledgement*, & *thankefullnesse*, which thou lookest for, after, accept my humble thankes, both for thy 15 *Mercy*, and for this particular *Mercie*, that in thy *Judgement* I can discerne thy *Mercie*, and find *comfort* in thy *corrections*. I know, O *Lord*, the ordinary *discomfort* that accompanies that phrase, *That the house is visited*, And that, *that thy markes, and thy tokens are upon the patient*; But what a wretched, and disconsolate *Hermitage* is that 20 *House*, which is not *visited* by thee, and what a *Wayve*, and *Stray* is that *Man*, that hath not thy *Markes* upon him? These heates, O *Lord*, which thou hast broght upon this *body*, are but thy chafing of the *wax*, that thou mightest *seale* me to thee; These *spots* are but the *letters*, in which thou hast written thine owne *Name*, and conveyed thy selfe to 25 mee; whether for a *present possession*, by taking me now, or for a future *reversion*, by glorifying thy selfe in my stay here, I limit not, I condition not, I choose not, I wish not, no more then the house, or land that passeth by any *Civill* conveyance. Onely be thou ever present to me, O *my God*, and this *bed-chamber*, & thy bed-chamber 30 shal be all one roome, and the closing of these bodily *Eyes* here, and the opening of the *Eyes* of my *Soule*, there, all one *Act*.

9 place,] place 1624(2), 1626   27 *reversion* 1624(2), 1626: *renersion* 1624(1)

14. Idque notant Criticis, Medici, evenisse Diebus.

*The Phisicians observe these accidents to have
fallen upon the criticall dayes.*

14. MEDITATION

5 I would not make *Man* worse then hee is, Nor his Condition more
miserable then it is. But could I though I would? As a Man cannot
flatter God, nor over prayse him, so a Man cannot *injure* Man, nor
undervalue him. Thus much must necessarily be presented to his
remembrance, that those *false Happinesses*, which he hath in this
10 World, have their *times*, & their *seasons*, and their *Critical dayes*, &
they are *Judged*, and *Denominated* according to the times, when they
befall us. What poore *Elements* are our *happinesses* made off, if *Tyme*,
Tyme which wee can scarce consider to be *any thing*, be an essential
part of our hapines? All things are done in some *place*; but if we
15 consider *place* to be no more, but the next hollow *Superficies* of the
Ayre, *Alas*, how thinne, & fluid a thing is *Ayre*, and how thinne a
filme is a *Superficies*, and a *Superficies* of *Ayre*? All things are done in
time too; but if we consider *Tyme* to be but the *Measure of Motion*,
and howsoever it may seeme to have three *stations*, *past*, *present*, and
20 *future*, yet the *first* and *last* of these *are* not (one is not, now, & the
other is not yet) And that which you call *present*, is not *now* the same
that it was, when you began to call it so in this *Line*, (before you
found that word, *present*, or that *Monosyllable*, *now*, the present, &
the *Now* is past,) if this *Imaginary halfe-nothing*, *Tyme*, be of the
25 Essence of our *Happinesses*, how can they be thought *durable*? *Tyme*
is not so; How can they bee thought to be? Tyme is not so; not so,
considered in any of the *parts* thereof. If we consider *Eternity*, into
that, *Tyme* never Entred; *Eternity* is not an everlasting flux of
Tyme; but Tyme is as a short *parenthesis* in a longe *period*; and
30 *Eternity* had bin the same, as it is, though time had never beene; If
we consider, not *Eternity*, but *Perpetuity*, not that which had no *tyme*

---

1 Medici, *Ed.*: Medici all edd.   15 more,] more 1624(2), 1626   23 *Mono-syllable*] Monasyllable 1624(2), 1626   24 *Imaginary*] Imaginary, 1624(2), 1626
24 *Tyme, A, S*: Tyme all edd.   26 so;] so, 1626   29 is as a] is a 1624(2), 1626
30 had never] never had 1626

to beginne in, but which shall out-live *Tyme* and be, when *Tyme shall bee no more*, what A *Minute* is the life of the Durablest *Creature*, compared to that? And what a Minute is Mans life in respect of the Sunnes, or of a tree? and yet how little of our *life is Occasion, opportunity* to receyve good in; and how little of that *occasion*, doe 5 wee apprehend, and lay hold of? How busie, and perplexed a *Cobweb*, is the *Happinesse* of Man here, that must bee made up with a *Watchfulnesse*, to lay hold upon *Occasion*, which is but a little peece of that, which is *Nothing, Tyme*? And yet the best things are *Nothing* without that. *Honors, Pleasures, Possessions*, presented to us, out of 10 time, in our decrepit, and distasted, & unapprehensive *Age*, loose their *office*, & loose their *Name*; They are not *Honors* to us, that shall never appeare, nor come abroad into the Eyes of the people, to receive *Honor*, from them who give it: Nor *pleasures* to us, who have lost our sense to taste them; nor *possessions* to us, who are departing 15 from the possession of them. Youth is their *Criticall Day*; that *Judges* them, that *Denominates* them, that *inanimates*, and *informes* them, and makes them *Honors*, and pleasures, and *possessions*, & when they come in an unapprehensive *Age*, they come as a *Cordiall* when the bell rings out, as a *Pardon*, when the Head is off. We rejoyce in the 20 Comfort of *fire*, but does any Man cleave to it at *Midsomer*; Wee are glad of the freshnesse, & coolenes of a *Vault*, but does any Man keepe his *Christmas* there; or are the pleasures of the *Spring* acceptable in *Autumne*? If happinesse be in the *season*, or in the *Clymate*, how much happier then are *Birdes* then *Men*, who can change the *Climate*, 25 and accompanie, and enjoy the same season ever.

14. EXPOSTULATION

Dan. 7.9

Mat. 20.6

6.34

My *God*, my *God* wouldest thou cal thy selfe the *Ancient of dayes*, if we were not to call our selves to an account for our *dayes*? wouldest thou chide us for *standing idle heere all the day*, if we were sure to have 30 more dayes, to make up our harvest? When thou biddest us *take no thought for tomorrow; for sufficient unto the day* (to every day) *is the evill thereof*, is this truely, absolutely, to put off all that concernes the

---

11 distasted,] distasted 1626   21 *Midsomer*;] *Midsomer*? 1624(2), 1626   25 *Climate* 1624(1) *corrected: Climate* 1624(1) L³ *originally*   *Margin* 7,9 1624(1) *corrected:* 7.6 1624(1) Y, C *originally*   33 off 1624(2), 1626, *S:* of 1624(1)

present life? When thou reprehendest the *Galatians* by thy Message
to them, *That they observed dayes, and Moneths, and Tymes, and Yeares,*   4.10
when thou sendest by the same *Messenger,* to forbid the Colossians all   2.16
Criticall dayes, Indicatory dayes, Let no Man Judge you, in respect of a
5 *holy-day, or of a new Moone, or of a Saboth,* doest thou take away all
Consideration, all destinction of *dayes*? Though thou remove them
from being of the *Essence* of our *Salvation,* thou leavest them for
assistances, and for the *Exaltation* of our *Devotion,* to fix our selves, at
certaine *periodicall,* & *stationary times,* upon the consideration of those
10 things, which thou hast done for us, and the *Crisis,* the *triall,* the
judgment, how those things have wrought upon us, and disposed us
to a spirituall recovery, and convalescence. For there is to every man
a day of salvation, Now is the accepted time, now is the day of salvation,   2 Cor. 6.2
And there is *a great day of thy wrath,* which no man shal be able to   Apoc. 6.17
15 stand in; And there are *evill dayes before,* and therfore thou warnest
us, and armest us, *Take unto you the whole armor of God, that you may*   Eph. 6.13
be able to stand in the evill day. So far then our daies must be *criticall* to
us, as that by consideration of them, we may make a *Judgment* of our
spiritual health; for that is the *crisis* of our *bodily health;* Thy beloved   3.Joh.
20 servant *S. Joh* wishes to *Gaius, that he may prosper in his health, so as*   v. 2
his soule prospers; for if the *Soule* be leane, the marrow of the *Body*
is but water; if the *Soule* wither, the verdure and the good estate of
the *body,* is but an illusion, & the *goodliest man, a fearefull ghost.* Shall
wee, O my *God,* determine our thoughts, & shal we never determin
25 our disputations upon our *Climactericall yeares,* for particular men,
and *periodical yeres,* for the life of *states* and *kingdoms,* and never
consider these in our *long life,* & our interest in the *everlasting king-*
dome? We have exercisd our *curiosity* in observing that *Adam,* the
eldest of the eldest world, died in his *climactericall yere,* & *Sem* the
30 eldest son of the next world, in his; *Abraham the father of the faithfull,*
in his, & the blessed *Virgin Mary,* the garden, where the root of faith
grew, in hers. But they whose *Climacteriques* wee observe, imployd
their observation upon their *critical dayes,* the working of thy promise
of a *Messias* upon them. And shall we, O my *God,* make lesse use of
35 those *dayes,* who have more of them? We, who have not only the

3 *Messenger,*] *Messenger* 1624(2), 1626   10 things,] things 1626   *Margin* 6.13
Ed.: 6.1 all edd.   16 *God,*] *God* 1624(2), 1626   20 *health,* 1624(2), 1626, *S:*
health 1624(1)

Heb. 1.2

1 Thes. 5.8

Mat. 23.30

Mat. 22.15,
17

v. 23

v. 35

v. 46

Gen. 32.26

2 Pet. 3.8

day of the *Prophets*, the first dayes, but the last daies, in which thou
hast spoken unto us, by thy *Son*? *We are the children of the day*, for
thou hast shind in as ful a Noone, upon us, as upon the *Thessalonians*;
They who were of the *night*, (a *Night*, which they had superinduc'd
upon themselves) the *Pharises*, pretended, *That if they had bin in their* 5
Fathers daies, (those *indicatory*, and *iudicatory*, those *Criticall dayes*) *they*
would not have been partakers of the bloud of the Prophets; And shal we
who are in the *day*, these *Daies*, not of the *Prophets*, but of the *Son*,
stone those *Prophets* againe, and crucifie that *Son* againe, for all those
evident *Indications*, and *critical Iudicatures* which are afforded us? 10
Those oppos'd adversaries of thy *Son*, the *pharises* with the *Herodians*,
watch'd a *Critical day*; Then when the *State* was incens'd against him,
they came to tempt him in the dangerous question of Tribute. They left
him; & that day was the *Critical day* to the *Saduces*; *The same day*,
saies thy *Spirit*, in thy word, *the Saduces came to him to question him* 15
about the Resurrection; and them hee silenc'd; They left him; & this
was the *Criticall day* for the *Scribe*, expert in the *Law*, who thoght
himselfe learneder then the *Herodian*, the *Pharise* or *Saduce*; and he
tempted him *about the great Commandement*; & him *Christ* left without
power of replying. When all was done, & that they went about to 20
begin their *circle* of vexation, and tentation again, *Christ* silences
them so, that, as they had taken their *Criticall dayes*, to come, in *That*,
and in *that* day, so *Christ* imposes a *Criticall* day upon them; *From*
that day forth, saies thy *Spirit, no man durst aske him any more questions*.
This, *O my God*, my most blessed *God*, is a fearefull *Crisis*, a fearefull 25
Indication, when we will study, and seeke, and finde, what *dayes* are
fittest to forsake thee in; To say, Now, *Religion* is in a *Neutralitie* in
the *world*, and this is my *day*, the day of *libertie*; Now I may make
new friends by changing my *old religion*, and this is my *day*, the *day of*
advancement. But *O my God*, with thy servant *Jacobs* holy boldnes, 30
who *though thou lamedst him, would not let thee goe, till thou hadst given*
him a blessing, Though thou have laid me upon my *hearse*, yet thou
shalt not depart from mee, from this bed, till thou have given me a
Crisis, a *Judgment* upon my selfe this *day*. Since *a day is as a thousand*
yeres with thee, Let, *O Lord*, a *day*, be as a *weeke* to me; and in this one, 35

Margin 1 Thes. *S*: 2 Thes. all edd.   5 *Pharises*, *S*: *Pharises*; all edd.   *Margin*
23.30] 13.30 1626   *Margin* 22.15,17: *Ed.*: 22.15: all edd.   14 him;] him 1624(2),
1626   14 *Saduces*; Ed.: *Saduces*, all edd.   *Margin v.* 35 Ed.: *v.* 34 all edd.
22 *That*] that 1624(2), 1626   23 them; *Ed.*: them, all edd.   *Margin* 3.8] 2.8
1626   35 Let,] Let 1624(2), 1626

let me consider *seven daies*, seven *critical daies*, and *judge my selfe, that I be not judged by thee*. First, this is the day of thy *visitation*, thy comming to me; and would I looke to be welcome to thee, and not entertaine thee in thy comming to me? We measure not the *visitations* of great
5 persons, by their *apparel*, by their *equipage*, by the *solemnity* of their comming, but by their very comming; and therefore, howsoever thou come, it is a *Crisis* to me, that thou wouldest not loose me, who seekst me by any means. This leads me from my *first day*, thy *visitation* by sicknes, to a *second*, to the light, and testimony of my
10 *Conscience*. There I have an *evening*, & a *morning*; a sad guiltinesse in my *soule*, but yet a cheerfull rising of thy *Son* to; Thy *Evenings* and *Mornings* made *dayes* in the *Creation*, and there is no mention of *Nights*; My sadnesses for *sins* are *evenings*, but they determin not in *night*, but deliver me over to the *day*, the day of a *Conscience* dejected,
15 but then rectified, accused, but then acquitted, by thee, by him, who speaks thy word, & who is thy word, thy *Son*. From this *day*, the *Crisis* and examination of my *Conscience*, breakes out my *third day*, my day of preparing, & fitting my selfe for a more especial *receiving* of thy *Sonne*, in his institution of the *Sacrament*: In which *day* though
20 there be many dark passages, & slippry steps, to them who wil entangle, and endanger themselves, in unnecessary disputations, yet there are light houres inough, for any man, to goe his whole *journey* intended by thee; to know, that that *Bread* and *Wine*, is not more really assimilated to my *body*, & to my *blood*, then the *Body* and
25 *blood* of thy *Sonne*, is communicated to me in that action, and participation of that *bread*, and that *wine*. And having, O *my God*, walkd with thee these *three dayes*, The day of thy *visitation*, the day of my *Conscience*, The day of *preparing* for this seale of *Reconciliation*, I am the lesse afraid of the clouds or storms of my *fourth day*, the day
30 of my *dissolution & transmigration* from hence. Nothing deserves the name of *happines*, that makes the remembrance of *death* bitter; And *O death, how bitter is the remembrance of thee, to a man that lives at rest,*   Ecclus. 41.1 *in his possessions, the Man that hath Nothing to vexe him, yea unto him, that is able to receive meat?* Therefore hast thou, O *my God*, made this
35 *sicknes*, in which I am not able to receive meate, my *fasting day*, my

8 means] meanes 1624(2), 1626   30 *dissolution*] dissolution, 1624(2), 1626   32
O death, 1624(2), 1626, S: *O death* 1624(1)   32 *rest*,] rest 1624(2), 1626

75

Eve, to this great *festival*, my *dissolution*. And this *day* of *death* shall deliver me over to my *fift day*, the day of my *Resurrection*; for how long a *day* soever thou make that *day* in the *grave*, yet there is no *day* between that, and the *Resurrection*. Then wee shall all bee invested, reapparelled in our owne *bodies*; but they who have made just use of 5 their former *dayes*, be super-invested with *glorie*, wheras the others, condemned to their *olde clothes*, their *sinfull bodies*, shall have *Nothing* added, but *immortalitie* to *torment*. And this *day* of awaking me, and reinvesting my *Soule*, in *my body*, and my *body* in the body of *Christ*, shall present mee, *Bodie*, and *Soule*, to my *sixt day*, *The day of* 10 *Judgement*; which is truely, and most literally, the *Critical*, the *Decretory day*; both because all *Judgement* shall bee manifested to *me* then, and *I* shall assist in judging the world then, and because then, that *Judgement* shall declare to me, and possesse mee of my *Seventh day*, my *Everlasting Saboth* in *thy rest, thy glory, thy joy, thy sight, thy* 15 *selfe*; and where I shall live as long, without reckning any more *Dayes* after, as thy *Sonne*, and thy *Holy Spirit* lived with thee, before you three made any *Dayes* in the *Creation*.

14. PRAYER

O eternall and most gracious *God*, who though thou didst permit 20 *darknesse* to be before *light* in the *Creation*, yet in the making of *light*, didst so multiplie that *light*, as that it enlightned not the *day* only, but the *night* too, though thou have suffered some *dimnesse*, some clouds of *sadnesse* & disconsolatenesse to shed themselves upon my *soule*, I humbly blesse, and thankfully glorifie thy holy name, that thou hast 25 afforded mee the *light* of thy *spirit*, against which the *prince of dark-nesse* cannot prevaile, nor hinder his illumination of our darkest nights, of our saddest thoughts. Even the visitation of thy most blessed *Spirit*, upon the blessed *Virgin*, is called an *overshadowing*. There was the presence of the *Holy Ghost*, the fountaine of all *light*, 30 and yet an *overshadowing*; Nay except there were some *light*, there could bee no *shadow*. Let thy mercifull providence so governe all in

15 *thy rest* 1624(1) *corrected: thy thy rest* 1624(1) L³, C *originally*   16 long,] long 1626   24 *sadnesse*] sadnes, 1626   25 blesse, 1624(2), 1626, S: blesse 1624(1) 27 nor] not 1626

this *sicknesse*, that I never fall into utter *darknesse, ignorance of thee*, or *inconsideration of my selfe*; and let those *shadowes* which doe fall upon mee, *faintnesses of Spirit*, and *condemnations of my selfe*, bee overcome by the power of thine irresistible *light*, the *God* of *consolation*; that

5 when those *shadowes* have done their office upon mee, to let me see, that of my selfe, I should fall into irrecoverable darknesse, thy *spirit* may doe his *office* upon those *shadowes*, and disperse them, and establish mee in so bright a *day* here, as may bee a *Criticall day* to me, *a day wherein*, and *whereby* I may give thy *Judgement* upon my selfe,

10 and that the words of thy *sonne*, spoken to his *Apostles*, may reflect upon me, *Behold, I am with you alwaies, even to the end of the world.*   Mat. 28.20

15. Interea insomnes noctes Ego duco, Diesque.

I sleepe not day nor night.

15. MEDITATION

15 Naturall Men have conceived a twofold use of *sleepe*; That it is a *refreshing* of the body in this life; That it is a *preparing* of the *soule* for the next; That it is a *feast*, and it is the *Grace* at that feast; That it is our *recreation*, and cheeres us, and it is our *Catechisme*, and instructs us; wee lie downe in a hope, that wee shall rise the stronger; and we

20 lie downe in a knowledge, that wee may rise no more. *Sleepe* is an *Opiate* which gives us *rest*, but such an *Opiate*, as perchance, being under it, we shall wake no more. But though naturall men, who have induced secondary and figurative considerations, have found out this second, this *emblematicall* use of *sleepe*, that it should be a

25 *representation of death*, God, who wrought and perfected his worke, before *Nature* began, (for *Nature* was but his *apprentice*, to learne in the first *seven daies*, and now is his *foreman*, and works next under him) *God*, I say, intended *sleepe* onely for the *refreshing* of man by bodily rest, and not for a *figure of death*, for he intended not *death* it

7 *office*] *office*, 1626   12 Interea *S*: Intereà all edd.   26 began,] began 1624(2), 1626

77

selfe then. But *Man* having induced *death* upon himselfe, *God* hath taken *Mans Creature*, *death*, into his hand, and mended it; and where-as it hath in it selfe a fearefull forme and aspect, so that Man is afraid of his own *Creature*, *God* presents it to him, in a *familiar*, in an *assiduous*, in an *agreeable*, and *acceptable* forme, in *sleepe*, that so when 5 hee awakes from *sleepe*, and saies to himselfe, shall I bee no otherwise when I am dead, than I was even now, when I was asleep, hee may bee ashamed of his waking *dreames*, and of his *Melancholique* fancying out a horrid and an affrightfull figure of that *death* which is so like sleepe. As then wee need *sleepe* to live out our *threescore and ten* 10 *yeeres*, so we need *death*, to live that *life* which we cannot *out-live*. And as *death* being our *enemie*, *God* allowes us to defend our selves against it (for wee *victuall* our selves against *death*, *twice* every day, as often as we *eat*) so *God* having so sweetned *death* unto us, as hee hath in *sleepe*, wee put our selves into our *Enemies* hands *once* every 15 day, so farre, as *sleepe* is *death*; and *sleepe* is as much *death*, as *meat* is *life*. This then is the *misery* of my *sicknesse*, That death as it is produced from mee, and is mine owne *Creature*, is now before mine *Eies*, but in that forme, in which *God* hath mollified it to us, and made it acceptable, in *sleepe*, I cannot see it: how many *prisoners*, who have 20 even hollowed themselves their *graves* upon that *Earth*, on which they have lien long under heavie fetters, yet at this *houre*, are *asleepe*, though they bee yet working upon their owne *graves*, by their owne *waight*? hee that hath seene his *friend* die to *day*, or knowes hee shall see it to *morrow*, yet will sinke into a sleepe betweene. I cannot; and 25 oh, if I be entring now into *Eternitie*, where there shall bee no more distinction of *houres*, why is it al my businesse now *to tell Clocks*? why is none of the *heavinesse* of my *heart*, dispensed into mine *Eie-lids*, that they might fall as my heart doth? And why, since I have lost my delight in all *objects*, cannot I discontinue the facultie of seeing them, 30 by closing mine Eies in *sleepe*? But why rather, being entring into that presence, where I shall wake continually and never sleepe more, doe I not interpret my continuall waking here, to bee a *parasceve*, and a *preparation* to that?

16 day, *A*: day; all edd.   24 hee that] Hee that 1624(2), 1626   29 fall] fall, 1624(2), 1626   31 rather, *Ed.*: rather all edd.

15. EXPOSTULATION

My *God*, my *God*, I know, (for thou hast said it) *That he that keepeth*   Psa. 121.4
Israel, shall neither slumber, nor sleepe: But shall not that *Israel*, over
whom thou watchest, sleepe? I know, (for thou hast said it) that
5 there are Men, *whose damnation sleepeth not*; but shall not they to   2 Pet. 2.3
whom thou art *Salvation*, sleepe? or wilt thou take from them that
evidence, and that *testimony*, that they are thy *Israel*, or thou their
salvation? *Thou givest thy beloved sleepe*. Shall I lacke that *seale* of thy   Psa. 127.2
love? You shall lie downe, and none shall make you afraid; Shal I bee   Lev. 26.6
10 *outlawd* from that *protection*? *Jonas slept in one dangerous storme*, and   Jon. 1.5
thy blessed Sonne in another. Shall I have no use, no benefit, no   Mat. 8.24
application of those great *Examples*? *Lord, if hee sleepe, he shall doe*   Jo. 11.12
well, say thy *Sonnes Disciples* to him, of *Lazarus*; And shall there bee
no roome, for that *Argument* in me? or shall I bee open to the
15 contrary? If I sleepe not, shall I not bee well, in their sense? Let me   Eccles. 8.16
not, O my *God*, take this too *precisely*, too *literally*: *There is that*
neither day nor night seeth sleepe with his eies, saies thy wise servant
Solomon; and whether hee speake that of *worldly Men*, or of Men
that *seeke wisdome*, whether in *justification* or *condemnation* of their
20 watchfulnesse, we can not tell: wee can tell, *That there are men, that*   Pro. 4.16
cannot sleepe, till they have done mischiefe, and then they can; and wee
can tell that *the rich man cannot sleepe, because his abundance will not let*   Eccles. 5.12
him. The tares were sowen when the husbandmen were asleepe; And the   Mat. 13.25
elders thought it a probable excuse, a credible lie, that the watchmen
25 which kept the Sepulchre, should say, *that the bodie of thy son was*   28.13
stolne away, when they were asleepe: Since thy blessed *Sonne* rebuked
his Disciples for *sleeping*, shall I murmure because I doe not sleepe?   26.40
If *Samson* had slept any longer in *Gaza*, he had beene taken; And   Jud. 16.3
when he did sleepe longer with *Delilah*, he was taken. *Sleepe* is as   *v. 19*
30 often taken for *naturall death* in thy *Scriptures*, as for *naturall rest*. Nay
sometimes *sleepe* hath so heavy a sense, as to bee taken for *sinne it*   Eph. 5.14
selfe, as well as for the punishment of *sinne, Death*. Much comfort is   1 Thes. 5.6
not in much sleepe, when the most fearefull and most irrevocable

Margin 121.4 *S*: 121.1 all edd.   4 know,] know 1624(2), 1626   *Margin* 127.2
Ed.: 127.1 all edd.   *Margin* 8.24] 8.14 1624(2), 1626   13 him,] him 1624(2),
1626   20 *men*,] men 1624(2), 1626

Jer. 51.39

Malediction is presented by thee, in a *perpetuall sleepe. I will make their feasts, and I will make them drunke, and they shall sleepe a perpetuall sleepe, and not wake.* I must therefore, O my God, looke farther, than into the very act of sleeping, before I mis-interpret my waking: for since I finde thy whole hand light, shall any *finger* of that hand seeme 5 heavy? since the whole sicknesse is thy *Physicke,* shall any accident in it, bee my poison, by my murmuring? The name of *Watchmen* belongs to our *profession*; Thy *Prophets* are not onely *seers* indued with a *power* of seeing, able to see, but *Watchmen,* evermore in the *Act* of seeing. And therefore give me leave, O my blessed *God,* to invert the 10

Can. 5.2

words of thy *Sonnes Spouse*; she said, *I sleepe, but my heart waketh*; I say, *I wake, but my heart sleepeth*; My body is in a sicke wearinesse, but my soule in a peacefull rest with thee; and as our *eies,* in our health, see not the *Aire,* that is next them, nor the *fire,* nor the *spheares,* nor stop upon any thing, till they come to *starres,* so my *eies,* that are 15 open, see nothing of this world, but passe through all that, and fix themselves upon thy *peace,* and *joy,* and *glory* above. Almost as soone

I Thes. 5.6
v. 10

as thy *Apostle* had said, *Let us not sleepe,* lest we should be too much discomforted, if we did, he saies againe, *whether we wake or sleepe, let us live together with Christ.* Though then this *absence of sleepe,* may 20 argue the *presence of death* (the *Originall* may exclude the *Copie,* the *life,* the *picture*) yet this gentle *sleepe,* and rest of my *soule* betroths mee to thee, to whom I shall bee married *indissolubly,* though by this way of *dissolution.*

15. PRAYER   25

O eternall and most gracious *God,* who art able to make, and dost make the *sicke bed* of thy servants, *Chappels of ease* to them, and the *dreames* of thy servants, *Prayers,* and *Meditations* upon thee, let not this continuall watchfulnes of mine, this inabilitie to sleepe, which thou hast laid upon mee, bee any *disquiet,* or *discomfort* to me, but 30 rather an argument, that thou wouldest not have me sleepe in thy *presence.* What it may indicate or signifie, concerning the state of my

Margin 51.39 *Ed.*: 51.59 all edd.   Margin 5.2 *Ed.*: 5.8 all edd.   13 *eies,*] *Eyes* 1624(2), 1626   22 *soule*] *Soule,* 1624(2), 1626

body, let them consider to whom that consideration belongs; doe thou, who onely art the *Physitian* of my *soule*, tell her, that thou wilt afford her such *defensatives* as that shee shall *wake* ever towards thee, and yet ever *sleepe* in *thee*; & that through all this sicknesse, thou wilt
5 either preserve mine understanding, from all decaies and distractions, which these watchings might occasion, or that thou wilt reckon, and account with me, from before those violences, and not call any peece of my *sicknesse*, a *sinne*. It is a heavy, and indelible sinne, that I brought into the world with me; It is a heavy and innumerable
10 multitude of sins, which I have heaped up since; I have sinned *behind thy backe* (if that can be done) by wilfull absteining from thy *Congregations*, and omitting thy *service*, and I have sinned *before thy face*, in my *hypocrisies* in Prayer, in my *ostentation*, and the mingling a respect of *my selfe*, in preaching thy Word; I have sinned in my
15 *fasting* by repining, when a penurious fortune hath kept mee low; And I have sinned even in that fulnesse, when I have been at thy table, by a negligent examination, by a wilfull prevarication, in receiving that heavenly *food* and *Physicke*. But, as I know, O my gracious *God*, that for all those sinnes committed since, yet thou
20 wilt consider me, as I was in thy *purpose*, when thou wrotest my name in the *booke of Life*, in mine *Election:* so into what deviations soever I stray, and wander, by occasion of this sicknes, O *God*, returne thou to that *Minute*, wherein thou wast pleased with me, and consider me in that *condition*.

25 ## 16. Et properare meum clamant, è Turre propinqua, Obstreperae Campanae aliorum in funere, funus.

From the bels of the church adjoyning, I am daily remembred of my buriall in the funeralls of others.

16. MEDITATION

30 We have a *Convenient Author*, who writ a *Discourse of Bells* when hee was Prisoner in *Turky*. How would hee have enlarged himselfe, if he

Magius.

---

4 *thee*;] *thee* 1624(2); *thee,* 1626   7 violencies] violences 1624(2), 1626   8 indelible] indelibly 1624(2), 1626   30 *Bells*] *Bells,* 1626   31 *Turky.*] *Turky,* 1626

had beene my *fellow Prisoner* in this *sicke bed*, so neere to that *steeple*, which never ceases, no more than the *harmony of the spheres*, but is more heard. When the *Turkes* tooke *Constantinople*, they melted the *Bells* into *Ordnance*; I have heard both *Bells* and *Ordnance*, but never been so much affected with those, as with these *Bells*, I have lien 5

Antwerp
Roan.

neere a *steeple*, in which there are said to be more than *thirty Bels*; And neere another, where there is one so bigge, as that the *Clapper* is said to weigh more than *six hundred pound*; yet never so affected as here. Here the *Bells* can scarse solemnise the funerall of any person, but that I knew him, or knew that hee was my *Neighbour*: we dwelt 10 in houses neere to one another before, but now hee is gone into that house, into which I must follow him. There is a way of correcting the *Children* of great persons, that other *Children* are corrected in their *behalfe*, and in their *names*, and this workes upon them, who indeed had more deserved it. And when these *Bells* tell me, that now 15 one, and now another is buried, must not I acknowledge, that they have the *correction* due to me, and paid the *debt* that I owe? There is a

Roccha.

story of a *Bell* in a *Monastery*, which, when any of the house was sicke to death, rung alwaies *voluntarily*, and they knew the inevitable-nesse of the danger by that. It rung once, when no man was sick; but 20 the next day one of the house, fell from the *steeple*, and died, and the *Bell* held the reputation of a *Prophet* still. If these *Bells* that warne to a *Funerall* now, were appropriated to none, may not I, by the houre of the *funerall*, supply? How many men that stand at an *execution*, if they would aske, for what dies that Man, should heare their owne 25 faults condemned, and see themselves executed, by *Atturney*? We scarce heare of any man *preferred*, but wee thinke of our selves, that wee might very well have beene that *Man*; Why might not I have beene that *Man*, that is carried to his *grave* now? Could I fit my selfe, to *stand*, or *sit* in any Mans *place*, & not to lie in any mans *grave*? I 30 may lacke much of the *good parts* of the meanest, but I lacke nothing of the *mortality* of the weakest; They may have acquired better *abilities* than I, but I was borne to as many *infirmities* as they. To be an *incumbent* by lying down in a *grave*, to be a *Doctor* by teaching *Mortification* by *Example*, by *dying*, though I may have *seniors*, others 35

8 *pound*;] *pound*, 1624(2), 1626   20 sick;] sick, 1624(2), 1626

may be *elder* than I, yet I have proceeded apace in a good *University*, and
gone a great way in a little time, by the furtherance of a vehement
fever; and whomsoever these *Bells* bring to the ground to day, if hee
and I had beene compared yesterday, perchance I should have been
5 thought likelier to come to this preferment, then, than he. *God* hath
kept the power of *death* in his owne hands, lest any Man should
bribe death. If man knew the *gaine of death*, the *ease of death*, he would
solicite, he would provoke death to assist him, by any hand, which
he might use. But as when men see many of their owne professions
10 preferd, it ministers a hope that that may light upon them; so when
these hourely *Bells* tell me of so many *funerals* of men like me, it
presents, if not a *desire* that it may, yet a *comfort* whensoever mine
shall come.

16. EXPOSTULATION

15 My *God*, my *God*, I doe not expostulate with *thee*, but with *them*,
who dare doe that: Who dare expostulate with *thee*, when in the
voice of thy *Church*, thou givest allowance, to this *Ceremony* of *Bells*
at *funeralls*. Is it enough to refuse it, because it was in use amongst the
Gentiles? so were *funeralls* too. Is it because some *abuses* may have
20 crept in, amongst *Christians*? Is that enough, that their ringing hath
been said to drive away *evill spirits*? Truly, that is so farre true, as
that the *evill spirit* is vehemently vexed in their ringing, therefore,
because that action brings the *Congregation* together, and unites *God*
and his *people*, to the destruction of that *Kingdome*, which the *evill*
25 *spirit* usurps. In the first *institution* of thy *Church*, in this world, in the
foundation of thy *Militant Church*, amongst the *Jewes*, thou didst
appoint the calling of the *assembly* in, to bee by *Trumpet*, and when   Num. 10.2
they were in, then thou gavest them the sound of *Bells*, in the   Exo. 18.33
garment of thy *Priest*. In the *Triumphant Church*, thou imploiest both
30 too, but in an inverted *Order*; we enter into the *Triumphant Church* by
the sound of Bells (for we *enter* when we *die*;) And then we receive
our further *edification*, or *consummation*, by the sound of *Trumpets*, at
the *Resurrection*. The sound of thy *Trumpets* thou didst impart to

---

3 *fever*;] Fever, 1624(2), 1626   17 allowance,] allowance 1624(2), 1626   18 Is
it] It is 1624(2), 1626   20 in,] in 1626   *Margin* 10.2 S: 10.1 all edd.   28
sound] sonnd 1626   *Margin* 18.33 S: 18 all edd.   31 ;)] ;(1626

secular and *civill* uses too, but the sound of *Bells* onely to *sacred*; Lord
let us not breake the *Communion of Saints*, in that which was intended
for the *advancement* of it; let not that pull us asunder from one
another, which was intended for the assembling of us, in the *Militant*,
and associating of us to the *Triumphant Church*. But he for whose 5
funerall these *Bells* ring now, was at *home*, at his journies end,
yesterday; why ring they now? A *Man*, that is a world, is all the
things in the *world*; Hee is an *Army*, and when an *Army* marches, the
Vaunt may lodge to night, where the *Reare* comes not till to morrow.
A man extends to his *Act* and to his *example*; to that which he *does*, 10
and that which he *teaches*; so doe those things that concerne him, so
doe these *bells*; That which rung yesterday, was to convay him out
of the *world*, in his *vaunt*, in his *soule*: that which rung to day, was to
bring him in his *Reare*, in his *body*, to the *Church*; And this continuing of ringing after his *entring*, is to bring him to mee in the 15
application. Where I lie, I could heare the *Psalme*, and did joine with
the *Congregation* in it; but I could not heare the *Sermon*, and these
latter *bells* are a *repetition Sermon* to mee. But, O my *God*, my *God*, doe
I, that have this *feaver*, need other *remembrances* of my *Mortalitie*? Is not
mine owne *hollow voice*, voice enough to pronounce that to me? 20
Need I looke upon a *Deaths-head* in a *Ring*, that have one in my *face*?
or goe for *death* to my *Neighbours* house, that have him in my *bosome*?
We cannot, wee cannot, O my *God*, take in too many *helps* for
religious *duties*; I know I cannot have any better *Image* of *thee*, than
thy *Sonne*, nor any better *Image* of *him*, than his *Gospell*: yet must not 25
I, with thanks confesse to thee, that some *historicall pictures* of his,
have sometimes put mee upon better *Meditations* than otherwise I
should have fallen upon? I know thy *Church* needed not to have
taken in from *Jew* or *Gentile*, any supplies for the exaltation of thy
glory, or our *devotion*; of *absolute necessitie* I know shee needed not; 30
But yet wee owe thee our thanks, that thou hast given her leave to
doe so, and that as in making us *Christians*, thou diddest not destroy
that which wee were before, *naturall men*, so in the exalting of our
religious devotions now we are *Christians*, thou hast beene pleased
to continue to us those *assistances* which did worke upon the affections 35

4 for] for for 1624(2)   11 *teaches*;] *teaches*, 1624(2), 1626   13 *soule*:] *soule*,
1626   21 *Deaths-head*] *Deatheshead* 1626   22 house,] house 1626   25 *Gospell*:] *Gospel*; 1626   27 *Meditations*] *Meditations*, 1626   33 *men*,] *men*,, 1626

of *naturall men* before: for thou lovest a *good man*, as thou lovest a *good Christian*: and though *Grace* bee meerely from thee, yet thou doest not plant Grace but in *good natures*.

16. PRAYER

5 O eternall and most gracious *God*, who having consecrated our living *bodies*, to thine owne *Spirit*, and made us *Temples of the holy Ghost*, doest also require a respect to bee given to these *Temples*, even when the *Priest* is gone out of them; To these *bodies*, when the *soule* is departed from them; I blesse, and glorifie thy *Name*, that as thou
10 takest care in our life, of every haire of our head, so doest thou also of every graine of *ashes* after our death. Neither doest thou only doe good to us all, in *life* and *death*, but also wouldest have us doe good to one another, as in a holy *life*, so in those things which accompanie our *death*: In that Contemplation I make account that I heare this
15 dead brother of ours, who is now carried out to his *buriall*, to speake to mee, and to *preach* my *funerall Sermon*, in the voice of these *Bells*. In him, O *God*, thou hast accomplished to mee, even the request of *Dives* to *Abraham*; *Thou hast sent one from the dead to speake unto mee.* He speakes to mee aloud from that *steeple*; hee whispers to mee at
20 these *Curtaines*, and hee speaks thy words; *Blessed are the dead which die in the Lord, from henceforth.* Let this *praier* therfore, O my *God*, be as my *last gaspe*, my *expiring*, my *dying* in *thee*; That if this bee the houre of my *transmigration*, I may die the *death* of a *sinner*, drowned in my *sinnes*, in the *bloud* of thy *Sonne*; And if I live longer, yet I may
25 now *die* the *death* of the *righteous, die to sinne*; which *death* is a *resurrection* to a new *life. Thou killest and thou givest life*: which soever comes, it comes from *thee*; which way soever it comes, let mee come to *thee*.

Apoc. 14.13

6 *bodies*,] bodies 1624(2), 1626   26 *life*.] life: 1626   27 *thee*;] thee, 1626

17. Nunc lento sonitu dicunt, Morieris.

*Now, this Bell tolling softly for another, saies to
me, Thou must die.*

17. MEDITATION

Perchance hee for whom this *Bell* tolls, may bee so ill, as that he 5
knowes not it *tolls* for him; And perchance I may thinke my selfe so
much better than I am, as that they who are about mee, and see my
state, may have caused it to toll for mee, and I know not that. The
Church is *Catholike, universall,* so are all her *Actions; All* that she does,
belongs to *all.* When she *baptizes a child,* that action concernes mee; 10
for that child is thereby connected to that *Head* which is my *Head*
too, and engraffed into that *body,* whereof I am a *member.* And when
she *buries a Man,* that action concernes me; All *mankinde* is of one
Author, and is one *volume;* when one Man dies, one *Chapter* is not
torne out of the *booke,* but *translated* into a better *language;* and every 15
Chapter must be so *translated; God* emploies severall *translators;* some
peeces are translated by *Age,* some by *sicknesse,* some by *warre,* some
by *justice;* but *Gods* hand is in every *translation;* and his hand shall
binde up all our scattered leaves againe, for that *Librarie* where every
booke shall lie open to one another: As therefore the *Bell* that rings 20
to a *Sermon,* calls not upon the *Preacher* onely, but upon the *Congrega-*
tion to come; so this *Bell* calls us all: but how much more *mee,* who
am brought so neere the *doore* by this *sicknesse.* There was a *contention*
as farre as a *suite,* (in which both *pietie* and *dignitie, religion,* and
estimation, were mingled) which of the religious *Orders* should ring 25
to *praiers* first in the *Morning;* and it was *determined,* that *they should*
ring first that rose earliest. If we understand aright the *dignitie* of this
Bell, that tolls for our *evening prayer,* wee would bee glad to make it
ours, by rising early, in that *application,* that it might bee ours, as wel
as his, whose indeed it is. The *Bell* doth toll for him that *thinkes* it 30
doth; and though it *intermit* againe, yet from that *minute,* that that

3 *die.*] *die:* 1626   9 does,] does 1624(2), 1626   29 *application*] *apylycation*
1624(2)

occasion wrought upon him, hee is united to *God*. Who casts not up his *Eie* to the *Sunne* when it rises? but who takes off his *Eie* from a *Comet*, when that breakes out? who bends not his *eare* to any *bell*, which upon any occasion rings? but who can remove it from that
5 *bell*, which is passing a *peece of himselfe* out of this *world*? No Man is an *Iland*, intire of it selfe; every man is a peece of the *Continent*, a part of the *maine*; if a *Clod* bee washed away by the *Sea*, *Europe* is the lesse, as well as if a *Promontorie* were, as well as if a *Mannor* of thy *friends*, or of *thine owne* were; Any Mans *death* diminishes *me*,
10 because I am involved in *Mankinde*; And therefore never send to know for whom the *bell* tolls; It tolls for *thee*. Neither can we call this a *begging* of *Miserie* or a *borrowing* of *Miserie*, as though we were not miserable enough of our selves, but must fetch in more from the next house, in taking upon us the *Miserie* of our *Neighbours*. Truly it
15 were an excusable *covetousnesse* if wee did; for *affliction* is a *treasure*, and scarce any Man hath *enough* of it. No Man hath *affliction* enough, that is not matured, and ripened by it, and made fit for *God* by that *affliction*. If a Man carry *treasure* in *bullion*, or in a *wedge of gold*, and have none coined into *currant Monies*, his *treasure* will not defray him
20 as he travells. *Tribulation* is *Treasure* in the *nature* of it, but it is not *currant money* in the use of it, except wee get nearer and nearer our *home*, *heaven*, by it. Another Man may be *sicke* too, and sicke to *death*, and this *affliction* may lie in his *bowels*, as *gold* in a *Mine*, and be of no use to him; but this *bell* that tels mee of his *affliction*, digs out,
25 and applies that *gold* to *mee*: if by this consideration of anothers danger, I take mine owne into Contemplation, and so secure my selfe, by making my recourse to my *God*, who is our onely securitie.

17. EXPOSTULATION

My *God*, my *God*, Is this one of thy waies, of *drawing light out of*
30 *darknesse*, To make *him* for whom this *bell* tolls, now in this dimnesse of his sight, to become a *superintendent*, an *overseer*, a *Bishop*, to as many as heare his *voice*, in this *bell*, and to give us a *confirmation* in

---

12 *Miserie*] misery, 1624(2), 1626   16 enough,] enough; 1626

this action? Is this one of thy waies *to raise strength out of weaknesse*, to make him who cannot rise *from his bed*, nor stirre *in his bed*, come *home* to *me*, and in this sound, give mee the strength of *healthy* and vigorous *instructions*? O my *God*, my *God*, what *Thunder* is not a *well-tuned Cymball*, what *hoarsenesse*, what *harshnesse* is not a cleare 5 *Organ*, if thou bee pleased to set *thy voice* to it? and what *Organ* is not well plaied on, if thy *hand* bee upon it? Thy *voice*, thy *hand* is in this *sound*, and in this *one sound*, I heare this *whole Consort*. I heare thy

Gen. 49.1

Jaacob call unto his *sonnes*, and say: *Gather your selves together, that I may tell you what shall befall you in the last daies*: He saies, *That which I* 10 *am now, you must bee then.* I heare thy *Moses* telling mee, and all

Deut. 33.1

within the *compasse* of this *sound, This is the blessing wherewith I blesse you before my death*; This, that before your death, you would consider

2 Reg. 20.1

your owne in mine. I heare thy *Prophet* saying to *Ezechias, Set thy house in order, for thou shalt die, and not live*; Hee makes us of his 15 *familie*, and calls this a setting of *his* house in order, to compose *us* to

2 Pet. 1.13, 14

the *meditation* of *death*. I heare thy *Apostle* saying, *I thinke it meet to put you in remembrance, knowing that shortly I must goe out of this Tabernacle.* This is the *publishing* of his *will*, & this *bell* is our *legacie*, the applying of *his present condition* to our use. I heare that which makes al sounds 20 *musique*, and all *musique* perfit; I heare thy *Sonne* himselfe saying, *Let*

Joh. 14.1

not your hearts be troubled; Only I heare this *change*, that whereas thy *Sonne* saies there, *I goe to prepare a place for you*, this man in this *sound* saies, *I send to prepare you for a place, for a grave.* But, O my *God*, my *God*, since *heaven* is *glory* and *joy*, why doe not *glorious* and *joyfull* 25 things leade us, induce us to *heaven*? Thy *legacies* in thy first *will*, in thy *old Testament* were *plentie* and *victorie*; *Wine* and *Oile, Milke* and *Honie*, *alliances of friends, ruine of enemies, peacefull hearts*, & *cheerefull countenances*, and by these *galleries* thou broughtest them into thy *bed-chamber*, by these *glories* and *joies*, to the *joies* and *glories* of 30 *heaven*. Why hast thou changed thine old way, and carried us, by the waies of *discipline* and *mortification*, by the *waies* of *mourning* and *lamentation*, by the waies of *miserable ends*, and *miserable anticipations* of those miseries, in appropriating the *exemplar* miseries of others to our selves, and *usurping* upon their *miseries*, as our owne, to our owne 35

10 *daies*:] *dayes*, 1626   17 *death*.] *death* 1626   *Margin* 1.13,14 *Ed.*: 2.13 all edd.   27 *thy old*] *the old* 1624(2), 1626   27 *Testament*] *Testament*, 1624(2), 1626   31 *us*,] *us* 1624(2), 1626

prejudice? Is the *glory* of *heaven* no perfecter in it selfe, but that it needs a *soile* of *depression* and *ingloriousnesse* in this *world*, to set it off? Is the *joy* of *heaven* no perfecter in it selfe, but that it needs the *sourenesse* of this *life* to give it a *taste*? Is that *joy* and that *glory* but a
5 *comparative glory* and a *comparative joy*? not such in *it selfe*, but such in *comparison* of the *joilesnesse* and the *ingloriousnesse* of this *world*? I know, my *God*, it is farre, farre otherwise. As thou thy selfe, who art *all*, art made of no *substances*, so the *joyes* & glory which are with thee, are made of none of these *circumstances*; *Essentiall joy*, and *glory*
10 *Essentiall*. But why then, my *God*, wilt thou not *beginne* them *here*? pardon O *God*, this *unthankfull rashnesse*; I that aske why thou *doest not*, finde even now in *my selfe*, that thou *doest*; such *joy*, such *glory*, as that I conclude upon *my selfe*, upon *all*, They that finde not *joy* in their *sorrowes*, *glory* in their *dejections* in this *world*, are in a fearefull
15 *danger* of missing both in the *next*.

17. PRAYER

O eternall and most gracious *God*, who hast beene pleased to *speake* to us, not onely in the *voice* of *Nature*, who speakes in our *hearts*, and of thy *word*, which speakes to our *eares*, but in the speech of *speech-*
20 *lesse Creatures*, in *Balaams Asse*, in the speech of *unbeleeving men*, in the confession of *Pilate*, in the speech of the *Devill* himselfe, in the *recognition* and *attestation* of thy *Sonne*, I humbly accept thy *voice*, in the sound of this sad and funerall *bell*. And first, I blesse thy glorious name, that in this *sound* and *voice*, I can heare thy *instructions*, in
25 *another mans* to consider *mine owne condition*; and to know, that this *bell* which *tolls* for another, before it come to *ring out*, may take in me too. As *death is the wages of sinne*, it is *due* to mee; As death is *the end of sicknesse*, it belongs to *mee*; And though so disobedient a *servant* as I, may be afraid to *die*, yet to so mercifull a *Master* as thou, I cannot be
30 afraid to *come*; And therefore, *into thy hands*, O my *God*, *I commend my spirit*; A *surrender*, which I know thou wilt accept, whether I *live* or *die*; for thy *servant David* made it, when he put himselfe into thy

Psa. 31.5

---

9 thee,] thee 1624(2), 1626   10 then,] then 1626   11 this] his 1626   19 *word*,] *word* 1626   22 *Sonne*,] *Sonne*; 1626   30 *I commend* 1624(2), 1626, S: I *commend* 1624(1)

protection for his life; and thy blessed *Sonne* made it, when hee delivered up his *soule* at his *death*; declare thou thy will upon mee, O *Lord*, for *life* or *death*, in thy time; receive my *surrender* of my selfe now, *Into thy hands, O Lord I commend my spirit.* And being thus, O my *God*, prepared by thy *correction*, mellowed by thy chastisement, and conformed to thy will, by thy *Spirit*, having received thy *pardon* for my *soule*, and asking no *reprieve* for my *body*, I am bold, O *Lord*, to bend my *prayers* to thee, for his *assistance*, the voice of whose *bell* hath called mee to this *devotion*. Lay hold upon his *soule*, O *God*, till that *soule* have throughly considered his *account*, and how few minutes soever it have to remaine in that *body*, let the power of thy *Spirit* recompence the shortnesse of time, and perfect his *account*, before he passe away: present his *sinnes* so to him, as that he may *know* what thou forgivest, & not doubt of thy *forgivenesse*; let him *stop* upon the *infinitenesse* of those sinnes, but *dwell* upon the *infinitenesse* of thy *Mercy*: let him discerne his owne *demerits*, but wrap himselfe up in the *merits* of thy *Sonne, Christ Jesus*: Breath inward *comforts* to his *heart*, and affoord him the power of giving such outward *testimonies* thereof, as all that are about him may derive comforts from thence, and have this *edification*, even in this *dissolution*, that though the *body* be going the way of all *flesh*, yet that *soule* is going the way of all *Saints*. When thy *Sonne* cried out upon the *Crosse, My God, my God, Why hast thou forsaken me*? he spake not so much in his *owne Person*, as in the person of the *Church*, and of his afflicted *members*, who in deep distresses might feare thy *forsaking*. This *patient*, O most blessed *God*, is one of *them*; In his behalfe, and in his name, heare thy *Sonne* crying to thee, *My God, my God, Why hast thou forsaken me*? and forsake him not; but with thy *left hand* lay his *body* in the *grave*, (if that bee thy *determination* upon him) and with thy *right hand* receive his *soule* into thy *Kingdome*, and unite *him* & *us* in one *Communion of Saints*. Amen.

5

10

15

20

25

30

4 *hands*,] hands 1626   17 *Sonne*,] Son 1624(2), 1626

18. At inde, Mortuus es, Sonitu celeri, pulsuque agitato.

The bell rings out, and tells me in him, that I am dead.

18. MEDITATION

5 The *Bell* rings out; the *pulse* thereof is changed; the *tolling* was a *faint*, and *intermitting pulse*, upon one side; this *stronger*, and argues *more* and *better life*. His *soule* is gone out; and as a Man who had a lease of 1000. *yeeres* after the expiration of a short one, or an *inheritance* after the *life* of a Man in a *Consumption*, he is now entred into
10 the possession of his *better estate*. His *soule* is gone; *whither*? Who saw it *come in*, or who saw it *goe out*? *No body*; yet every body is sure, he *had one*, and *hath none*. If I will aske meere *Philosophers*, what the *soule* is, I shall finde amongst them, that will tell me, it is nothing, but the *temperament* and *harmony*, and *just and equall composition of the*
15 *Elements in the body*, which produces all those *faculties* which we ascribe to the *soule*; and so, in it selfe is *nothing*, no *seperable substance*, that overlives the *body*. They see the *soule* is nothing else in other *Creatures*, and they affect an *impious humilitie*, to think *as low of Man*. But if my *soule* were no more than the soule of a *beast*, I could not
20 thinke so; that *soule* that can *reflect* upon it selfe, *consider* it selfe, is *more* than so. If I will aske, not meere *Philosophers*, but *mixt* Men, *Philosphicall Divines, how* the *soule*, being a *separate substance*, enters into *Man*, I shall finde some that will tell me, that it is by *generation*, & *procreation* from *parents*, because they thinke it hard, to charge the
25 *soule* with the guiltinesse of *Originall* sinne, if the *soule* were infused into a *body*, in which it must necessarily grow *foule*, and contract *originall sinne*, whether it *will* or no; and I shall finde some that will tell mee, that it is by *immediate infusion from God*, because they think it hard, to maintaine an *immortality* in such a *soule*, as should be
30 begotten, and derived with the *body* from *Mortall parents*. If I will aske, not *a few men*, but almost *whole bodies, whole Churches*, what

1 inde, *Ed.*: inde all edd.   1 celeri] celari 1624(2), 1626   5 out;] out 1624(2), 1626   10 gone;] gone, 1626   16 *substance*,] *substance*; 1626   30 begotten,] begotten 1626

becomes of the *soules* of the *righteous*, at the *departing* thereof from the *body*, I shall bee told by some, *That they attend an expiation, a purification in a place of torment*; By some, that *they attend the fruition of the sight of God, in a place of rest; but yet, but of expectation*; By some, *that they passe to an immediate possession of the presence of God. S.* 5 *Augustine* studied the *Nature* of the *soule*, as much as any thing, but the *salvation of the soule*; and he sent an expresse *Messenger* to Saint *Hierome*, to consult of some things concerning the *soule*: But he satisfies himselfe with this: *Let the departure of my soule to salvation be evident to my faith, and I care the lesse, how darke the entrance of my soule,* 10 *into my body, bee to my reason.* It is the *going out*, more than the *coming in*, that concernes us. This *soule*, this *Bell* tells me is *gone out*; *Whither*? Who shall tell mee that? I know not *who* it is; much lesse *what* he was; The condition of the Man, and the course of his life, which should tell mee *whither* hee is gone, I know not. I was not there, in 15 his *sicknesse*, nor at his *death*; I saw not his *way*, nor his *end*, nor can aske them, who did, thereby to *conclude*, or *argue*, whither he is gone. But yet I have one neerer mee than all these, mine owne *Charity*; I aske that; & that tels me, *He is gone to everlasting rest*, and *joy*, and *glory*: I owe him a good *opinion*; it is but *thankfull charity* in mee, 20 because I received *benefit* and *instruction* from him when his *Bell* told: and I, being made the fitter to *pray*, by that disposition, wherein I was assisted by his occasion, did *pray* for him; and I *pray* not without *faith*; so I doe *charitably*, so I do *faithfully* beleeve, that that *soule* is gone to everlasting *rest*, and *joy*, and *glory*. But for the *body*, How 25 poore a wretched thing is *that*? wee cannot expresse it *so fast*, as it growes *worse* and *worse*. That *body* which scarce *three minutes* since was such a *house*, as that that *soule*, which made but one step from thence to *Heaven*, was scarse thorowly content, to leave that for *Heaven*: that *body* hath lost the *name* of a *dwelling house*, because none 30 dwels in it, and is making haste to lose the name of a *body*, and dissolve to *putrefaction*. Who would not bee affected, to see a cleere & sweet *River* in the *Morning*, grow a *kennell* of muddy land water by *noone*, and condemned to the saltnesse of the *Sea* by *night*? And how lame a *Picture*, how faint a *representation*, is that, of the precipitation 35

15 there,] there 1624(2), 1626   18 these, *Ed.*: these; all edd.   19 that;] that, 1624(2), 1626   19 rest,] rest 1624(2), 1626   19 joy,] joy 1624(2), 1626   22 I,] I 1626   32 affected, 1624(1) *corrected*: affected 1624(1) O¹², HN *originally*, 1624(2), 1626

of mans body to *dissolution*? *Now* all the parts built up, and knit by a lovely *soule*, *now* but a *statue* of *clay*, and *now*, these limbs melted off, as if that *clay* were but *snow*; and now, the whole *house* is but a *handfull of sand*, so much *dust*, and but *a pecke of Rubbidge*, so much

5 *bone*. If *he*, who, as this *Bell* tells mee, is gone now, were some *excellent Artificer*, who comes to him for a *clocke*, or for a *garment* now? or for *counsaile*, if hee were a *Lawyer*? If a *Magistrate*, for *justice*? Man before hee hath his *immortall soule*, hath a *soule of sense*, and a *soule* of *vegitation* before that: This *immortall soule* did not for-

10 bid other *soules*, to be in us before, but when this *soule* departs, it carries all with it; no more *vegetation*, no more *sense*: such a *Mother in law* is the *Earth*, in respect of our *naturall Mother*; in her *wombe* we grew; and when she was delivered of us, wee were planted in some *place*, in some *calling* in the *world*; In the wombe of the Earth, wee

15 *diminish*, and when shee is *delivered* of us, our *grave* opened for another, wee are not *transplanted*, but *transported*, our *dust* blowne away with *prophane dust*, with every wind.

18. EXPOSTULATION

My *God*, my *God*, if *Expostulation* bee too bold a word, doe thou

20 *mollifie* it with another; let it be *wonder* in my selfe; let it bee but *probleme* to others; but let me aske, why wouldest thou not suffer those, that serve thee in *holy services*, to doe any *office* about the *dead*,   Levit. 21.1 nor *assist* at their *funerall*? Thou hadst no *Counsellor*, thou needest none; thou hast no *Controller*, thou admittest none. Why doe I aske?

25 In *Ceremoniall things* (as that was) any *convenient reason* is enough; who can bee sure to propose that *reason*, that moved thee in the institution thereof? I satisfie my selfe with this; that in those *times*, the *Gentiles* were overfull, of an over-reverent respect to the *memory of the dead*: a great part of the *Idolatry* of the *Nations*, flowed

30 from that; an *over-amorous devotion*, an *over-zealous celebrating*, and *over-studious preserving* of the *memories*, and the *Pictures* of some *dead persons*: And by *the vaine glory of men, they entred into the world*; and   Sap. 14.14

2 *now*,] *now* 1626   2,3 off,... *clay*] off... *clay*, 1624(2), 1626   16 *dust*] *dust*, 1626   25 In 1624(2), 1626, S: in 1624(1)

93

their *statues*, and *pictures* contracted an opinion of *divinity*, by *age*: that which was at first, but a *picture* of a *friend*, grew a *God* in time, as

Sap. 13.10 the *wise man* notes, *They called them Gods, which were the worke of an ancient hand*. And some have assigned a *certaine time*, when a *picture* should come out of *Minority*, and bee at *age*, to bee a *God*, in 60. 5 yeeres after it is made. Those *Images* of *Men*, that had *life*, and some *Idols* of other things, which never had any *being*, are by one common name, called promiscuously, *dead*; and for that the *wise man* repre-

Sap. 13.18
Esay 8.19 hends the *Idolatrer; for health he praies to that which is weake, and for life he praies to that which is dead. Should we doe so*, saies thy *Prophet;* 10 *should we goe from the living to the dead?* So much ill then, being occasioned, by so much religious *complement* exhibited to the *dead*: thou *ô God*, (*I think*) wouldest therefore inhibit thy *principall holy servants*, from contributing any thing at all to this dangerous *intimation of Idolatry*; and that the people might say, surely those *dead men*, 15 are not so much to bee magnified, as men mistake, since *God* will not suffer his *holy officers*, so much as to *touch* them, not to *see* them. But those dangers being removed, thou, O my *God*, dost certainly allow, that we should doe *offices* of *piety* to the *dead*, and that we should draw *instructions* to *piety*, from the *dead*. Is not this, O my *God*, a holy 20 kinde of *raising up seed to my dead brother*, if I, by the meditation of his *death*, produce a better *life* in my selfe? It is the blessing upon

Deu. 33.6 *Reuben, Let Reuben live, & not die, and let not his men be few*; let him
Zechar. 11.9 propagate *many*. And it is a *Malediction, That that dieth, let it die*; let it
Jud. 12 doe no good in dying: for *Trees without fruit*, thou by thy *Apostle* 25 callst, *twice dead*. It is a *second death*, if none live the better, by me, after my *death*, by the *manner* of my *death*. Therefore may I justly

Exo. 12.30 thinke, that thou madest that a way to convay to the *Ægyptians*, a *feare* of *thee*, and a *feare* of *death*, that *there was not a house, where there was not one dead*; for therupon the *Ægyptians* said, *we are all dead* 30

Apo. 1.5 *men*; the *death* of *others*, should *catechise* us to *death*. Thy *Sonne Christ Jesus* is the *first begotten of the dead*; he rises first, the *eldest brother*, and he is my *Master* in this *science* of *death*: but yet, for *mee*, I am a *younger brother* too, to this *Man*, who *died now*, and to every man whom I see, or heare to die before *mee*, and all they are *ushers* to mee 35

3 *wise man*] *wiseman* 1624(2), 1626   *Margin* 13.10 *Ed.*: 13.9 all edd.   9 *Idolatrer;*] *Idolatrer* 1624(2), 1626   *Margin* 8.19 *S*: 8.14 all edd.   10 *Prophet;*] *Prophet,* 1626   13 *ô*] *O* 1624(2), 1626   17 *officers,*] *officers* 1624(2), 1626   20 *instructions*] *instructions,* 1626   20 *God,*] *God* 1626

in this *schoole* of *death*. I take therefore that which thy servant *Davids*
wife said to *him*, to bee said to *me*; *If thou save not thy life to night, to
morrow thou shalt bee slaine*. If the death of this man worke not upon
mee now, I shall die worse, than if thou hadst not afforded me this
5 helpe: for thou hast sent *him* in this *bell* to mee, as thou didst send to
the *Angell* of *Sardis*, with *commission to strengthen the things that remaine,*   Apoc. 3.2
and that are ready to die; that in this weaknes of *body*, I might receive
spiritual strength, by these occasions. This is my *strength*, that
whether thou say to mee, as thine *Angell* said to *Gedeon, Peace bee*   Jud. 6.23
10 *unto thee, feare not, thou shalt not die*, or whether thou say, as unto
Aaron, Thou shalt die there; yet thou wilt preserve that which is *ready*   Num. 20.26
to die, my *soule*, from the worst *death*, that of *sinne*. *Zimrie died for his*   1 Reg. 16.
sinnes, saies thy *Spirit, which he sinned in doing evill*; and *in his sinne,*   18, 19
which he did to make Israel sinne. For his *sinnes*, his *many sinnes*; and
15 then in *his sinne*, his *particular sinne*: for my *sinnes* I shall die, whensoever I die, for *death is the wages of sinne*; but I shall die in my *sinne*,
in that particular *sinne* of resisting thy *spirit*, if I *apply* not thy
assistances. Doth it not call us to a particular consideration, That thy
blessed *Sonne* varies his *forme* of Commination, and *aggravates* it in
20 the variation, when hee saies to the *Jewes*, (because they refused the   Joh. 8.21
light offered) *you shall die in your sinne*; And then when they proceeded to farther disputations, and vexations, and tentations, hee
addes, *you shall die in your sinnes*; he *multiplies* the former expressing,   *v.* 24
to a *plurall*: In *this sinne*, and in *all your sinnes*; doth not the resisting
25 of thy particular *helps* at last, draw upon us the guiltinesse of all our
former sinnes? May not the neglecting of this *sound* ministred to mee
in this *mans death*, bring mee to that miserie, as that I, whom the *Lord
of life* loved so, as to die for me, shall *die*, and a *Creature* of mine
owne shall be *immortall*; that I shall die, and the *worme of mine owne*   Esay 66.24
30 conscience shall never *die*?

18. PRAYER

O eternall and most gracious *God*, I have a new occasion of *thanks*,
and a new occasion of *prayer* to *thee*, from the *ringing* of this *bell*.

6 *Sardis*,] *Sardis* 1624(2), 1626   8 strength,] strength 1624(2), 1626   9
Gedeon, A: Gedeon; all edd.   10 say,] say 1626   *Margin* 16.18,19 *Ed.*: 16.18
all edd.   16 *sinne*;] *sin*, 1626   24 *plurall*: *A, S*: *plurall*. all edd.   29 *immortall*;] immortall, 1626   *Margin* 66.24 *S*: 66.14 all edd.

Thou toldst me in the other *voice*, that I was *mortall*, and approaching to *death*; In this I may heare thee say, that I am *dead*, in an *irremediable*, in an *irrecoverable* state for bodily health. If that bee thy *language* in this *voice*, how infinitely am I bound to thy heavenly *Majestie*, for speaking so plainly unto mee? for even that *voice*, that I *must die now*, is not 5 the voice of a *Judge*, that speaks by way of *condemnation*, but of a *Physitian*, that presents health in that: Thou presentest mee *death* as the *cure* of my *disease*, not as the *exaltation* of it; if I mistake thy voice herein, if I over-runne thy pace, and prevent thy hand, and imagine *death* more instant upon mee than thou hast bid him bee, yet the 10 voice belongs to me; *I am dead*, I was *borne dead*, and from the first laying of these *mud-walls* in my *conception*, they have *moldred* away, and the whole course of *life* is but an *active death*. Whether this *voice instruct* mee, that I am a *dead man now*, or *remember* me, that I have been a *dead man* all this while, I humbly thanke thee for speaking in 15 this *voice* to my *soule*, and I humbly beseech thee also, to accept my prayers in his behalfe, by whose occasion this *voice*, this sound is come to mee. For though hee bee by *death* transplanted to thee, and so in possession of inexpressible happinesse there, yet here upon earth thou hast given us such a portion of heaven, as that though men 20 dispute, whether thy *Saints* in heaven doe *know* what we in earth in particular doe stand in need of, yet without all disputation, wee upon earth doe know what thy *Saints* in heaven lacke yet, for the *consummation* of their *happinesse*; and therefore thou hast affoorded us the *dignitie*, that wee may pray for them. That therefore this *soule* now 25 newly departed to thy *Kingdome*, may quickly returne to a joifull *reunion* to that *body* which it hath left, and that *wee* with *it*, may soone enjoy the full *consummation* of all, in *body* and *soule*, I humbly beg at thy hand, O our most mercifull *God*, for thy Sonne *Christ Jesus sake*: That that blessed *Sonne* of thine, may have the *consummation* of his 30 *dignitie*, by entring into his *last office*, the office of a *Judge*, and may have *societie* of humane *bodies* in *heaven*, as well as hee hath had ever of *soules*; And that as thou hatest *sinne* it selfe, thy *hate* to *sinne* may bee expressed in the abolishing of all *instruments of sinne*, The *allurements* of this *world*, and the *world* it selfe; and all the temporarie 35

7 Thou] Thon 1624(2)   29 *sake: Ed.:* sake. all edd.   35 *world,*] *world* 1626

revenges of *sinne*, the *stings* of *sicknesse* and of *death*; and all the *castles*, and *prisons*, and *monuments* of *sinne*, in the *grave*. That *time* may bee swallowed up in *Eternitie*, and *hope* swallowed in *possession*, and *ends* swallowed in *infinitenesse*, and *all men* ordained to *salvation*, in *body*

5 and *soule*, be *one intire* and *everlasting sacrifice* to thee, where thou mayest receive *delight* from them, and they *glorie* from thee, for evermore. *Amen.*

19. Oceano tandem emenso, aspicienda resurgit Terra; vident, iustis, medici, iam cocta mederi

10 ### se posse, indiciis.

At last, the Physitians, after a long and stormie voyage, see land;
They have so good signes of the concoction of the disease,
as that they may safely proceed to purge.

19. MEDITATION

15 All this while the *Physitians* themselves have beene *patients*, patiently attending when they should see any *land* in this *Sea*, any *earth*, any *cloud*, any *indication* of *concoction* in these *waters*. Any *disorder* of mine, any *pretermission* of theirs, exalts the disease, accelerates the rages of it; no *diligence* accelerates the *concoction*, the *maturitie* of the *disease*;

20 they must stay till the *season* of the sicknesse come, and till it be ripened of it selfe, and then they may put to their hand, to *gather* it, before it *fall* off, but they cannot hasten the *ripening*. Why should wee looke for it in a *disease*, which is the *disorder*, the *discord*, the *irregularitie*, the *commotion*, and *rebellion* of the *body*? It were scarce a *disease*, if it

25 could bee *ordered*, and made obedient to our *times*. Why should wee looke for that in *disorder*, in a *disease*, when we cannot have it in *Nature*, who is so *regular*, and so *pregnant*, so forward to bring her worke to perfection, and to light? yet we cannot awake the *July-flowers* in *Januarie*, nor retard the *flowers* of the *spring* to *Autumne*. We

1 *sicknesse*] sicknesse, 1626   8 aspicienda] aspicianda 1624(2), 1626   10 in-
diciis] indicis 1626   11 *Physitians*,] Physicians 1624(2), 1626   26 *disease*,]
disease 1626

cannot bid the *fruits* come in *May*, nor the *leaves* to sticke on in December. A *woman* that is weake, cannot put off her *ninth moneth* to a *tenth*, for her *deliverie*, and say shee will stay till shee bee *stronger*; nor a *Queene* cannot hasten it to a *seventh*, that shee may bee ready for some other pleasure. *Nature* (if we looke for *durable* and *vigorous* 5 effects) will not admit *preventions*, nor *anticipations*, nor *obligations* upon her; for they are *precontracts*, and she will bee left to her *libertie*. *Nature* would not be spurred, nor forced to mend her pace; nor *power*, the *power of man*; *greatnesse* loves not that kinde of *violence* neither. There are of *them* that will *give*, that will doe *justice*, that will 10 *pardon*, but they have their owne *seasons* for al these, and he that knowes not *them*, shall *starve* before that gift come, and *ruine*, before the Justice, and *dye* before the pardon save him: some *tree* beares no fruit, except much *dung* be laid about it, and *Justice* comes not from some, till they bee richly manured: some *trees* require much *visiting*, 15 much *watring*, much *labour*; and some men give not their *fruits* but upon *importunitie*; some *trees* require *incision*, and *pruning*, and *lopping*; some men must bee *intimidated* and *syndicated* with *Commissions*, before they will deliver the fruits of *Justice*; some *trees* require the *early* and the *often* accesse of the *Sunne*; some men *open* not, but upon 20 the *favours* and *letters* of *Court mediation*; some *trees* must bee *housd* and kept within doores; some men locke up, not onley their *liberalitie*, but their *Justice*, and their *compassion*, till the sollicitation of a *wife*, or a *sonne*, or a *friend*, or a *servant* turne the *key*. *Reward* is the *season* of one man, and *importunitie* of another; *feare* the *season* of 25 one man, and *favour* of another; *friendship* the *season* of one man, and *naturall affection* of another; and hee that knowes not their *seasons*, nor cannot *stay* them, must lose the *fruits*; As *Nature* will not, so *power* and *greatnesse* will not bee put to change their *seasons*; and shall wee looke for this *Indulgence* in a *disease*, or thinke to shake it off before it 30 bee *ripe*? All this while therefore, we are but upon a *defensive warre*, and that is but a *doubtfull state*: Especially where they who are *besieged* doe know the *best* of their *defences*, and doe not know the worst of their *enemies power*; when they cannot mend their *works within*, and the *enemie* can increase his *numbers without*. O how many 35

9 *man*;] *man*, 1624(2), 1626   32 *state*:] *state*; 1626

farre more miserable, and farre more worthy to be lesse miserable than I, are besieged with this *sicknesse*, and lacke their *Sentinels*, their *Physitians* to *watch*, and lacke their *munition*, their *cordials* to *defend*, and perish before the *enemies* weaknesse might invite them to *sally*, 5 before the *disease* shew any *declination*, or admit any way of *working* upon it selfe? In me the *siege* is so farre slackned, as that we may come to *fight*, and so die in the *field*, if I *die*, and not in a *prison*.

19. EXPOSTULATION

My *God*, my *God*, Thou art a *direct God*, may I not say, a *literall God*, 10 a *God* that wouldest bee understood *literally*, and according to the *plaine sense* of all that thou saiest? But thou art also (*Lord* I intend it to thy *glory*, and let no *prophane mis-interpreter* abuse it to thy *diminution*) thou art a *figurative*, a *metaphoricall God* too: A *God* in whose words there is such a height of *figures*, such *voyages*, such 15 *peregrinations* to fetch remote and precious *metaphors*, such *extentions*, such *spreadings*, such *Curtaines* of *Allegories*, such *third Heavens* of *Hyperboles*, so *harmonious eloquutions*, so *retired* and so *reserved expressions*, so *commanding perswasions*, so *perswading commandements*, such *sinewes* even in thy *milke*, and such *things* in thy *words*, as all 20 *prophane Authors*, seeme of the seed of the *Serpent*, that *creepes*; thou art the *dove*, that flies. O, what words but thine, can expresse the inexpressible *texture*, and *composition* of thy *word*; in which, to one Man, that *argument* that binds his faith to beleeve that to bee the Word of *God*, is *the reverent simplicity* of the Word, and to another, 25 the *majesty* of the Word; and in which two men, equally pious, may meet, and one wonder, that all should not understand it, and the other, as much, that any man should. So, *Lord*, thou givest us the same *Earth*, to labour on, and to lie in; a *house*, and a *grave*, of the same *earth*; so *Lord*, thou givest us the same *Word* for our *satisfaction*, 30 and for our *Inquisition*, for our *instruction*, and for our *Admiration* too; for there are places, that thy servants *Hierom* and *Augustine* would scarce beleeve (when they grew warm by mutual *letters*) of one

5 *declination*,] *declination* 1624(2), 1626   7 in a *prison*] in *prison* 1626   9 Thou] thon 1624(2)   20 *creepes*; *Ed.*: *creepes*, all edd.   27 much,] much 1624(2), 1626

another, that they understood them, and yet both *Hierome* and *Augustine* call upon persons, whom they knew to bee farre weaker, than they thought one another (*old women & young maids*) to read thy *Scriptures*, without confining them, to these or those places. Neither art thou thus a *figurative*, a *Metaphoricall God*, in thy *word* 5 only, but in thy *workes* too. The *stile* of thy *works*, the *phrase* of thine *Actions*, is *Metaphoricall*. The *institution* of thy whole *worship* in the *old Law*, was a continuall *Allegory*; *types & figures* overspread all; and *figures* flowed into *figures*, and powred themselves out into *farther figures*; *Circumcision* carried a *figure* of *Baptisme*, & *Baptisme* 10 carries a *figure* of that *purity*, which we shall have in *perfection* in the *new Jerusalem*. Neither didst thou *speake*, and *worke* in this *language*, onely in the time of thy *Prophets*; but since thou spokest in thy *Son*, it is so too. How often, how much more often doth thy *Sonne* call himselfe a *way*, and a *light*, and a *gate*, and a *Vine*, and *bread*, than the 15 *Sonne* of *God*, or of *Man*? How much oftner doth he exhibit a *Metaphoricall Christ*, than a *reall*, a *literall*? This hath occasioned thine ancient *servants*, whose delight it was to write after thy *Copie*, to proceede the same way in their *expositions* of the *Scriptures*, and in their composing both of *publike liturgies*, and of *private prayers* to 20 thee, to make their accesses to thee in such a kind of *language*, as thou wast pleased to speake to them, in a *figurative*, in a *Metaphoricall language*; in which manner I am bold to call the comfort which I receive now in this *sicknesse*, in the *indication* of the *concoction* and *maturity* therof, in certaine *clouds*, and *residences*, which the *Physitians* 25 observe, a discovering of *land* from *Sea*, after a long, and tempestuous *voyage*. But wherefore, O my *God*, hast thou presented to us, the *afflictions* and *calamities* of this life, in the name of *waters*? so often in the name of *waters*, and *deepe waters*, and *Seas* of *waters*? must we looke to bee *drowned*? are they *bottomlesse*, are they *boundles*? Thats 30 not the *dialect* of thy *language*; thou hast given a *Remedy* against the deepest *water*, by *water*; against the *inundation* of sinne, by *Baptisme*; and the first *life*, that thou gavest to any *Creatures*, was in *waters*; therefore thou doest not threaten us, with an *irremediablenesse*, when our *affliction* is a *Sea*. It is so, if we consider *our selves*; so thou callest 35

4 thy] the 1624(2), 1626   4 them,] them 1624(2), 1626   23 *language*;] *language*, 1626   24 sicknesse,] sicknesse 1624(2), 1626   26 long,] long 1624(2), 1626

Gennezareth, which was but a lake, and not *salt*, a *Sea*, so thou callest the *Mediterranean Sea*, still the *great Sea*, because the *inhabitants* saw no other *Sea*; they that dwelt there, thought a *Lake*, a *Sea*, and the others thought a *little Sea*, the *greatest*, and wee that know not the

5 *afflictions* of others, call our owne the *heaviest*. But, O my *God*, that is *truly great*, that overflowes the *channell*; that is *really a great affliction*, which is above my *strength*, but, thou, O *God*, art my *strength*, and then what can bee above it? *Mountaines shake with the swelling of thy*   Psa. 46.3 *Sea, secular Mountaines*; men *strong in power, spirituall mountaines*,

10 men *strong in grace*, are shaked with *afflictions*; but *thou laiest up thy*   Psa. 33.7 *sea in store-houses*; even thy *corrections* are of thy *treasure*, and thou wilt not waste thy *corrections*; when they have done their *service*, to humble thy *patient*, thou wilt call them in againe; for, *thou givest the*   Prov. 8.29 *Sea thy decree, that the waters should not passe thy Commandement*. All   Jos. 3.17

15 our *waters* shal run into *Jordan*, & *thy servants passed Jordan dry foot*; they shall run into the red *Sea* (the *Sea* of thy *Sons bloud*) & the red *Sea*, that red *Sea*, drownes none of *thine*. But, *they that saile in the*   Ecclus. 43.24 *Sea, tell of the danger thereof*; I that am yet in this affliction, owe thee the *glory* of *speaking* of it; But, as the wise man bids me, I say, I may

20 *speak much, and come short*; *wherefore in summe, thou art all*. Since thou   *v.* 27 art so, O my *God*, and *affliction is a Sea*, too deepe for us, what is our *refuge*? thine *Arke*, thy *ship*. In all other *Seas*, in all other *afflictions*, those *meanes* which thou hast ordained; In this *Sea*, in *Sicknesse*, thy *Ship* is thy *Physitian*. *Thou hast made a way in the Sea, and a safe path*   Sap. 14.3, 4

25 *in the waters, shewing that thou canst save from all dangers; yea, though a man went to Sea without art*; yet where I finde all that, I finde this added, *Neverthelesse thou wouldest not, that the worke of thy wisdome should be idle*. Thou canst save without *means*; but thou hast told no man that thou *wilt*: Thou hast told every man, that thou *wilt not*.

30 When the *Centurion* beleeved the *Master* of the *ship* more than Saint   Act. 27.11 *Paul*, they were all opened to a great danger; this was a *preferring of* thy *meanes*, before thee, the *Author* of the *meanes* but, my *God*, though thou beest *every where*, I have no promise of *appearing* to me, but in thy *ship*: Thy blessed *Sonne preached out of a Ship*: The *meanes*   Luc. 5.3

35 is preaching, he did that; and the *Ship* was a *type* of the *Church*; hee

2 *great Sea*, 1624(2), 1626, *A, S: great Sea*; 1624(1)   5 But,] But 1624(2), 1626
9 *Mountaines*; *A: Mountaines*, all edd.   13 againe;] again, 1624(2), 1626
Margin Prov. *S*: Psa. all edd.   14 Commandement.] commandement 1626   17
Sea, drownes] sea drownes 1624(2), 1626   *Margin* 14.3,4 *Ed.*: 14.3 1624 (1&2);
143 1626   *Margin* 27.11 *S*: 17.11 all edd.

Act. 27.24

did it there. *Thou gavest* S. *Paul the lives of all them, that saild with him*; If they had not beene in the *Ship* with him, the gift had not extended to them. *As soone as thy Son was come out of the ship, immediatly there met him out of the tombes, a man with an uncleane spirit, and no man could hold him, no not with chaines.* Thy *Sonne* needed no use of *meanes*; 5 yet there wee apprehend the *danger* to us; if we leave the ship, the *meanes*; in this case, the *Physitian*. But as they are *Ships* to us in those *Seas*, so is there a *Ship* to them too, in which they are to stay. Give mee leave, O my *God*, to assist my selfe with such a *construction* of these words of thy servant *Paul*, to the *Centurion*, when the *Mariners* 10 would have left the *Ship: Except these abide in the Ship, you cannot bee safe.* Except they who are our *ships*, the *Physitians*, abide in that which is theirs, and our *ship*, the *truth*, and the *sincere* and *religious worship of thee*, and thy *Gospell*, we cannot promise our selves, so good *safety*; for though we have our *ship*, the *Physitian*, he hath not 15 his *ship*, *Religion*; And meanes are not meanes, but in their *concatenation*, as they *depend*, and are *chained* together. *The ships are great*, saies thy *Apostle*, *but a helme turnes them*; the *men* are *learned*, but their *religion* turnes their *labours* to good: And therefore it was a heavy *curse*, *when the third part of the ships perished*: It is a heavy case, where 20 either *all Religion*, or *true Religion* should forsake many of these *ships*, whom thou hast sent to convey us over these *Seas*. But, O my *God*, my *God*, since *I have my ship*, and *they theirs*, I have *them*, and they have *thee*, why are we yet no neerer land? As soone as thy *Sonnes Disciple* had taken *him* into the *ship*, *immediatly the ship was at the* 25 *land, whither they went.* Why have not *they* and *I* this dispatch? Every thing is *immediatly* done, which is done when *thou* wouldst have it done. Thy purpose *terminates* every action, and what was *done* before that, is *undone* yet. Shall that slacken my *hope*? Thy *Prophet* from *thee*, hath forbid it. *It is good that a man should both hope, and quietly wait for* 30 *the salvation of the Lord.* Thou puttest off many *judgements*, till the *last* day, many passe this life without any; and shall not I endure the putting off thy *mercy* for a day? and yet, O my *God*, thou puttest me not to that; for, the *assurance* of *future mercy*, is *present mercy*. But what is my *assurance* now? What is my *seale*? It is but a *cloud*; that which 35

Mar. 5.2, 3

Act. 27.31

Jac. 3.4

Apo. 8.9

Jo. 6.21

Lam. 3.26

1 *them*,] them 1624(2), 1626   *Margin* 5.2,3 *Ed*.: 5.2 all edd.   9 leave,] leave 1624(2), 1626   11,12 *Ship*: . . . *safe. Ed.*: *Ship*, . . . *safe*; all edd.   34 for,] for 1624(2), 1626

my *Physitians* call a *cloud*, is *that*, which gives them their *Indication*. But a *Cloud*? Thy *great Seale* to all the world, the *raine-bow*, that secured the *world* for ever, from *drowning*, was but a *reflexion upon a cloud*. A *cloud* it selfe was a *pillar* which guided the *church*, and *the glory of God*, not only *was*, but *appeared in a cloud*. Let me returne, O my *God*, to the consideration of thy *servant Eliahs* proceeding, in a time of *desperate drought*; he bids them look towards the *Sea*; They looke, and see *nothing*. He bids them *againe* and *againe*, *seven times*: and at the *seventh time*, they saw a little *cloud* rising out of the *Sea*; and presently they had their desire of *raine*. *Seven dayes*, O my *God*, have we looked for this *cloud*, and now we have it; none of thy *Indications* are *frivolous*; thou makest thy *signes*, *seales*; and thy *Seales*, *effects*; and thy *effects*, *consolation*, and *restitution*, whersoever thou maiest receive *glory* by that way.

Margin:
Exo. 13.21
16.10

1 Reg. 18.43

19. PRAYER

O eternall and most gracious *God*, who though thou passedst over infinite millions of generations, before thou camest to a *Creation* of this *world*, yet when thou beganst, didst never intermit that *worke*, but continuedst *day* to *day*, till thou hadst perfited all the *worke*, and deposed it in the hands and rest of a *Sabbath*, though thou have beene pleased to glorifie thy selfe in a long exercise of my *patience*, with an *expectation* of thy *declaration* of thy selfe in this my *sicknesse*, yet since thou hast now of thy goodnesse afforded that, which affords us some hope, if that bee still *the way* of thy *glory*, proceed in *that way*, and perfit *that worke*, and establish me in a *Sabbath*, and *rest* in *thee*, by this thy *seale* of *bodily restitution*. Thy *Priests* came up to thee, by *steps* in the *Temple*; Thy *Angels* came *downe* to *Jaacob*, by *steps* upon the *ladder*; we finde no *staire*, by which thou *thy selfe* camest to *Adam* in *Paradise*, nor to *Sodome* in thine *anger*; for *thou*, and *thou onely* art able to doe all at once. But, O *Lord*, I am not *wearie* of thy *pace*, nor *wearie* of mine owne *patience*. I provoke thee not with a *praier*, not with a *wish*, not with a *hope*, to more haste than consists with thy

1 is *that* S: in *that* all edd.   3 ever,] ever 1624(2), 1626   5 Let] Le 1624(2)
Margin 18.43 S: 19.43 all edd.

purpose, nor looke that any other thing should have entred into thy *purpose*, but thy *glory*. To *heare* thy steps comming *towards* mee, is the same comfort, as to see thy face present with mee; whether thou doe the *worke* of a *thousand yeere* in a *day*, or extend the *worke of a day*, to a *thousand yeere*, as long as *thou workest*, it is *light*, and *comfort*. 5 *Heaven* it selfe is but an *extention* of the same joy; and an *extention* of this *mercie*, to proceed at thy *leisure*, in the way of *restitution*, is a *manifestation* of *heaven* to me here upon *earth*. From that *people*, to whom thou appearedst in *signes*, and in *Types*, the *Jewes*, thou art departed, because they trusted in them; but from thy *Church*, to 10 whom thou has appeared in *thy selfe*, in *thy Sonne*, thou wilt never depart; because we cannot trust *too much* in *him*. Though thou have afforded me these *signes* of *restitution*, yet if I *confide* in *them*, and beginne to say, all was but a *Naturall accident*, and *nature* begins to *discharge* her selfe, and shee will *perfit* the whole *worke*, my *hope* shall 15 vanish because it is not in *thee*. If thou shouldest take thy *hand* utterly from me, and have nothing to doe with me, *Nature* alone were able to *destroy* mee; but if thou withdraw thy *helping hand*, alas how frivolous are the helps of *Nature*, how impotent the assistances of *Art*? As therefore the *morning dew*, is a *pawne* of the *evening fatnesse*, 20 so, O *Lord*, let *this daies* comfort be the *earnest* of to *morrowes*, so farre as may *conforme* me entirely to thee, to what *end*, and by what *way* soever thy *mercie* have appointed mee.

20. Id agunt.

Upon these Indications of digested matter,   25
they proceed to purge.

20. MEDITATION

Though *counsel* seeme rather to consist of *spirituall parts*, than *action*, yet *action* is the *spirit* and the *soule* of *counsell*. *Counsels* are not alwaies

3 comfort,] comfort 1624(2), 1626   5 *light*,] *light* 1624(2), 1626   16 thou] thon 1626   20 *evening* 1624(1) *corrected*, 1624(2), 1626: *evenings* 1624(1) C, C³ *originally*   26 *proceed*] preceed 1624(2)

determined in *Resolutions*; Wee cannot alwaies say, *this was concluded*; *actions* are alwaies determined in *effects*; wee can say *this was done*. Then have *Lawes* their *reverence*, and their *majestie*, when wee see the *Judge* upon the *Bench* executing them. Then have *counsels of*

5 *warre* their *impressions*, and their *operations*, when we see the *seale* of an *Armie* set to them. It was an ancient way of celebrating the *memorie* of such as deserved well of the *State*, to afford them that kinde of *statuarie representation*, which was then called *Hermes*; which was, *the head and shoulders of a man, standing upon a Cube*, but those *shoulders*

10 without *armes* and *hands*. All together it figured a *constant supporter of the state*, by his *counsell*: But in this *Hierogliphique*, which they made without *hands*, they passe their consideration no farther, but that the *Counsellor* should bee without *hands*, so farre, as *not to reach out his hand to forraigne tentations of bribes, in matters of Counsell*, and, that it

15 was not necessary, that the *head* should employ *his owne hand*; that *the same men* should serve in the *execution*, which assisted in the *Counsell*; but that there should not belong *hands* to every *head*, *action* to every *counsell*, was never intended, so much as in *figure*, and *representation*. For, as *matrimonie* is scarce to bee called *matrimonie*,

20 where there is a *resolution* against the *fruits of matrimonie*, against the having of *Children*, so *counsels* are not *counsels*, but *illusions*, where there is from the beginning no purpose to execute the determinations of those *counsels*. The *arts* and *sciences* are most properly referred to the *head*; that is their proper *Element* and *Spheare*; But yet the *art* of

25 proving, *Logique*, and the *Art* of *perswading*, *Rhetorique*, are deduced to the *hand*, and *that* expressed by a *hand* contracted into a *fist*, and *this* by a *hand* enlarged, and expanded; and evermore the *power of man*, and the *power of God* himselfe is expressed so, *All things are in his hand*; neither is *God* so often presented to us, by names that carry our

30 consideration upon *counsell*, as upon *execution of counsell*; he is oftner called the *Lord of Hosts*, than by all other *names*, that may be referred to the other signification. Hereby therefore wee take into our *meditation*, the slipperie condition of *man*, whose *happinesse*, in any kinde, the defect of *any one thing*, conducing to that *happinesse*, may

35 *ruine*; but it must have *all the peeces* to make it up. Without *counsell*, I

August.

30 is oftner] oftner is 1624(2), 1626

had not got thus farre; without *action* and *practise*, I should goe no farther towards *health*. But what is the present necessary *action*? *purging*: A *withdrawing*, a violating of *Nature*, a *farther weakening*: O *deare price*, & O *strange* way of *addition*, to doe it by *substraction*; of *restoring* Nature, to *violate Nature*; of *providing strength*, by *increasing* 5 *weaknesse*. Was I not *sicke* before? And is it a *question* of *comfort* to be asked now, Did *your Physicke make you sicke*? Was that it that my *Physicke* promised, to make me *sicke*? This is another *step*, upon which we may stand, and see farther into the *miserie of man*, the *time*, the *season* of his *Miserie*; It must bee done *now*: O *over-cunning*, *over-* 10 *watchfull*, *over-diligent*, and *over-sociable misery* of *man*, that seldome comes alone, but then when it may accompanie other *miseries*, and so put one another into the higher *exaltation*, and better *heart*. I am ground even to an *attenuation*, and must proceed to *evacuation*, all waies to exinanition and annihilation. 15

20. EXPOSTULATION

My *God*, my *God*, the *God of Order*, but yet not of *Ambition*, who assignest *place* to every one, but not *contention* for place, when shall it be thy pleasure to put an *end* to all these *quarrels*, for *spirituall precedences*? when shall men leave their uncharitable *disputations*, 20 which is *to take place*, *faith* or *repentance*, and which, when we consider *faith*, and *works*? The *head* and the *hand* too, are required to a *perfit naturall man*; *Counsell* and *action* too, to a *perfit civill man*; *faith* and *works* too, to him that is *perfitly spirituall*. But because it is easily said, I *beleeve*, and because it doth not easily *lie in proofe*, nor is easily 25 demonstrable by any *evidence* taken from my *heart*, (for who sees that, who searches those *Rolls*?) whether I doe *beleeve*, or no, is it not therefore, O my *God*, that thou dost so *frequently*, so *earnestly*, referre us to the *hand*, to the *observation* of *actions*? There is a little *suspition*, a little *imputation* laid upon *over-tedious* and *dilatorie counsels*. Many 30 good occasions slip away in long *consultations*; and it may be a *degree* of *sloth*, to be too long in *mending nets*, though *that* must bee

5 Nature,] Nature: 1624(2), 1626   10 *Miserie*;] *Misery*: 1626   22 *faith*,] *faith* 1624(2), 1626

done. *He that observeth the wind, shall not sow, and he that regardeth the* Eccles. 11.4
clouds, shall not reape; that is, he that is too *dilatorie*, too *superstitious* in
these *observations*, and studies but the *excuse* of his *owne idlenesse* in
them; But, that which the same *wise* and *royall servant* of thine, saies
5 in another place, all accept, and aske no *comment* upon it, *He* Prov. 10.4
becommeth poore, that dealeth with a slacke hand; but the hand of the
diligent maketh rich; All *evill* imputed to the *absence*, all *good* attributed
to the *presence* of the *hand*. I know, my *God*, (and I blesse thy name
for knowing it; for all good *knowledge* is from thee) that thou
10 considerest the *heart*; but thou takest not off thine *eie*, till thou come
to the *hand*. Nay, my *God*, doth not thy *spirit* intimate, that thou
beginnest where wee *beginne*, (at least, that thou allowest us to *beginne*
there) when thou orderest thine owne answer to thine owne question,
Who shall ascend into the hill of the Lord? Thus, *he that hath cleane hands*, Psa. 24.3, 4
15 *and a pure heart*? Doest thou not (at least) *send us*, first to the *hand*?
And is not the *worke* of their *hands*, that declaration of their *holy*
zeale, in the present execution of manifest *Idolatrers*, called a *consecra-* Exod. 32.29
tion of themselves, by thy *holy Spirit*? Their *hands* are called *all*
themselves: for, even *counsell* it selfe goes under that *name*, in thy
20 *word*, who knowest best how to give right *names*: because the
counsell of the Priests assisted *David, Saul* saies, *the hand* of the *Priest* is 1 Sam. 22.17
with *David*: And that which is often said by *Moses*, is very often
repeated by thy other *Prophets, These* and *these* things *the Lord spake*, Levit. 8.36
and the *Lord said*, and the *Lord commanded*, not by the *counsels*, not by
25 the *voice*, but by the *hand of Moses*, and by the *hand of the Prophets*:
Evermore we are referred for our *Evidence*, of *others*, and of *our*
selves, to the *hand*, to *action*, to *works*. There is something *before* it,
beleeving; and there is something *after* it, *suffering*; but in the most
eminent, and obvious, and conspicuous place, stands *doing*. Why
30 then, O my *God*, my blessed *God*, in the waies of my *spirituall*
strength, come I so slow to *action*? I was whipped by thy *rod*, before I
came to *consultation*, to consider my state; and shall I goe no farther?
As hee that would describe a *circle* in paper, if hee have brought that
circle within one *inch* of finishing, yet if he remove his *compasse*, he
35 cannot make it up a perfit *circle*, except he fall to worke againe, to

6 *hand*;] *hand*, 1624(2), 1626   8 *hand*.] *hand* 1624(2), 1626   *Margin* 24.3,4
Ed: 24.3 all edd.   14 *Thus*,] *Thus* 1626   14 *hands*,] *hands*. 1626   *Margin*
32.29 *S*: 31.29 all edd.   *Margin* 22.17] 21.29 1624(2), 1626   22 *David*:] *David*.
1624(2); *David*, 1626   24 *commanded* 1624(2), 1626: *comman-manded* 1624(1)

finde out the same *center*, so, though setting that *foot* of my *compasse* upon *thee*, I have gone so farre, as to the *consideration* of my selfe, yet if I depart from *thee*, my *center*, all is unperfit. This proceeding to *action* therefore, is a returning to *thee*, and a *working* upon *my selfe* by thy *Physicke*, by thy *purgative physicke*, a free and entire evacuation of my *soule* by *confession*. The working of *purgative physicke*, is *violent* and contrary to *Nature*. O Lord, I decline not this *potion of confession*, how ever it may bee contrary to a *naturall man*. To take *physicke*, and *not according to the right method, is dangerous*. O *Lord*, I decline not that *method* in this *physicke*, in things that burthen my *conscience*, to make my *confession* to *him*, into whose hands thou hast put the *power* of *absolution*. I know that *Physicke may be made so pleasant, as that it may easily be taken; but not so pleasant as the vertue and nature of the medicine bee extinguished*; I know, I am not submitted to such a *confession* as is a *racke* and *torture* of the *Conscience*; but I know I am not exempt from all. If it were meerely *problematicall*, left meerely indifferent, whether we should take this *Physicke*, use this *confession*, or no, a great *Physitian* acknowledges this to have beene his *practise*, *To minister many things, which hee was not sure would doe good, but never any other thing, but such as hee was sure would doe no harme*. The use of this spirituall *Physicke* can certainly doe no *harme*; and the *Church* hath alwaies thought that it might, and doubtlesse, many humble *soules* have found, that it hath done them *good*. I will *therefore take the cup of Salvation, and call upon thy Name*; I will fill this *Cup* of *compunction*, as full as I have formerly filled the *Cups* of worldly *confections*, that so I may scape the *cup of Malediction*, and irrecoverable destruction that depends upon that. And since thy blessed and glorious *Sonne*, being offered in the way to his *Execution*, a Cup of *Stupefaction*, to take away the sense of his *paine*, (a charity afforded to condemned persons ordinarily in those places, and times) refused that *ease*, and embraced the whole *torment*, I take not this *Cup*, but this *vessell* of mine owne *sinnes*, into my *contemplation*, and I powre them out here according to the *Motions* of thy *holy Spirit*, and *any where*, according to the ordinances of thy *holy Church*.

Galen.

Galen.

Galen.

Psa. 116.13

Mar. 15.23

5

10

15

20

25

30

1 *center*, 1624(2), 1626, *A*, *S*: center; 1624(1)   12 *absolution.*] absolution, 1626
15 know] know, 1624(2), 1626   18 *practise.*] practise; 1626   23 found,]
found 1626   *Margin* 116.13 *Ed.*: 106.12 1624(1&2); 162.12 1626

20. PRAYER

O eternall, and most gracious *God*, who having married *Man* and
Woman together, and made them one *flesh*, wouldest have them also,
5 to become one *soule* so, as that they might maintaine a *simpathy* in
their *affections*, and have a *conformity* to one another, in the *accidents* of
this *world*, good or bad, so having married this soule and this body
in me, I humbly beseech thee, that my soule may looke, and make
her use of thy mercifull proceedings towards my *bodily restitution*, &
10 goe the same way to a *spirituall*. I am come by thy goodnesse, to the
use of thine ordinary meanes for my *body*, to wash away those
peccant humors, that endangered it. I have, *O Lord*, a *River* in my *body*,
but a *Sea* in my *soule*, and a *Sea* swoln into the depth of a *Deluge*,
above the *Sea*. Thou hast raised up certaine *hils* in *me* heretofore, by
15 which I might have stood safe, from these *inundations* of *sin*. Even
our *Naturall faculties* are a *hill*, and might preserve us from *some sinne*.
Education, study, observation, example, are *hills* too, and might
preserve us from *some*. Thy *Church*, and thy *Word*, and thy *Sacraments*, and thine *Ordinances*, are *hills*, above these; thy *Spirit* of
20 *remorse*, and *compunction*, & *repentance* for former *sin*, are *hills* too;
and to the *top* of all these *hills*, thou hast brought mee heretofore;
but this *Deluge*, this *inundation*, is got above all my *Hills*; and I have
sinned and sinned, and multiplied *sinne* to *sinne*, after all these thy
assistances against *sinne*, and where is there *water* enough to wash away
25 this *Deluge*? There is a *red Sea*, greater than this *Ocean*; and there is a
little spring, through which this *Ocean*, may powre it selfe into that
red Sea. Let thy *Spirit* of true *contrition*, and *sorrow* passe all my *sinnes*
through these *eies*, into the *wounds* of thy *Sonne*, and I shall be cleane,
and my *soule* so much better purged than my *body*, as it is ordained
30 for a *better*, and a *longer* life.

8 looke,] look; 1626   11 for my] of my 1626   19 *Ordinances*,] *Ordinances*
1624(2), 1626   20 too;] too, 1626   23 sinned,] sinned. 1626   26 *Ocean*,]
Ocean 1624(2), 1626   27 *contrition*,] *contrition* 1626   30 for a *better*] for *better*
1624(2), 1626

21. Atque annuit Ille, Qui, per eos, clamat, Linquas iam, Lazare, lectum.

God prospers their practise, and he, by them, calls Lazarus *out of his tombe, mee out of my bed.*

21. MEDITATION   5

If man had beene left *alone* in this *world*, at first, shall I thinke, that he would not have *fallen*? If there had beene no *Woman*, would not *Man* have served, to have beene his owne *Tempter*? When I see him now, subject to infinite weakenesses, fall into *infinite sinne*, without any *forraine tentations*, shall I thinke, hee would have had *none*, if hee 10 had beene *alone*? GOD saw that Man needed a *Helper*, if hee should bee well; but to make *Woman* ill, the *Devill* saw, that there needed no *third*. When *God*, and *wee* were *alone*, in *Adam*, that was not enough; when the *Devill* and *wee* were *alone*, in *Eve*, it was enough. O what a *Giant* is *Man*, when hee fights against himselfe, and what a 15 *dwarfe*, when hee *needs*, or *exercises* his owne assistance for himselfe? I cannot *rise* out of my bed, till the *Physitian enable* mee, nay I cannot tel, that I am able to rise, till *hee tell* me so. I *doe* nothing, I *know* nothing of my selfe: how little, and how impotent a peece of the *world*, is any *Man* alone? and how much lesse a peece of *himselfe* is 20 *that Man*? So little, as that when it falls out, (as it falls out in some cases) that more *misery*, and more *oppression*, would bee an *ease* to a *man*, he cannot give himselfe that *miserable addition*, of *more misery*; A *man* that is *pressed to death*, and might be eased by more *weights*, cannot lay those more *weights* upon himselfe: Hee can sinne *alone*, 25 and suffer *alone*, but not *repent*, not bee *absolved*, without *another*. Another tels mee, I *may rise*; and I *doe* so. But is every *raising* a *preferment*? or is every present *preferment* a *station*? I am readier to fall to the *Earth* now I am up, than I was when I *lay* in the bed: O *perverse way, irregular motion* of *Man*; even *rising* it selfe is the way to 30 *Ruine*. How many *men* are raised, and then doe not *fill* the place they

5 21. *Ed.*: 21 all edd.   12 well;] well 1624(2), 1626   13 *God*,] God 1626

are raised to? No *corner* of any place can bee *empty*; there can be no *vacuity*; If that *Man* doe not fill the place, *other men* will; complaints of his *insufficiency* will *fill* it; Nay, such an abhorring is there in *Nature*, of *vacuity*, that if there be but an *imagination of not filling*, in

5 any *man*, that which is but *imagination*, neither will *fill* it, that is, *rumor* and *voice*, and it will be *given out*, (upon no ground, but *Imagination*, and no man knowes, *whose imagination*) that hee is *corrupt* in his place, or *insufficient* in his place, and another prepared to *succeed* him in his place. A man *rises*, sometimes, and *stands* not,

10 because hee doth not, or is not beleeved to *fill* his place; and sometimes he *stands* not, because hee *over-fills* his place: Hee may bring so much *vertue*, so much *Justice*, so much *integrity* to the place, as shall *spoile* the place, *burthen* the place; his *integrity* may bee a *Libell* upon his *Predecessor*, and cast an *infamy* upon him, and a *burden* upon his

15 *successor*, to proceede by *example*, and to bring the place it selfe, to an *under-value*, and the *market* to an *uncertainty*. I am *up*, and I seeme to *stand*, and I goe *round*; and I am a *new Argument* of the *new Philosophie*, That the *Earth* moves round; why may I not beleeve, that the *whole earth* moves in a *round motion*, though that seeme to

20 mee to *stand*, when as I seeme to *stand* to my *Company*, and yet am carried, in a giddy, and *circular motion*, as I *stand*? Man hath no *center*, but *misery*; *there* and onely *there*, hee is *fixt*, and sure to finde himselfe. How little soever he bee *raised*, he *moves*, and moves in a *circle*, giddily; and as in the *Heavens*, there are but a few *Circles*, that goe

25 about the whole world, but many *Epicicles*, and other lesser *Circles*, but yet *Circles*, so of those men, which are *raised*, and put into *Circles*; few of them move from *place* to *place*, and passe through many and beneficiall places, but fall into little *Circles*, and within a step or two, are at their *end*, and not so well, as they were in the *Center*, from

30 which they were *raised*. Every thing serves to *exemplifie*, to *illustrate* mans *misery*; But I need goe no farther, than *my selfe*; for a long time, I was not able to *rise*; At last, I must bee *raised* by others; and now I am *up*, I am ready to sinke *lower* than before.

---

1 *empty*;] emptie, 1626   5 *imagination*, neither *A*: *imagination* neither, 1624(1&2);
imagination neither 1626   8 prepared] perpared 1626   12 place,] place 1626
14 him,] him; 1626   16 *uncertainty*.] uncertainty 1626   17 *round*;] *round*,
1624(2), 1626   20 *stand*, when] *stand* when 1626   23 *circle*,] *circle* 1624(2),
1626   26 *Circles*; Ed.: *Circles*, all edd.

21. EXPOSTULATION

My *God*, my *God*, how large a *glasse* of the next *World* is *this*? As wee
have an *Art*, to cast from one *glasse* to another, and so to carry the
Species a great way off, so hast thou, that way, much more; wee shall
have a *Resurrection* in *Heaven*; the knowledge of that thou castest by 5
another *glasse* upon us here; we *feele* that wee have a *Resurrection*
from *sinne*; and that by another *glasse* too; wee see wee have a
Resurrection of the *body*, from the *miseries* and *calamities* of this life.
This *Resurrection* of my *body*, shewes me the *Resurrection* of my *soule*;
and both *here* severally, of both together hereafter. Since thy *Martyrs* 10
under the *Altar*, presse thee with their solicitation for the *Resurrection*
of the *body* to *glory*, thou wouldest pardon mee, if I should presse thee
by *Prayer*, for the accomplishing of this *Resurrection*, which thou hast
begunne in me to *health*. But, O my *God*, I doe not *aske*, where I
might aske amisse, nor begge that which perchance might bee worse 15
for mee. I have a *Bed* of *sinne*; *delight* in *Sinne*, is a *Bed*; I have a *grave*
of *sinne*; *senselesnesse* in *sinne*, is a *grave*; and where *Lazarus* had
beene *foure daies*, I have beene *fifty yeeres*, in this *putrifaction*; Why dost
thou not call mee, as thou diddest him, *with a loud voice*, since my
Soule is as dead as his *Body* was? I need thy *thunder*, O my *God*; thy 20
musicke will not serve me. Thou hast called thy *servants*, who are to
worke upon us, in thine *Ordinance*, by all these loud *Names*, *Winds*,
and *Chariots*, and *falls of waters*; where thou wouldest be heard, thou
wilt bee heard. When thy *Sonne* concurred with thee, to the making
of Man, there it is but a *speaking*, but a *saying*; There, O *blessed and* 25
glorious Trinity, was none to *heare*, but you *three*, and you easily
heare *one another*, because you say the *same things*. But when thy
Sonne came to the worke of *Redemption*, *thou spokest*, and they that
heard it, tooke it for *Thunder*; and thy *Sonne* himselfe *cried with a loud*
voice, upon the *Crosse*, twice, as hee, who was to prepare his com- 30
ming, *John Baptist*, was the *voice of a cryer*, and not of a *Whisperer*.
Still if it be *thy voice*, it is a *loud voice*; *These words*, saies thy *Moses*,
Thou spokest with a great voice, and *thou addest no more*, saies hee there;

Jo. 11.43 (margin, line ~19)

Jo. 12.28 (margin, line ~28)

Mat. 27.46, (margin, line ~31)
50
Deut. 5.22

5 *Resurrection*] resurrection 1624(2), *resurrecton* 1626   5 knowledge] knowledge,
1626   7 *sinne*;] sin, 1624(2), 1626   9 *body*,] body; 1626   *Margin* 11.43]
11.14 1626   28 *spokest*,] spakest 1626   29 it,] it 1626   30 *voice*,] voice
1624(2), 1626   30 twice, 1626, *S*: twice; 1624(1&2)   *Margin* 46,50] 49,50
1626   32 *words*,] words 1626

PAGE 113   *Margin* 22.14] 23.14 1626   6 heard;] heard: 1626   7 us,] us 1626

That which thou hast said, is *evident*, and it is evident, that none can speake so *loud*; none can binde us to heare him, as wee must *thee*. *The most high uttered his voice*: what was *his voice*? *The Lord thundred from heaven*, it might bee heard; But this voice, *thy voice*, is also a *mightie* 5 *voice*; not onely *mightie in power*, it may be heard, nor *mightie in obligation* it *should* be *heard*, but mightie in *operation*, it *will* bee heard; and therefore hast thou bestowed a whole *Psalme* upon us, to leade us to the consideration of thy *voice*. It is such a *voice*, as that thy *Sonne* saies, *the dead shall heare it*; and thats *my state*; And why, O *God*, doest 10 thou not speake to me, in that *effectuall loudnesse*? *Saint John heard a voice, and hee turned about to see the voice*: sometimes we are too curious of the *instrument*, by what man *God* speakes; but thou speakest loudest, when thou speakest to the *heart*. *There was silence, and I heard a voice*, saies one, to thy *servant Job*. I hearken after *thy* 15 *voice, in thine Ordinances*, and I seeke not a *whispering* in *Conventicles*; but yet, O my *God*, speake *louder*, that so, though I doe heare thee now, then I may heare *nothing but thee*. My *sinnes* crie aloud; *Cains murther* did so; my *afflictions* crie aloud; *The flouds have lifted up their voice*, (and *waters* are *afflictions*) but thou, O *Lord, art mightier than the* 20 *voice of many waters*; than many *temporall*, many *spirituall afflictions*; than *any* of *either* kinde; and why doest thou not speak to me in *that voice*? *What is man, and whereto serveth he*? *what is his good, and what is his evill*? My *bed* of *sinne* is not *evill*, not desperatly evill, for thou doest call mee out of it; but my rising out of it is not *good*, (not 25 perfitly good) if thou call not *louder*, and hold me now I am *up*. O my *God*, I am afraid of a fearefull application of those words, *when a man hath done, then hee beginneth*; when his *body* is unable to *sinne*, his *sinfull memory* sinnes over his old sinnes againe; and that which thou wouldest have us to remember for *compunction*, we remember with 30 *delight. Bring him to me in his bed, that I may kill him*, saies *Saul* of *David*; Thou hast not said so, that is not *thy* voice. *Joash his owne servants slew him, when hee was sicke in his bed*; Thou hast not suffered that, that my *servants* should so much as *neglect* mee, or be *wearie* of mee, in my *sicknesse*. Thou threatnest, *that as a shepheard takes out of* 35 *the mouth of the Lion, two legs, or a peece of an eare, so shall the children of*

2 Sam. 22.14
Psa. 68.33

Psa. 29
Jo. 5.25

Apo. 1.12

Job 4.16

Psa. 93.3, 4

Ecclus. 18.8

Ibid. v. 7

1 Sam. 19.15
2 Chro.
24.25

Amos 3.12

9 *it*;] it? 1626   9 why,] why 1626   14 hearken] heaken 1626   17 aloud] alond 1626   19 *mightier*] *mightier*, 1626   20 *afflictions*;] *afflictions*, 1624(2), 1626   *Margin* 18.8 *Ed.*: 8.8 all edd.   22 *good*,] *good* 1624(2), 1626   24,25 *good*, (...) if] *good*, ... *if* 1626   25 *up*.] *up*, 1626   27 his *body*] this *body* 1624(2)   30 *him*,] *him* 1626   *Margin* 19.15] 26.15 1626   *Margin* 24.25] 26.25 1626   34 *mee*,] *me* 1624(2), 1626   34 threatnest,] threatnest; 1626

Israel, that dwell in Samaria, in the corner of a bed, and in Damascus, in a couch bee taken away: That even they that are *secure* from danger, shall perish; How much more might I, who was in the *bed of death, die*? But thou hast not dealt so with mee. As *they brought out sicke persons in beds, that thy servant Peters shadow might over-shadow them*; Thou hast, O my *God*, over-shadowed mee, refreshed mee: But when wilt thou doe *more*? when wilt thou doe *all*? when wilt thou speake in thy *loud voice*? when wilt thou bid mee *take up my bed and walke*? As my bed is my *affections*, when shall I beare them so as to *subdue* them? As my *bed* is my *afflictions*, when shall I beare them so, as not to *murmure* at them? When shall *I take up my bed and walke*? not *lie downe* upon it, as it is my *pleasure*, not *sinke under* it, as it is my *correction*? But, O my *God*, my *God*, the *God* of all *flesh*, and of all *spirit* too, let me bee content with that in my *fainting spirit*, which thou declarest in this *decaied flesh*, that as this body is content to *sit still*, that it may learne to *stand*, and to learne by *standing* to *walke*, and *by walking* to travell, so my *soule* by obeying this *thy voice*, of *rising*, may by a farther and farther growth of thy *grace*, proceed so, and bee so established, as may remove all *suspitions*, all *jealousies* betweene *thee* and *mee*, and may *speake* and *heare* in such a *voice*, as that still I may bee acceptable *to thee*, and satisfied *from thee*.

Act. 5.15

Mat. 9.5, 6

5

10

15

20

21. PRAYER

O eternall and most gracious *God*, who hast made *little things* to signifie *great*, and convaid the *infinite merits* of thy *Sonne* in the *water* of *Baptisme*, and in the *Bread* and *Wine* of thy other *Sacrament*, unto us, receive the *sacrifice* of my humble thanks, that thou hast not onely afforded mee, the abilitie to rise out of this *bed* of *wearinesse & discomfort*, but hast also made this *bodily rising*, by thy *grace*, an *earnest* of a *second resurrection* from *sinne*, and of a *third*, to *everlasting glory*. Thy *Sonne*, himselfe, alwaies *infinite* in *himselfe*, & incapable of *addition*, was yet pleased to grow in the *Virgins* wombe, & to grow in *stature*, in the sight of men. Thy good purposes upon mee, I know,

25

30

3 might] migh 1626   4 dealt so] so dealt 1624(2), 1626   4,5 out . . . beds,] our . . . beds 1626   6 mee:] me, 1626   *Margin* Mat. 9.5,6 *Ed.*: Mat. 9.6 1624(1); Ma. 9.6 1624(2), 1626   11 *up*] *uy* 1624(2)   13 But,] But 1624(2), 1626   14 too,] too 1624(2)   18 *grace*,] *grace* 1624(2), 1626   21 *thee*,] *thee* 1624(2), 1626   21 *thee*.] *thee* 1626

have their *determination* and *perfection*, in thy holy *will* upon mee; there thy *grace* is, and there I am *altogether*; but manifest them so unto me in thy *seasons*, and in thy *measures* and *degrees*, that I may not onely have that *comfort* of knowing *thee* to be *infinitely good*, but that
5 also of finding thee to bee every day *better* and *better* to mee: and that as thou gavest *Saint Paul*, the *Messenger of Satan*, to *humble* him, so for my *humiliation*, thou maiest give me *thy selfe*, in this knowledge, that what *grace* soever thou afford mee *to day*, yet I should perish *to morrow*, if I had not *to morrowes grace too*. Therefore I begge of thee,
10 *my daily bread*; and as thou gavest mee the *bread* of *sorrow* for many daies, and since the *bread* of *hope* for some, and this day the *bread* of *possessing*, in *rising* by that strength, which thou the *God* of all strength, hast infused into me, so, O *Lord*, continue to mee the *bread of life*; the *spirituall bread of life*, in a faithfull assurance in *thee*; the
15 *sacramentall bread of life*, in a worthy receiving of *thee*; and the *more reall bread of life*, in an everlasting *union to thee*. I know, O *Lord*, that when thou hadst created *Angels*, and they saw thee produce *fowle*, and *fish*, and *beasts*, and *wormes*, they did not importune thee, and say, shall wee have no better *Creatures* than these, no better *companions*
20 than these; but staid thy *leisure*, and then had *man* delivered over to them, no much inferiour in *nature* to themselves. No more doe I, O *God*, now that by thy *first mercie*, I am able to *rise*, importune thee for present confirmation of *health*; nor now, that by thy *mercie*, I am brought to see, that thy *correction* hath wrought *medicinally* upon mee,
25 presume I upon that *spirituall strength* I have; but as I acknowledge, that my *bodily strength* is subject to every *puffe of wind*, so is my *spirituall strength* to every *blast of vanitie*. Keepe me therefore still, O my gracious *God*, in a such a *proportion* of both *strengths*, as I may still have something to thanke thee for, which I *have received*, & still
30 something to *pray for*, and aske at thy hand.

---

3 me] me, 1624(2), 1626   4 *infinitely*] *infinietly* 1624(2)   6 him, so] him so 1624(2); him so, 1626   9 had not] had not had 1624(2), 1626   9 thee,] thee 1624(2), 1626   11 some,] some; 1626   13 strength,] strength 1624(2), 1626   16 *thee.*] *thee,* 1626   17 hadst] hast 1624(2), 1626   18 say,] say 1624(2), 1626

22. Sit morbi fomes tibi cura;

*The Physitians consider the root and occasion, the embers, and
coales, and fuell of the disease, and seeke to purge or correct that.*

22. MEDITATION

How *ruinous* a *farme* hath *man* taken, in taking *himselfe*? how ready is 5
the *house* every day to fall downe, and how is all the *ground* overspread with *weeds*, all the *body* with *diseases*? where not onely every
turfe, but every *stone*, beares *weeds*; not onely every *muscle* of the
flesh, but every *bone* of the *body*, hath some *infirmitie*; every little
flint upon the *face* of this *soile*, hath some *infectious weede*, every *tooth* 10
in our *head*, such a paine, as a *constant man* is afraid of, and yet
ashamed of that *feare*, of that sense of the paine. How *deare*, and how
often a *rent* doth Man pay for this *farme*? hee paies *twice a day*, in
double *meales*, and how little time he hath to *raise his rent*? How
many *holy daies* to call him from his labour? Every day is *halfe-holy* 15
day, halfe spent in *sleepe*. What *reparations*, and *subsidies*, and *contri-
butions* he is put to, besides his *rent*? What *medicines*, besides his *diet*?
and what *Inmates* he is faine to take in, besides his owne *familie*, what
infectious diseases, from other men. *Adam* might have had *Paradise* for
dressing and *keeping* it; and *then* his *rent* was not *improved* to such a 20
labour, as would have made his *brow sweat*; and yet he gave it over;
how farre greater a *rent* doe wee pay for this *farme*, this *body*, who
pay *our selves*, who pay the *farme it selfe*, and cannot *live* upon it?
Neither is our *labour* at an end, when wee have cut downe some *weed*,
as soone as it sprung up, corrected some *violent* and dangerous 25
accident of a *disease*, which would have destroied *speedily*; nor when
wee have pulled up that *weed*, from the very *root*, recovered *entirely*
and *soundly*, from that *particular disease*; but the whole *ground* is of an
ill nature, the whole *soile ill disposed*; there are inclinations, there is a
propensnesse to *diseases* in the *body*, out of which without any other 30
disorder, *diseases* will grow, and so wee are put to a continuall labour

2 embers,] embers 1624(2), 1626   6 downe, and how] downe; how 1626   8
stone,] stone 1624(2), 1626   13 this] his 1624(2), 1626   15,16 *halfe-holy day*]
halfe holy-day 1624(2), 1626   16 reparations,] reperations 1626   17 medicines,]
medicines 1626   19 diseases,] diseases 1624(2), 1626   21 over;] over, 1624(2),
1626   27 weed,] weed 1626

upon this *farme*, to a continuall studie of the whole *complexion* and *constitution* of our *body*. In the *distempers* and *diseases* of *soiles, sourenesse, drinesse, weeping,* any kinde of *barrennesse,* the *remedy* and the *physicke,* is, for a great part, sometimes in *themselves*; sometimes the very
5   *situation* releeves them, the *hanger* of a *hill,* will purge and vent his owne *malignant moisture*; and the burning of the upper *turfe* of some ground (as *health* from *cauterizing*) puts a *new* and a *vigorous youth* into that *soile,* and there rises a kinde of *Phoenix* out of the *ashes,* a *fruitfulnesse* out of that which was *barren* before, and *by that,* which is
10 the barrennest of all, *ashes.* And where the *ground* cannot give it selfe *physicke,* yet it receives *Physicke* from other grounds, from other soiles, which are not the worse, for having contributed that helpe to them, from *Marle* in other *hils,* or from *slimie sand* in other *shoares*: *grounds* helpe *themselves,* or hurt not other *grounds,* from whence they
15 receive *helpe.* But I have taken a *farme* at this *hard rent,* and upon those *heavie covenants,* that it can afford it selfe no *helpe*; (no part of my *body,* if it were cut off, would *cure* another part; in some cases it might *preserve* a sound part, but in no case *recover* an infected) and, if my *body* may have my *Physicke,* any *Medicine* from another *body,*
20 one *Man* from the flesh of another *Man* (as by Mummy, or any such *composition,*) it must bee from a man that is dead, and not, as in other *soiles,* which are never the worse for contributing their *Marle,* or their fat slime to my *ground.* There is nothing in the same *man,* to helpe *man,* nothing in *mankind* to helpe *one another,* (in this sort, by way of
25 *Physicke*) but that hee who *ministers* the *helpe,* is in as ill case, as he that *receives* it would have beene, if he had not had it; for hee, from whose *body* the *Physicke* comes, is *dead.* When therefore I tooke this *farme,* undertooke this body, I undertooke to *draine,* not a *marish,* but a *moat,* where there was, not water *mingled* to offend, but all was
30 *water*; I undertooke to *perfume dung,* where no one part, but all was equally *unsavory*; I undertooke to make such a thing *wholsome,* as was not *poison* by any manifest quality, *intense heat,* or *cold,* but *poison* in the *whole substance,* and in the *specifique forme* of it. To cure the *sharpe accidents* of *diseases,* is a great worke; to cure the *disease it*
35 *selfe,* is a greater; but to cure the *body,* the *root,* the *occasion* of *diseases,*

---

1 *farme,*] *farme*; 1626   4 *part,*] *part*; 1624(2), 1626   4 sometimes the *S*: sometime the all edd.   9 *fruitfulnesse*] *fruitfulnes,* 1624(2), 1626   .15 *helpe.*] *helpe,* 1626   23 *ground.*] *ground,* 1626   27 *comes,*] *comes* 1624(2), 1626   33 *substance,*] *substance* 1626

is a worke reserved for the great *Physitian*, which he doth never any other way, but by *glorifying* these *bodies* in the next world.

22. EXPOSTULATION

My *God*, my *God*, what am I put to, when I am put to *consider*, and *put off*, the *root*, the *fuell*, the *occasion* of my *sicknesse*? What *Hypo-* 5
crates, what *Galen*, could shew mee that in my *body*? It lies deeper than so; it lies in my *soule*: And deeper than so; for we may wel consider the *body*, before the *soule* came, before *inanimation*, to bee *without sinne*; and the *soule* before it come to the *body*, before that *infection*, to be *without sinne*; *sinne* is the *root*, and the *fuell* of all 10
sicknesse, and yet that which destroies *body* & *soule*, is in *neither*, but in *both together*; It is in the *union* of the *body* and *soule*; and, O my *God*, could I *prevent* that, or can I *dissolve* that? The *root*, and the *fuell* of my *sicknesse*, is my *sinne*, my *actuall sinne*; but even that *sinne* hath another *root*, another *fuell*, *originall sinne*; and can I *devest* that? 15
Wilt thou bid me to separate the *leven*, that a lumpe of Dowe hath received, or the *salt*, that the water hath contracted, from the *Sea*? Dost thou looke, that I should so looke to the *fuell*, or *embers* of *sinne*, that I never take fire? The whole world is *a pile of fagots*, upon which wee are laid, and (as though there were no other) *we* are the 20

Lev. 5.2

Num. 15.24

Rom. 1.32

bellowes. *Ignorance* blowes the *fire*, *He that touched any uncleane thing,*
though he knew it not, became uncleane, and a sacrifice was required,
(therefore a *sin* imputed) *though it were done in ignorance*. *Ignorance*
blowes this *Coale*; but then *knowledge* much more; for, *there are that*
know thy judgements, and yet not onely doe, but have pleasure in others, 25
that doe against them. *Nature* blowes this *Coale*; *By nature wee are the*

Eph. 2.3

children of wrath: And the *Law* blowes it; thy *Apostle*, Saint *Paul*, found, *That sinne tooke occasion by the Law,* that therefore because it is forbidden, we do some things. If wee breake the *Law*, wee *sinne*;

1 Jo. 3.4
Rom. 7.23

Jer. 6.7

Sinne is the transgression of the Law; And *sinne it selfe becomes a Law in* 30
our *members*. Our *fathers* have imprinted the *seed*, infused a *spring* of *sinne* in us: *As a fountaine casteth out her waters, wee cast out our*

3 22.] 22 1626   14 my *sinne*,] my *sinne* 1626   *Margin* 15.24 *S*: 15.22 all edd.
23 *ignorance*.] *ignorance*? 1626   27 it; *S*: it, all edd.   27 *Apostle*,] *Apostle*
1624(2), 1626   32 *our*] *her* 1626   *Margin* 6.7] 67. 1626

wickednesse; *but we have done worse than our fathers.* We are open to   7.26
infinite *tentations*, and yet, as though we lacked, *we are tempted of our*   Jacob 1.14
owne lusts. And not satisfied with that, as though we were not
powerfull enough, or *cunning* enough, to demolish, or undermine our
5   selves, when wee our selves have no pleasure in the *sinne*, we *sinne*   Gen. 3.6
for others sakes. When *Adam* sinned for *Eves* sake, and *Salomon* to   1 Reg. 11.3
gratifie his wives, it was an *uxorious* sinne: When the *Judges* sinned   1 Reg. 21.11
for *Jezabels* sake, and *Joab* to obey *David*, it was an *ambitious* sinne: 2 Sam. 11.
When *Pilat* sinned to *humor the people*, and *Herod* to *give farther*   16, 21
10 *contentment to the Jewes*, it was a *popular* sinne: Any thing serves, to   Luc. 23.23
occasion sin, at *home*, in my bosome, or *abroad*, in my *Marke*, and   Act. 12.3
aime; that which *I am*, and that which *I am not*, that which I *would*
be, proves *coales*, and *embers*, and *fuell*, and *bellowes* to *sin*; and dost
thou put me, O my *God*, to discharge my selfe, of *my selfe*, before I
15 can be *well*? When thou bidst me *to put off the old Man*, doest thou   Eph. 4.22
meane, not onely my old *habits* of *actuall sin*, but the *oldest of all*,
originall sinne? When thou biddest me *purge out the leven*, dost thou   1 Cor. 5.7
meane, not only the sowrenesse of mine owne ill contracted *customes*,
but the innate *tincture* of sin, imprinted by *Nature*? How shall I doe
20 that which thou requirest, and not *falsifie* that which thou hast *said*,
that sin is gone over all? But, O my *God*, I presse thee not, with *thine*
owne text, without *thine owne comment*; I know that in the state of my
body, which is more *discernible*, than that of my soule, thou dost
effigiate my *Soule* to me. And though no *Anatomist* can say, in dis-
25 secting a *body*, here lay the *coale*, the *fuell*, the *occasion* of all *bodily*
diseases, but yet *a man* may have such a knowledge of his owne
constitution, and bodily inclination to *diseases*, as that he may *prevent*
his *danger* in a great part: so though wee cannot assigne the *place* of
originall sinne, nor the *Nature* of it, so *exactly*, as of *actuall*, or by any
30 diligence *devest* it, yet having *washed it* in the water of thy *Baptisme*,
wee have not onely so cleansed it, that wee may the better look upon
it, and *discerne* it, but so *weakned* it, that howsoever it may retaine
the *former nature*, it doth not retaine the *former force*, and though it
may have the *same name*, it hath not the same *venome*.

Margin 21.11 *Ed.*: 21 all edd.   Margin 2 Sam. 11.16,21 *S*: 1 *Par.* 22.3 all edd.
13 *coales*,] coales 1624(2), 1626   Margin 4.22] 4,2.2 1626   29 it,] it 1624(2),
1626

22. PRAYER

O eternall and most gracious *God*, the *God* of *securitie*, and the *enemie* of *securitie* too, who wouldest have us alwaies *sure* of thy *love*, and yet wouldest have us alwaies *doing something* for it, let mee alwaies so apprehend *thee*, as *present* with me, and yet to *follow* after thee, as 5 though I had not apprehended thee. Thou enlargedst *Ezechias* lease for *fifteene yeeres*; Thou renewedst *Lazarus* his lease, for a time, which we know not: But thou didst never so put out any of these *fires*, as that thou didst not rake up the *embers*, and wrap up a *future mortalitie*, in that *body*, which thou hadst then so *reprieved*. Thou proceedest no 10 otherwise in our *soules*, O our *good*, but *fearefull God*: Thou pardonest no *sinne* so, as that that *sinner* can sinne no more; thou makest no *man* so *acceptable*, as that thou makest him *impeccable*. Though therefore it were a *diminution* of the *largenesse*, and *derogatorie* to the *fulnesse* of thy *mercie*, to looke backe upon those sinnes which in a true 15 *repentance*, I have buried in the wounds of thy *Sonne*, with a *jealous* or *suspicious eie*, as though they were now *my sinnes*, when I had so transferred them upon thy *Sonne*, as though they could now bee *raised* to life againe, to condemne mee to death, when they are dead in *him*, who is the *fountaine of life*; yet were it an *irregular anticipation*, 20 and an *insolent presumption*, to thinke that thy *present mercie* extended to all my *future sinnes*, or that there were no *embers*, no *coales of future sinnes* left in mee. Temper therefore thy *mercie* so to my *soule*, O my *God*, that I may neither *decline* to any faintnesse of spirit, in suspecting thy *mercie* now, to bee lesse *hearty*, lesse *sincere*, than it used to be, to 25 those who are perfitly reconciled to thee, nor *presume* so of it, as either to thinke this *present mercie* an *antidote* against *all poisons*, and so *expose* my selfe to *tentations*, upon confidence that this thy *mercie* shall *preserve* mee, or that when I doe cast my selfe into *new sinnes*, I may have *new mercie* at *any time*, because thou didst so *easily* afford mee 30 *this*.

3 *securitie* too] *secutity* too 1624(2)   6 enlargedst] inlargest 1624(2), 1626   7 renewedst] renewest 1626   9 *mortalitie*,] *mortality* 1624(2), 1626   19 condemne 1624(2), 1626: con-*demne* 1624(1)   20 *life*; 1626, *A*: *life*, 1624(1&2)   24 any] my 1626   25 used *Ed.*: uses all edd.

23. Metusque Relabi.

They warne mee of the fearefull danger of relapsing.

23. MEDITATION

It is not in *mans body*, as it is in the *Citie*, that when *the Bell* hath rung,
5 to cover your *fire*, and rake up the *embers*, you may lie downe, and
sleepe without feare. Though you have by *physicke* and *diet*, raked up
the *embers* of your *disease*, stil there is a feare of a *relapse*; and the
greater *danger* is in that. Even in *pleasures*, and in *paines*, there is a
propriety, a *Meum & Tuum*; and a man is most affected with that
10 *pleasure* which is *his*, *his* by former enjoying and experience, and
most intimidated with those *paines* which are *his*, *his* by a wofull
sense of them, in former afflictions. A *covetous* person, who hath pre-
occupated all his senses, filled all his capacities, with the *delight* of
gathering, wonders how any man can have *any taste* of *any pleasure* in
15 *any opennesse*, or *liberalitie*; So also in *bodily paines*, in a fit of the
stone, the patient wonders why any man should call the *Gout* a *paine*:
And hee that hath felt neither, but the *tooth-ach*, is as much afraid of a
fit of that, as either of the other, of either of the other. *Diseases*,
which we never *felt* in our selves, come but to a *compassion* of others
20 that have endured them; Nay, *compassion* it selfe, comes to no great
degree, if wee have not *felt*, in some *proportion*, in *our selves*, that
which wee lament and condole in another. But when wee have had
those torments in their *exaltation*, *our selves*, wee tremble at a *relapse*.
When wee must *pant* through all those *fierie heats*, and *saile*
25 thorow all those *overflowing sweats*, when wee must *watch* through all
those long *nights*, and *mourne* through all those long *daies*, (*daies* and
nights, so *long*, as that *Nature* her selfe shall seeme to be *perverted*, and
to have put the *longest day*, and the *longest night*, which should bee
six moneths asunder, into one *naturall, unnaturall day*) when wee must
30 stand at the same *barre*, expect the returne of *Physitians* from their
consultations, and not bee sure of the same *verdict*, in any good

---

1 Metusque *Ed.*: Metusque, all edd.   5 rake] take 1626   9 *propriety*] pro-
prietary 1624(2), 1626   23 at a *relapse*] at *Relapse* 1624(2), 1626   26 *daies*,] *daies*
1624(2), 1626   27 *long*,] *long* 1626

Indications, when we must goe the same *way* over againe, and not see the same *issue*, this is a *state*, a *condition*, a *calamitie*, in respect of which, any other *sicknesse* were a *convalescence*, and any *greater*, *lesse*. It addes to the *affliction*, that *relapses* are, (and for the most part justly) imputed to *our selves*, as occasioned by some *disorder* in us; and so we are not 5 onely *passive*, but *active*, in our owne *ruine*; we doe not onely stand under a *falling house*, but *pull it* downe upon us; and wee are not onely *executed*, (that implies *guiltinesse*) but wee are *executioners*, (that implies *dishonor*;) and *executioners of our selves*, (and that implies *impietie*.) And wee fall from that *comfort* which wee might have in 10 our first *sicknesse*, from that *meditation*, *Alas, how generally miserable is Man, and how subject to diseases*, (for in that it is some degree of *comfort*, that wee are but in the state *common* to all) we fall, I say, to this *discomfort*, and *selfe accusing*, & *selfe condemning*; *Alas, how unprovident, and in that, how unthankfull to God and his instruments am I,* 15 *in making so ill use of so great benefits, in destroying so soone, so long a worke, in relapsing, by my disorder, to that from which they had delivered mee*; and so my *meditation* is fearefully transferred from the *body* to the *minde*, and from the consideration of the *sicknesse*, to *that sinne*, that sinfull *carelesnesse*, by which I have occasioned my *relapse*. And 20 amongst the many *weights* that aggravate a *relapse*, this also is one, that a *relapse* proceeds with a more violent dispatch, and more *irremediably*, because it finds the *Countrie weakned*, and *depopulated* before. Upon a *sicknesse*, which as yet appeares not, wee can scarce fix a *feare*, because wee know not what to feare; but as *feare* is the 25 *busiest* and *irksomest affection*, so is a *relapse* (which is still *ready to come*) into that, which is but newly gone, the *nearest object*, the *most immediate* exercise of that *affection* of *feare*.

23. EXPOSTULATION

My *God*, my *God*, my *God*, thou mightie *Father*, who hast beene my 30 *Physitian*; Thou glorious *Sonne*, who hast beene my *physicke*; Thou blessed *Spirit*, who hast *prepared* and *applied* all to mee, shall *I alone*

---

14 *discomfort*,] discomfort 1624(2), 1626   15 *I*,] I 1624(2), 1626   26 (which]; which 1626   30 *Father*,] Father; 1626

bee able to overthrow the worke of *all you*, and *relapse* into those *spirituall sicknesses*, from which your infinite *mercies* have withdrawne me? Though thou, O my *God*, have filled my *measure* with *mercie*, yet my *measure* was not so *large*, as that of thy *whole people*, 5 the *Nation*, the *numerous* and *glorious nation of Israel*; and yet how often, how often did they fall into *relapses*? And then, where is my *assurance*? how easily thou passedst over many other sinnes in them, and how vehemently thou insistedst in those, into which they so often *relapsed*; Those were their *murmurings* against thee, in thine *Instru-* 10 *ments*, and *Ministers*, and their turnings upon other *gods*, and embracing the *Idolatries* of their *neighbours*. O my *God*, how *slipperie* a way, to how *irrecoverable* a bottome, is *murmuring*? and how neere *thy selfe* hee comes, that *murmures* at *him*, who comes from *thee*? The *Magistrate* is the *garment* in which thou apparellest *thy selfe*; and hee 15 that shoots at the *cloathes*, cannot say, hee meant no ill to the *man*: Thy *people* were feareful *examples* of that; for, how often did their *murmuring* against thy *Ministers*, end in a *departing* from *thee*? when they would have *other officers*, they would have *other gods*; and still *to daies murmuring*, was *to morrowes Idolatrie*; As their *murmuring* 20 induced *Idolatrie*, and they *relapsed* often into *both*, I have found in my selfe, O my *God*, (O my *God*, thou hast found it in me, and thy finding it, hath shewed it to me) such a *transmigration* of *sinne*, as makes mee afraid of *relapsing too*. The *soule* of *sinne*, (for wee have made *sinne immortall*, and it must have a *soule*) The *soule* of *sinne*, is *dis-* 25 *obedience* to thee; and when one *sinne* hath beene *dead* in mee, that *soule* hath passed into another *sinne*. Our *youth* dies, and the *sinnes* of our *youth* with it; some *sinnes* die a *violent death*, and some a *naturall*; *povertie, penurie, imprisonment, banishment*, kill some sinnes in us, and some die of *age*; many waies wee become *unable* to doe that *sinne*; 30 but still the *soule* lives, and passes into another *sinne*; and that, that was *licentiousnesse*, growes *ambition*, and that comes to *indevotion*, and *spirituall coldnesse*; wee have *three lives*, in our *state of sinne*; and where the *sinnes of youth* expire, those of our *middle yeeres* enter; and those of our *age* after them. This *transmigration of sinne*, found in my selfe, 35 makes me afraid, O my *God*, of a *Relapse*: but the *occasion* of my

2 which your infinite] which infinit 1624(2), 1626   15 *man*:] *man.* 1626   29 *sinne*;] *sin*, 1626

feare, is more *pregnant* than so; for, I have *had*, I have *multiplied Relapses* already. Why, O my *God*, is a *relapse* so odious to thee? Not so much their *murmuring*, and their *Idolatry*, as their *relapsing* into those *sinnes*, seemes to affect thee, in thy disobedient people. *They limited the holy one of Israel*, as thou complainest of them: That was a 5 *murmuring*; but before thou chargest them with the *fault it selfe*, in the same place, thou chargest them, with the *iterating*, the *redoubling* of that *fault*, before the *fault* was named; *How oft did they provoke mee in the Wildernesse; and grieve me in the Desart*? That which brings thee to that exasperation against them, as to say, that *thou wouldest* 10 *breake thine owne oath*, rather than leave them *unpunished*, (*They shall not see the land, which I sware unto their fathers*) was because *they had tempted thee ten times*, infinitely; upon that, thou threatnest with that *vehemencie, if ye do in any wise goe backe, know for a certainty, God will no more drive out any of these Nations from before you; but they shall be* 15 *snares, and traps unto you, and scourges in your sides, and thornes in your eies, till ye perish.* No *tongue*, but *thine owne*, O my GOD, can expresse thine indignation, against a *Nation relapsing to Idolatry. Idolatry* in any *Nation* is *deadly*; but when the *disease* is *complicated* with a *relapse* (a *knowledge* and a *profession* of a *former recoverie*) it is *desperate*: And 20 thine *anger* workes, not onely where the *evidence* is *pregnant*, and without *exception*, (so thou saiest, *when it is said, That certaine men in a Citie, have withdrawne others to Idolatrie, and that inquirie is made, and it is found true, the Citie, and the inhabitants, and the Cattell are to bee destroied*) but where there is but a *suspicion*, a *rumor*, of such a *relapse* 25 to *Idolatrie*, thine *anger* is awakened, and thine *indignation* stirred. In the government of thy servant *Josua, there was a voice, that Reuben and Gad, with those of Manasseh, had built a new altar. Israel* doth not *send* one to enquire; but *the whole congregation gathered to goe up to warre against them*; and *there went a Prince of every Tribe*: And they 30 *object* to them, not so much their present declination to *Idolatry*, as their *Relapse; is the iniquity of* Peor *too little for us*? An *idolatry* formerly committed, and punished with the slaughter of *twenty foure thousand delinquents.* At last *Reuben*, and *Gad* satisfie them, *that that Altar was not built for Idolatry*, but built as *a patterne of theirs, that* 35

Psa. 78.41

Num. 14.22, 23

Jos. 23.12

Deut. 13.12–15

Jos. 22.11

v. 12

Num. 25.9

Margin 22,23 *Ed.*: 22 all edd.   12 *fathers*)] *fathers*(1624(2), 1626   14 *ye*] *you* 1624(2), 1626   *Margin* 13.12–15 *Ed.*: 13.12 1624(1); 23.12 1624(2), 1626 *Margin v.* 12 *S*: 1.12 all edd.   *Margin* 25.9 *Ed.*: 25.4 all edd.

they might thereby *professe* themselves to bee of the *same profession*, that they were; and so the *Army* returned without bloud. Even where it comes not so farre, as to an *actuall Relapse* into *Idolatry*, Thou, O my GOD, becommest sensible of it; though thou, who

5 seest the heart all the way, preventedst all *dangerous effects*, where there was no *ill meaning*, how ever there were *occasion* of *suspicious rumours*, given to thine *Israel*, of *relapsing*. So *odious* to thee, & so *aggravating* a weight upon *sinne*, is a *relapse*. But, O my *God*, why is it so? *so odious*? It must bee so, because hee that hath *sinned*, and then

10 *repented*, hath *weighed God* and the *Devill* in a *ballance*; hee hath *heard God* and the *Devill plead*; and after *hearing*, given *Judgement* on   *Tertull.* that *side*, to which he *adheres*, by his *subsequent practise*; if he returne to his *sinne*, hee *decrees* for *Satan*; he prefers *sinne* before *grace*, and *Satan* before *God*; and in *contempt* of *God*, declares the *precedency* for

15 his *adversary*: And a contempt wounds deeper than an injury; a *relapse* deeper, than a *blasphemy*. And when thou hast told me, that a *relapse* is more *odious* to *thee*, neede I aske why it is more *dangerous*, more *pernitious* to *me*? Is there any other *measure* of the greatnesse of my *danger*, than the greatnesse of thy *displeasure*? How *fitly*, and how

20 *fearefully* hast thou expressed my *case*, in a *storm at Sea*, if I relapse? (*They mount up to Heaven, and they goe downe againe to the depth*:) My *Psa.* 107.26 *sicknesse* brought mee to *thee* in *repentance*, and my *relapse* hath cast mee farther from thee: *The end of that man shall be worse than the* *Mat.* 12.45 *beginning*, saies thy *Word*, thy *Sonne*; My *beginning* was *sicknesse*,

25 *punishment* for *sin*; but *a worse thing may follow*, saies he also, if I *sin*, *Jo.* 5.14 againe: not onely *death*, which is an *end*, worse than *sicknesse*, which was the *beginning*, but *Hell*, which is a *beginning* worse than that *end*. Thy *great servant* denied thy *Sonne*, and he *denied* him againe; but all *Mar.* 14.70 before *Repentance*; here was no *relapse*. O, if thou haddest ever re-

30 admitted *Adam* into *Paradise*, how *abstinently* would hee have walked by that *tree*? and would not the *Angels*, that *fell*, have *fixed* themselves upon thee, if thou hadst once *re-admitted* them to thy *sight*? They never *relapsed*; If I doe, must not my case be as desperate? Not so desperate, for, *as thy Majestie, so is thy Mercie*, both *infinite*: and thou *Ecclus.* 2.18

35 who hast commanded me *to pardon my brother seventy times seven*, hast

5 preventedst *Ed.*: preventest all edd. 13 *Satan*;] Satan, 1624(2), 1626 24 *beginning*,] beginning 1626 *Margin* 5.14 *S*: 8.14 all edd. *Margin* 14.70] 1.70 1626 35 *seventy times seven Ed.*: *seventy seven times* all edd.

limited thy selfe to no *Number*. If *death* were ill in it *selfe*, thou wouldest never have *raised* any *dead Man*, to life againe, because that man must necessarily *die againe*. If thy *Mercy*, in *pardoning*, did so farre *aggravate a Relapse*, as that there were no more *mercy* after it, our case were the worse for that *former Mercy*; for who is not under, even 5 a *necessity of sinning*, whilst hee is here, if wee place this *necessity* in our own *infirmity*, and not in thy *Decree*? But I speak not this, O my *God*, as preparing a way to my *Relapse* out of *presumption*, but to *preclude* all accesses of *desperation*, though out of *infirmity*, I should *Relapse*.

23. PRAYER   10

O eternall and most gracious *God*, who though thou beest *ever infinite*, yet *enlargest* thy selfe, by the *Number* of our prayers, and takest our *often petitions* to thee, to be an *addition* to thy *glory*, and thy *greatnesse*, as *ever* upon all occasions, so now, O my *God*, I come to thy *Majestie* with *two Prayers, two Supplications*. I have *Meditated* 15 upon the *Jelouzie*, which thou hast of thine owne *honour*; and considered, that Nothing can come neerer a *violating* of that *honor*, neerer to the *Nature* of a *scorne* to thee, then to sue out thy *Pardon*, and receive the *Seales* of *Reconciliation* to thee, and then *returne* to that *sinne*, for which I *needed*, and *had* thy pardon before. I know that this 20 comes to neare, to a making thy holy *Ordinances*, thy *Word*, thy *Sacraments*, thy *Seales*, thy *Grace, instruments* of my *Spirituall Fornications*. Since therefore thy *Correction* hath brought mee to such a *participation of thy selfe (thy selfe,* O my *God,* cannot bee *parted*) to such an *intire possession* of thee, as that I durst deliver my selfe over to thee 25 this *Minute,* If this *Minute* thou wouldst accept my *dissolution, preserve* me, O my *God* the *God* of *constancie,* and *perseverance,* in this state, from all *relapses* into those *sinnes,* which have induc'd thy *former Judgements* upon me. But because, by too lamentable *Experience,* I know how slippery my *customs* of *sinne,* have made my *wayes* of 30 *sinne,* I presume to adde this *petition* too, That if my *infirmitie* over- take mee, thou *forsake* mee not. Say to my *Soule, My Sonne, thou hast*

Ecclus. 21.1

---

8 *presumption,*] presumption 1624(2), 1626   9 *desperation,*] desperation; 1626   12 selfe,] selfe 1624(2), 1626   16 *honour*;] honour, 1624(2), 1626   17 can come] come 1624(2), 1626   22 thy *Seales*] the *Seales* 1626   24 *selfe*] selfe, 1624(2), 1626   27 my *God*] my *God*, 1624(2), 1626   29 I 1624(2), 1626, S: I I 1624(1) *Margin* 21.1] 1.21 1624(2), 1626

sinned, doe so no more; but say also, that though I doe, thy *Spirit* of *Remorce*, and *Compunction* shall never *depart* from mee. Thy holy *Apostle, Saint Paul*, was shipwrackd *thrice*; & yet *stil saved*. Though   2 Cor. 11.25
the *rockes*, and the *sands*, the *heights*, and the *shallowes*, the *prosperitie*,
5   and the *adversitie* of this *world* do diversly threaten mee, though mine
owne *leakes* endanger mee, yet, O *God*, let mee never put my selfe
aboard with *Hymeneus*, nor *make shipwracke of faith, and a good*   1 Timo. 1.19
Conscience; and then thy *long-livd*, thy *everlasting Mercy*, will visit
me, though *that*, which I most earnestly pray against, should fall
10   upon mee, a *relapse* into those *sinnes*, which I have *truely repented*, and
thou hast *fully pardoned*.

FINIS.

Margin 1 Timo. *S*: Timo. all edd.   8 *Conscience*; *Ed.*: *Conscience*, all edd.

127

Commentary

PAGE 3

ll. 12–13 *the Father to the Father . . . the Sonne to the Sonne.* The reference is couched in a paradox typical of Donne but not all its elements are clear. Donne is most probably referring to his dedication to King James of his earlier prose work, *Pseudo-Martyr* (1610). If he is thinking of this dedication, his paradox creates a parallel between two fathers (himself as father of *Pseudo-Martyr* and James as father of Prince Charles) and between two 'sonnes' (*Devotions*, his literary child, and Prince Charles, James' son).

ll. 15–16 *Examples of Good Kings are Commandements.* Donne is using the word 'example' with its contemporary meaning that a good human being is a better teacher of morals than books, a point that Ascham makes in *The Scholemaster* (1570), p. 20ᵛ.

l. 16 *Ezechiah writt the Meditations.* Ezechiah (Hezekiah or Ezekias), king of Judah, c. 727 to 696 B.C., recovered from a serious illness in the fourteenth year of his reign, and recorded a vision experienced by him during his sickness (Isa. 28:9–20). The biblical passage was obviously in the forefront of Donne's mind during the composition of *Devotions*, for he refers to it several times.

PAGE 7

ll. 8–11 *We study Health . . . a regular work.* In Renaissance health manuals, the plan for physical fitness was rather elaborate. Relying heavily on the tenets of the Ancients—particularly Hippocrates and Galen—it covered the whole day's diet, with a related program for exercises. Coghan's *Haven* and Elyot's *Castle* are cases in point. Coghan's book opens with a chapter on exercises for physical fitness and for cleaning the pores (p. 2); this is followed by a chapter on the equally important exercise of the mind to nourish the wit (p. 13), and later by a number of chapters on the quantities of each food to be eaten at set times of day in given seasons of the year, depending on the age of the person. The book then describes the best kinds and quantities of drink, from water (p. 206) to buttered beer (p. 236), and concludes with chapters on sleep (p. 236) and sexual intercourse (p. 245). Elyot speaks in a somewhat less organized way than Coghan, but his program is equally elaborate. He draws a number of close connections—which Donne himself implies in the grouping of his words—between the nature of exercise (a 'vehement motion' accompanied by 'alteration of the breath of mynde of a man', pp. 46a, b) and the ideal moment for this exercise—a little later than midway between meals ('when bothe the firste and seconde digestion is complete', p. 45).

l. 16 *put a coale*. Donne's specific use of *coale* does not occur in the Bible but the word recurs many times in the Old Testament with general connotations of spiritual life (Isa. 54:16; Ezek. 1:13).

ll. 24–25 *one hand askes . . . how we do*. In contemporary medical manuals, a change of pulse and discoloration of urine were the two chief symptoms of internal diseases. These symptoms augured a great number of illnesses (Elyot, p. 87b, 88; Gerarde, p. 1160; Hart, *Arraignment*, p. 21) both to laymen (Gerarde, p. 1082) and to doctors (Banister, *History*, VII, 95). For laymen like Donne, Elyot considered discoloration of urine the greater symptom of the two ('the most common judgement in sicknesse', p. 87).

ll. 31–32 *Is this the honour . . . a little world*. The honour Donne refers to is explained by Crooke in the introduction ('Of the dignitie and wonderfull Frame of Mans Body') of his *Description* (p. 2). Crooke describes the physical structure of man as a microcosmic 'little world' which alone among created things epitomizes all the good elements of the macrocosmic universe. Man's structure represents in a single cogent figure all the parts of God's image distributed only piecemeal in other things. In Donne's analogy, the honour for man is an ambiguous privilege. In an illness, man is subject to physical upheavals of the same breadth as that which planetary upheavals inflict on the universe. Crooke writes: 'The Body also . . . carieth the Image of God, not in figure . . . but because the admirable structure and accomplished perfection of the Body, carieth in it a representation of all the most glorious and perfect workes of God, as being an Epitome or compend of the whole Creation, by which he is rather signified then expressed. And hence it is, that Man is called a *Microcosme* or little world.'

PAGE 8

l. 9 *a hote fever in cold Melancholy*. The simultaneous occurrence of hot fever and cold melancholic humour was considered the symptom of a common cold known as hot 'rewme'. This 'rewme', which may have been pneumonia, stimulated 'a hot temperature' in the body that its accompanying 'cold' melancholy, in spite of its name, dangerously raised rather than decreased (Elyot, pp. 78, 78ᵛ). The cold melancholy was created by an excessive functioning of the blood with a 'cold drie substance' that sent vapours shooting up to the head. It warmed the body feverishly (Bright, pp. 1, 2, 5) and rendered the usual remedy of a cold diet for a hot cold useless (Elyot, 78ᵛ). Donne's reader thinks of the 'contraryes' of 'cold and hott' creating the 'fantastique Ague' in the imagery of Holy Sonnet XIX (ll. 1, 7, 13).

l. 16 *dust & ashes.* Abraham (Gen. 18:27) and Job (30:19) claim to be mere dust and ashes, while Donne, departing from the Bible, claims that he is more than that.

l. 26 *antidates.* An obsolete word for anticipates, originating in the practice of fixing an earlier date than a true one to a document.

PAGE 9

l. 12 *Job did not charge thee foolishly.* Job 1:22.

ll. 25–27 *prodigall sonnes . . . not bin denied it.* Luke 15:12.

PAGE 11

ll. 14–15 *It doth not only melt him . . . but to lime.* In the chemical lore of contemporary natural philosophy, atoms were hypothetically the minutest particles to which matter might be reduced. One of the chief ways of effecting this reduction was the alchemical process of 'calcination', the distillation of a thing to lime (Power, *Philosophy*, b1ᵛ, b2). In calcination, matter returned to the original disorganized state of 'vacuity' that characterized the atoms of its four constituent elements (water, earth, fire, and air) before it came into being (Langley, *Abridgement*, I, Fol. IVb). But *to lime* is probably an allusion to Isa. 33:12, as well as to contemporary chemistry.

ll. 22–23 *Angells . . . had a Ladder to goe to Heaven.* Isa. 28:12.

PAGE 12

ll. 1–2 *In the sweat of thy browes . . . bread.* Gen. 3:19.

l. 2 *it is multiplied to me.* Donne's use of the word 'multiplied' suggests his theory of 'numbers' and of 'singular' things in *Essays in Divinity* and in other passages of *Devotions.* His theory was that God expressed his divine greatness in creation by imaging his concept of multiplicity in the propagation of the human race (*Essays*, p. 54). Through propagation after the fall of Adam, the effects of original sin were multiplied to as great a number as there were men. God thereby extended to the punishment of man an element of multiplicity originally reserved to his existence before the fall.

Margin I Sam. 24:15. King James Bible; 24:14 Geneva Bible.

l. 18 *proportion to God.* The proportion in question was beyond social position and class. A slave had it as much as a king. Proportion was a generic word for the designs like the circles, rectangles, squares, and triangles that the symmetrical parts of the human body could alone be imagined as creating (Crooke, p. 6). These designs represented divine ideas imaged only individually in the shapes of other things in the universe. (Crooke used the example of a man lying on his back, making a five-pronged star-like figure with the equidistant points of his hands, feet, and head, p. 63). All created things had proportion, but only proportion in man had a figurative quality which raised him above other things in the universe. In 'Loves diet', Donne uses the term metaphorically. He describes himself as striving to keep his love for his mistress in symmetrical proportion by feeding it less.

ll. 18–19 *David Worthies.* 2 Sam. 21:15.

l. 19 *Gyants.* 2 Sam. 21:16. The word occurs in the King James but not in the Geneva Bible.

ll. 22–23 *God calls things that are not, as though they were.* Rom. 4:17.

l. 27 *Noahs time, 120 yeres.* Gen. 6:3.

ll. 27–28 *thou staidst . . . 40 yeares.* Num. 14:33.

PAGE 13

l. 4 *thou wast not wont to come in whirlwinds.* Job. 38:1, Nah. 1:3, Jer. 23:19.

l. 5 *breathed a Soule into mee.* Gen. 2:7

l. 6 *Thy breath in the Congregation.* Exod. 29:44.

l. 11 *all that afflicted Job.* Job 2:6.

l. 22 *Surgite Mortui, Rise yee dead.* The phrase is a rhetorical adaptation of the thought and imagery of numerous biblical passages (Eph. 5:14, 1 Thess. 4:16, Rev. 20:11–15, 1 Cor. 15:22). It was perhaps inspired by a passage of a Latin Mass, though belonging to no specific liturgy.

PAGE 14

l. 8 *the Supper of the Lamb, with thy Saints in heaven.* Rev. 19:9.

ll. 19–20 *a Light in a Bush, in the middest of these brambles, & thornes.* Exod. 3:4.

ll. 23–24 *crowned with thornes.* Matt. 27:29, Mark 15:17.

PAGE 15

ll. 16–18 *The Anchorites . . . immur'd themselves in hollow walls.* The 'Anchorites' or 'Anchorets' were recluses of both sexes living independently of all religious groups, and they inhabited quarters like the hollowed trunks of trees. In such dwellings, the sky coming through a hole above their heads was the only distraction that they allowed to break into their meditations (R. M. Clay, *The Hermits and Anchorites of England*, London, 1914, pp.1-2, passim).

l. 18   *That perverse man . . . in a Tubb.* Diogenes the Cynic (b. Sinope, 413 B.C., d. Corinth, 323), the philosopher popular in seventeenth-century proverbs, who inured himself to the vicissitudes of weather by living in a tub belonging to the temple of Cybele.

PAGE 16

ll. 10-11   *Lord, I am a child, and cannot speake.* Jer. 1:6.

PAGE 17

ll. 10-11   *not a Recusancie . . . but it is an Excommunication.* Recusancy was a voluntary refusal to attend religious services (in Donne's time, applied particularly to the refusal of Roman Catholics to acknowledge the rites of the Established Church), and, by contrast, Catholic excommunication was the canonical exclusion of a Catholic from Sacraments, life in the church, or both.

ll. 11-12   *thou art Lord of Hosts, & lovest Action.* Jer. 7:3, 4.

ll. 12-13   *in the grave no man shall praise thee.* Isa. 38:18.

ll. 18-19   *Thou couldst take me by the head, as thou didst Abacuc.* Abacuc is the form of the name of Habakkuk in 2 Esdras 1:40, but the reference is to the legend in the apocryphal work, Bel and the Dragon, 36, sometimes attached to the Book of Daniel.

ll. 23-24   *his Exaltation, as himselfe calls his Crucifying.* John 12:33.

l. 28   *suspends mee betweene Heaven and Earth, as a Meteor.* Donne is using the word 'suspended' metaphorically to describe his participation in the spiritual and earthly worlds simultaneously. He is imaging this participation as a creature in both worlds in the figure of the meteor which exists in the terrestial and astral worlds. In Renaissance astronomy books, the meteor was described as formed of the 'vapours' of water and the 'exhalations' of earth, and yet as moving like an astral or superterrestial body (Fulke, pp. 3a, b).

PAGE 18

ll. 8-9   *thy throne, the Heavens.* Matt. 5:34.

ll. 11–12 *the knees of my heart, which are bowed unto thee.* An image to occur
later (1633) in Herbert's 'Deniall' (l. 19).

l. 7 *Memory.* In the obsolete sense of posthumous reputation.

ll. 16–17 *those pieces were extended, and stretched out.* Extended: to lay out flat.
By contrast, see I, *Sermons* (1640), VII, p. 62; or I, *Sermons*, 5, p. 131: 'If I
extend this Sermon, if you extend your Devotion, or your Patience, beyond
the ordinary time.'

ll. 1–3 *Gyants: that reach from East to West, from earth to Heaven . . . span the
Sunn and Firmament.* Donne appears to be writing with a number of legendary
giants in mind; Colossus, the statue of Apollo that reputedly bestrode the
entrance of the harbor at Rhodes; and secondly (perhaps principally), Atlas,
the Greek Titan. In some versions of his legend, Atlas bore the earth on his
shoulders, and in others he held up the pillars of the universe. At the time of
the composition of *Devotions*, Atlas was passing into English vocabulary in
the title of a geography book often printed both in its original language and
in translation (Mercator's *Atlas, Containing his Cosmographicall Description of
the Fabricke and Figure of the World*). On the subject of Atlas, Blundeville's
A Plaine Treatise illuminates Donne's reference: 'Some say Atlas was the first
inventor [of the sciences of cosmography and geography], whom the Poets
faine to beare up the heavens with his shoulders, having his head placed in
the North Pole, and his feet in the South Pole, and his right hand bearing
the East part, and his left hand the West part of the world. Albeit that some
apply this fiction of the Poets to an high mountaine in Africa called Atlas,
which for his great height surmounting the clouds, is said to bear up the
skies' (p. 278).

ll. 13–15 *venimous, and infectious diseases, feeding & consuming diseases, and
manifold, and entangled diseases.* The three kinds of illnesses that Donne
mentions are described in contemporary medical books in terms of the animals and insects listed in his allusion a few lines earlier (serpents, vipers,
worms, caterpillars and 'monsters'). A venomous and infectious disease was
caused by a poisonous outside agent (Monardes, 1580, Fol. 115), such as the
bite of a serpent, that left its victim racked with 'paine, pricking, vehement
lyting, griefe' (Bannister, *Workes* II, 4, p. 175). The feeding and consuming
diseases were cancerous malignities implanted by worms that fed on the
body as worms and caterpillars fed on natural things (Gerarde, 952b; Lyte,
I, p. 6). Lastly, the manifold and entangled diseases, less precisely described,

were illnesses like the cold and fever that spread from one part of the body to the other, creating new forms of disorder on the way (Gabelhover, p. 9; Elyot, p. 79a). They made hybrid diseases out of different human and animal sicknesses (Topsell, pp. 263–64).

ll. 20–21 *Hercules against these Gyants, . . . the forces of the other world.* It is not entirely clear which of the twelve labours of Hercules Donne has in mind. Except for his statement that the physician treating him musters up the forces of the other world for his task to defeat 'Gyants', the reference is imprecise. The seventeenth-century uses of the word 'Gyant' were so varied that they might be made to cover practically all the monsters Hercules encountered in his labours. Donne is either using 'Gyants' to refer generally to all Hercules' foes, or to the twelfth labour alone, which is the only one that required Hercules to summon help from another world (Hermes and Athena from the Greek Olympus) to defeat Cerberus in Hades.

ll. 25–28 *The Hart . . . knowes an Herbe . . . The dog . . . knowes his grasse.* The herb in question was dittany, a 'hot and sharpe herbe' with hoary leaves which Gerarde says originated in Crete (*Herbale*, p. 651). The hart's predilection for this herb was proverbial (Topsell, p. 101: 'When they are wounded with a Dart', harts got 'it out of their body by eating Dittany'; and Gerarde, p. 652: 'deere . . . when they be wounded with arrowes, do shake them out by eating of this plant'). Other herbs like the stinking gladdon were medically good, generally speaking, for all animals (Lyte, pp. 37, 141; Gerarde, p. 53). However, the great majority of creatures, while possessed of the hart's natural taste for healing plants (Monardes, 1580, Fol. 114), lacked its precise instinct for a specific herb. For example, the dog that Donne mentions was reputed to refuse all food until he had satisfied his instinct to eat grass of any sort in order to vomit what was making him sick (Turberville, p. 224).

l. 30 *obvious and present Simples.* A simple was a medical preparation consisting of only one substance. Nicholas Culpepper, the seventeenth-century physician, lists 'Porrage, Bugloss, Marsh mallows, Mallows, Vervain, Violet Leaves and Flowers' as simples for the cure of a cold and dry brain, in his commentary on *Galen's Art of Physick* (p. 25). Donne discusses the melting down of simples on the body of a sick man briefly in 'To Mr. Rowland Woodward' (ll. 24–25).

PAGE 21

l. 1 *Meditations again, and bring it downe.* Sparrow changes 'Meditations' to the singular for grammatical conformity with the 'it', but the apposition of the two words is not necessary. By 'it' Donne appears to refer to the divine judgment on man suggested by his use of the verb 'bring downe', which the closing part of the meditation describes.

l. 29   *The Phisician cutteth off a long disease.* Ecclus. 38:7.

PAGE 22

l. 6   *that spirituall phisicke.* Donne refers to the third or 'judicial' form of absolution in 'The Visitation of the Sicke' in the Book of Common Prayer, given by the attending minister in response to the confession by the ill person (D3ᵛ).

l. 20   *Method.*   A medical prescription.

ll. 24–25   *Give a sweet savor, and a memoriall of fine flower, and make a fat offering, as not being.* Ecclus. 38:11.

PAGE 23

l. 8   *help to Man by the Ministery of man.* Ecclus. 38:1, 2.

PAGE 24

ll. 17–18   *thou be pleased to multiply seven dayes, (and seven is infinite).* In Donne's mystical theory of numbers, the variety of things in creation expressed the greatness of God's concept of multiplicity. Certain digits like ten and seven epitomized this greatness ('Seven is ever used to express infinite,' *Essays*, p. 59; 'three and foure are seven, and seven is infinite,' X, *Sermons*, 8, p. 180).

PAGE 25

ll. 2–4   *Meere vacuitie, the first Agent, God, the first instrument of God, Nature, will not admit.* In scholastic tradition and Greek philosophy, vacuity was a hypothesis suggesting that space could be voided of all matter. In reality, vacuity was impossible because space was meant to contain something, even if only air, according to a law of creation that even God himself could not contradict (Aristotle, *Works*, II, *Physics*, IV, 8, 216b; Aquinas, 'Treatise on the Divine Government', *Summa*, I, Q.CIV, a6, pp. 402–3). Donne took up the idea of 'vacuity' and 'nothing', coupled with the scholastic theory of 'quintessence' and 'privation', in 'A nocturnall upon S. Lucies Day.' In the imagery of the poem, the lover is transformed into an 'ordinary nothing' (l. 35).

l. 11   *pestiducts.* An archaic metaphor for conductors of the plague.

ll. 13–14   *Civilitie . . . working Charitie.* Donne's distinction between civility and charity is based on their current significance. Civility was the politic secular form of behaviour of the kind man among civilized beings, while the finest illustrations of charity were specifically Christian. Charity was 'the friendship of man for God' in the scholastic tradition from which Donne borrows the sense of the word (Aquinas, *Summa*, II, i, Q.XXIII, a5, p. 272). Thomas Morton made the same distinction between the two terms as Donne in his translation of Calvin's *The Institution of Christian Religion* (IV, XX, p. 733).

l. 19   *in that house many mansions.* John 14:2.

l. 22   *Militant, and Triumphant Church.* The Militant Church is the communion of Christians in a state of warfare against sin on earth, and the Triumphant Church is the congregation of saved souls that have passed out of the Church militant victoriously into heaven. In his poem, 'Epithalamion', VI (ll. 166–167), Donne describes the Triumphant Church as the fulfilment of the Militant. These images for the Church recur often in Christian tradition, in, for example, the Book of Common Prayer (before the Communion service, C3ᵛ), and are derived from numerous metaphors of the Bible (2 Cor. 2:14; Rev. 12:6–7, and 2:10–11).

l. 27   *hee made him a helper.* Gen. 2:18.

ll. 31–33   *their blessing was, Encrease ... there is no Phenix; nothing singular, nothing alone.* Donne's interest in the Phoenix legend is due as much to its contemporary interpretation as to its Greek origins. One branch of contemporary thinking marvels not so much at the resurrection of the bird out of its ashes in the Greek legend, as at the 'singleness' of its existence (*Pilgrimage of Perfection*, London, 1531, Fol. 202b). To be 'single' meant not to be propagated, and this singleness led some thinkers to deny the phoenix's existence. Only 'plural' things that propagated themselves existed in the created universe, and only spiritual beings like angels in another world than the earthly could exist in the 'singular,' independently of other like beings for their origin (*Essays*, pp. 52–53). Donne attributes the same 'singular' character to the phoenix in 'The Canonization': 'The Phoenix ridle hath more wit/By us, we two being one, are it' (ll. 23–24).

PAGE 26

ll. 7–8   *God hath two Testaments, two Wils.* In the sense of God's canons and decrees expressed in the two Books of Life, namely, the Register of the Elect and the Bible (*Essays*, pp. 6–8). Donne describes the fusion of God's 'two Wils' into 'one law' in 'The Litanie,' VIII (ll. 66–67).

l. 8   *Scedule ... Codicill.* The codicil was a general document which a testator appended to a will, while a schedule was a specific form of codicil designed to explain or change the main document itself.

ll. 21–22   *I know that he shal rise . . . at the last day.* John 11:24.

l. 28   *Two are better than one.* Eccles. 4:9.

PAGE 28

ll. 10–11   *calledst down fire from Heaven . . . but once.* Jer. 32:29; Amos 2:5; Ezek. 39:6; Hos. 8:14.

ll. 11–12   *openedst the Earth to swallow the Murmurers, but once.* Num. 16:30.

ll. 12–13   *threwst down the Tower of Siloe upon sinners, but once.* Luke 13:4.

PAGE 29

ll. 19–21   *the ill affections of the spleene . . . in every action, or passion of the mind.* The spleen, sometimes called the milt, was believed connected with the mind because it supposedly produced melancholy, and melancholy in turn produced fear. In the body's intricate network of humours, the spleen refined 'the more earthie' part of the blood which the liver could not, and it 'belched' out this blood in the form of melancholic humours if it was unable to absorb it into its own matter (Crooke, III, 2, pp. 126–27). These excess humours had a comparatively small effect on a healthy body. However, in a sick body like Donne's they made their way up to the head quickly, first causing physical disturbances in the brain, and then in the heart on their way back down. They left a trail of disorder among a man's thoughts and in the emotions generated by his heart (Bright, pp. 89–91). The chief emotion of the disordered heart was fear, mixed with sadness for the irrational conclusions of the brain.

ll. 21–22   *wind in the body . . . Stone, & seem the Gout.* Wind was considered to be an 'impostumation' or tumour of air collected in a blocked passage of the body (Barrough, 1613, p. 321; Alexis, IV, p. 37). It was easily confused with 'gout', which consisted of humidities like air pockets (Paynell, p. 8) or 'windie tumors' in the joints (Gerarde, p. 908); and, for less specific reasons, it was also mistaken for stone, because of the sharpness of its pain. Wind was cured by the dissolution of its foreign matter, often by the same herbs that eliminated gout and stone (Gerarde, p. 862; Lyte, pp. 214–15).

l. 27   *feare of loosing that.* Donne is describing the confusion of the emotions and thoughts in the worst kind of the known fits of melancholy (Bright, pp. 91, 97–98). In such a fit, all logical connection between reason and emotion was destroyed. A man laughed at what was sad, ridiculed what was sensible, and was depressed by what was good (p. 95).

PAGE 30

ll. 8–9 *every cold ayre, is not a dampe.* A damp originating in either cold air or a mist, infected people with a variety of plague known as the 'sweating sickness' (Coghan, 1584, p. 281).

PAGE 31

Margin *Luc. 11.5.* The reference appears wrongly in the place of the previous marginal note, Luke 18:1, in all edd. Sparrow relocates it correctly.

l. 8 *to morrow. to* is the last word on p. 124 of 1624(1), followed by the catchword *mor-* on the line below, which the compositor left out when he started p. 125, and merely printed the last syllable of the word, *row.*

PAGE 32

Margin *Ps. 53.5 . . . 14.5.* The notes were originally inverted, all edd.

ll. 19–20 *Joseph was his Disciple.* Joseph of Arimithea.

l. 31 *There is a feare, & there is a hope.* Job 27:8.

PAGE 33

l. 1 *my hope, is hope, and love, confidence, and peace.* Perhaps an echo of Job 4:6.

ll. 7–8 *Angels of the Resurrection, went from the sepulchre.* Matt. 28:8.

l. 11 *thy feare and thy love, are inseperable.* I Pet. 2:17.

l. 12 *in infinite places, to feare God.* Exod. 18:21; 20:20; Lev. 19:14; 25:17; Deut. 10:12; 2 Kings 17:39, and I Pet. 2:17.

l. 13 *Thou shalt love the Lord thy God.* Matt. 22:37.

l. 16 *his Sonne.* Solomon.

ll. 28–29 *it is a fearefull thing to fall into thy hands.* Heb. 10:31.

PAGE 34

l. 4 *supple, and conformable affections.* The 'conformable affections' of Donne's prayer were sane human feelings. These feelings were expended with 'conformity' through a balanced reaction of the humours, the understanding and the will to an external stimulus (as love for a lovable object or fear for something fearful: Wright, pp. 45, 149). By contrast, the emotions in Donne's fit of melancholy were due to a diseased 'fantasie' stimulated incoherently by bodily illness (Bright, p. 102).

ll. 9–10 *pretermit.* To overlook deliberately (as in I, *Sermons* (1640), XXV, p. 253, or IX, *Sermons*, 9, p. 212: 'God pretermits many times errours in circumstances'.

ll. 12–13 *thy most blessed Sonne himselfe.* Perhaps a reference to Christ in Gethsemane in Matt. 26:39, or Mark 14:35–36.

l. 27 *wardrope.* Wardrobe.

PAGE 35

l. 17 *to one Dictator.* The members of the thirty *curiae* of ancient Rome were headed by a common 'rex' or king, as chief of state. At the beginning of the republican and imperial period of Rome in 509 B.C., the king was replaced by two consuls. Finally, the institution of the two consuls gave way to the dictatorship of Julius Caesar in 49 B.C.

l. 23 *one anothers force, so.* The medical theory underlying Donne's metaphor of conspiracy was that a disease originally occurred in the body through an imbalance of the humours and became successively complicated by additional imbalances. These imbalances created an unchecked illness (Hart, p. 21) and a 'conspiracy' of diseases (a metaphor also used by the medical writer, Barrough, to describe pleurisy) that produced simultaneously violent physical and psychological effects (1639, pp. 82–83).

l. 29 *our best Antidote.* According to a definition common in the seventeenth century, an antidote was 'a medicine against poyson' and, more specifically, 'any medicine which serves to amend any distemper of the body' by re-dressing the balance of the humours (*Physical Dictionary*, B6, B6ᵛ). It was to be chosen with extreme caution to avoid creating one imbalance while redressing another.

l. 30 *Cordiall hath bene deadly poyson.* Prescribed by medical manuals for heart diseases, cordials had a mixed reputation. Like the cordial of marigold herb, they might 'strengthen ... the hart, and ... withstand poison'; but, as the herbist Gerarde suggested, like the cordial of *lapis lazuli*, they might also possess a fatal 'venemous qualitie' unless their side-effects were counter-acted by yet another antidote (pp. 603, 1160). In *Devotions*, Donne's know-ledge of the possible maladministration of medicine was as profound as in his other writings. In 'The Litanie' XXVI (ll. 227–30), he uses elaborate images of medical malpractice ('physicke' and 'invenom'd') to describe the breaking of civil and religious laws.

PAGE 36

ll. 1–5 *that Tiran Dyonisius ... was a good Poet.* Donne is confusing Dionysius I, the Elder, a man of lowly birth who ruled Syracuse from 405 to 367 B.C., with his son, Dionysius II, who was driven from his throne for misrule in 357 B.C. He is correct, however, in identifying Dionysius the Elder as a tragedian, the author of *Ransom of Hector*, who died of a drinking bout held to celebrate an award to him for his play.

ll. 5–6 *a Man may live of a litle.* The most likely proverb is a common one in the century: 'A little and good fills the trencher' (Stevenson, II, p. 1443).

l. 8 *with one Advocate.* According to the law of the Reformed English Church, a defendant in an ecclesiastical case could have as many as three so-called attorneys to defend him, the attorney being a legal expert in an ecclesiastical court, as opposed to the barrister and solicitor in a civil or common law court (A. K. R. Kiralfy, *Potter's Historical Introduction to English Law*, London, 1958, pp. 84, 85; *Constitutions*, 1604, CXXX, VI^v, a volume described by Keynes, 'Appendix IV, L 48, p. 212, as Donne's copy). The large number of attorneys possible in a single case, each of them handling the part of the law suit fitting him best, was due to their importance in the process assuring justice for the defendant (*Reformatio Legum Ecclesiasticarum, Ex Authoritate primum Regis Henrici 8, London*, 1571, 97, 97^v).

ll. 12–15 *Man of Stile . . . without a grave.* According to a popular history originally prepared for James I's son, Henry, Prince of Wales, William the Conqueror was extraordinarily cruel in subjugating the conquered English, but was admirably just once this subjugation was accomplished (John Hayward, *The Lives of three Norman Kings*, London, 1613, pp. 96–103, 107–10). However, at his death in Rouen on 9 September 1087, his chief men attending him were so afraid of the possible consequences of his passing that they scurried back to their estates for protection. Before doing so, they stripped the dead king of everything in his death room for booty: 'Thus the dead body was not onely abandoned, but left almost naked upon the ground: where it remained from prime until three of the clocke, neither guarded nor regarded by any man' (p. 117).

l. 24 *understanding with comfort.* Donne is drawing on ideas of apprehension, imagination, and understanding in contemporary psychology. The imagination created a 'fantasy' due to an obsession with a particular sense impression, and discoloured all subsequent sense impressions in the normal course of experience. Donne's doctors put an end to this vicious chain of fantasy in Donne by following recommended treatment. They 'broke' through 'the gates of the imagination' in the original distortion of sense experience (as one of his contemporaries put it) to the 'rational understanding' (Wright, p. 51). The narrator of Donne's *Ignatius His Conclave* willingly submits to the very disease of the imagination that he here describes (pp. 5, 7).

l. 22　*Receit.* A statement of the ingredients in a medical prescription.

l. 32　*Bill.* The bills of mortality posted weekly in every London parish from 1592.

PAGE 37

ll. 7–8　*Julip . . . Bezar enough.* Bezar was a stone and julep was a syrup taken as medicine to lower fevers and prevent thirst. Since Donne had a fever it is possible that his doctors prescribed both as remedies. The bezar, about the size of the pit of a fig, originated in the entrails of mountain goats and was considered 'excellent vertue against poyson' (*Physical Dictionary*, C1ᵛ). Its reputation spread with the description of its supposed cure of the 'Duchess of Bezar' in a book by the Spaniard Nicholas Monardes, *Ioyfull Newes*, in 1577 (Fols. 115, 120ᵛ, 131). Less exotic than the bezar, the julep was considered as medically effective. It was a 'pleasant cooling' drink commonly made 'of distill'd waters and syrups' (*Physical Dictionary*, H4ᵛ, H5). One variety composed of water and violets, listed in the medical commentator Llwyd's table of 'Comfortatives' (f 5), made with the bezar an excellent compound medicine. According to Gerarde's *Herbale*, compound medicines cleared away 'all inflammations especially of the sides and lungs, they take away the hoarseness of the chest [;] the ruggedness of the wind pipe and jaws' (pp. 701, 1082).

ll. 16–17　*some places of Genesis. Confessions,* XI, iii, p. 247.

ll. 18–21, and margin　*the Watchman tolde him . . . the word signifies so.* Donne is drawing a parallel between two Hebrew words written in very similar ways but having different meanings. The phonetic similarities between the two words are the basis for their relationship as 'type' and 'copy'. The words are 'good tidings', BESURAH and 'I depart', BESURI. Donne makes the first word a symbol for the meaning of the second ('good tidings' a figure of speech for the verb depart and its associated words like running) although the original Hebrew characters do not themselves appear in his text. Johannes Buxtorf, or Buxdor, cited in the *marginalia* (b. 1564, Kamen, Westphalia; d. 1629, Basle), an eminent scholar of oriental languages and a contemporary of Donne, glosses BESURI on p. 518 of his *Thesaurius Grammaticus Linguae Sanctae Hebraeae. . . . Basilea,* 1620; and Schindler, the grammarian of Hebrew Donne refers to (b. Oderan, [N.D.]; d. Helmstadt, 1604), glosses it in Column 1832d, of his *Lexicon Pentaglotton . . . Hanoviae,* 1612, published posthumously by his son.

　The 'translation' in Donne's marginal note is the King James version of the Bible. Unlike the lexicographic glosses of Buxdor and Schindler, this Bible makes no connection between 'good news' and 'running', either by translation, phonetics, or typology.

l. 27 *thy Apostle.* Paul.

ll. 30–31 *S. Paul laboured in.* Paul speaks of Luke's help in 2 Tim. 4:11, Philem. 24, and Col. 4:14.

PAGE 38

l. 3 *Moses father in law.* Jethro.

l. 23 *appoynted . . . in the Church heere.* The italicized words are a paraphrase of the mission of the seven angels in Rev. 1:20.

ll. 29–30 *Angels in the plurall.* Angels existed in a spiritual world in a plural number fixed at the time of their creation. There could never be more or less angels than God originally made. By contrast, God expressed his concept of multiplicity in the material side of creation through ever fluctuating numbers in the propagation of his creatures (*Essays*, pp. 54–55).

PAGE 39

l. 6 *of thy helps.* Donne is probably referring to 1 Cor. 12:28. Variant forms of the word 'multiplication' in the sense of increased help are common in the Bible (Jude 2; 1 Pet. 1:2). The word may appear in Donne's text coloured by his theory of numbers in *Essays* (p. 57).

l. 8 *earnest.* A pledge of something afterwards to be received in greater abundance.

ll. 13–14 *thy Word, with thy Sacrament.* Donne links the ideas of Word and Sacrament according to the theology of the *Thirty-Nine Articles*, XXVI (pp. 16–17). By 'word' he means the Biblical passage instituting the Sacrament of the Eucharist, which an officiating minister paraphrased at a service; and by Sacrament he implies Hooker's meaning: the communication of grace by the union of God's will (in his biblical Word) with the minister's performance of the outward sign of the Sacrament (*Laws* V, 57:4, p. 310).

l. 14 *Seale, with thy Patent.* The letter patent was a royal document with a general salutation and an announcement of the king's will in behalf of a suppliant. On the bottom margin the king affixed a fragment of the Great Seal (*A Formula Book of English Official Historical Documents, Part I, Diplomatic Documents*, ed. by Hubert Hall, Cambridge, 1908, pp. 53–54).

ll. 17–18 *Augustine . . . blessed Sonne.* Homily XXVI, No. XI, on John 6:41–59, in X, *Works*, Vol. I, pp. 374–75.

l. 25 *that man liked best.* A paraphrase of Exod. 16:16.

ll. 31–33 *As therefore . . . it cooles too.* Donne is not only referring to the general theory that the body was composed of the four elements in the universe—fire, hot and dry; water, cold and moist; earth, cold and dry; and air, hot and moist, (Elyot, p. 1ᵛ)—but also to the fact that each of these four elements possessed an elemental 'force', of drying, burning, wetting, or cooling, respectively. The body could therefore be described as composed of these elemental forces of heat, cold, dryness, and moisture, as well as elements (Jones, Bᵛ).

PAGE 40

l. 7 *circumstances . . . of the substance.* In scholastic philosophy the 'substance' of a thing was its essence and nature, giving it its individual existence. For their part, 'circumstances' were a kind of 'accident'; 'accidents' were the qualities of a substance distinguishing it from all other substances; and 'circumstances' was the generic name of 'accidents' characterizing human actions (*Summa* I, Ques. XC, a2, pp. 251–52, and II, i, Ques. VII, al, pp. 104–105). Such terminology was common in contemporary writings (ll. 253–54 of Sir John Davies' 'Of the Soule of Man', *Nosce Teipsum*, 1622, p. 19).

l. 25 *his owne Phisician.* Bald (p. 452) agrees with Sparrow (p. 154) that James sent the Swiss-born French-educated Sir Theodore de Mayerne, who was appointed his physician in 1611, to examine Donne. Mayerne left behind vivid accounts of the illnesses of James and members of the royal family (Norman Moore, pp. 93–111).

PAGE 41

ll. 1–2 *tenant, but of misery the free-holder.* According to English law, the tenant of a farm held property loosely and could lose its fruits easily to the crown, while the freeholder held property usually for life, with a large amount of control over both the land and the distribution of its fruits (Francis Bacon, *Uses of the Law*, London, 1636, p. 44).

l. 2 *usufructuary.* One enjoying the fruits, profits, and temporary use of an estate, benefice, or office legally belonging to another or others.

l. 8 *lead enough.* A lump of lead hung onto a line by sailors and sometimes by fishermen to measure the depth of water.

l. 17 *God is called angry.* The 'affections' in Donne's list of God's emotions are anger, sorrow, dejection, and sadness. They correspond to the items that he describes in the categories of infirmities elsewhere in the passage, and they were all derived from hate. In the scholastic division of the 'affections', hate headed one of the two main branches of emotions. The other branch

unmentioned by Donne in this particular moment of his trial, was headed
by love (Bright, p. 80; Wright, p. 22).

ll. 19–22 *gods of the Heathen . . . asleepe.* 1 Kings 18:27.

l. 22 *Jupiter.* The chief Roman deity was incapable of infirmities.

l. 22 *an Aesculapius.* Aesculapius, the son of Apollo and Coronis, learned the
art of medicine from his father and died at the hand of Zeus for interfering
with his decrees by restoring Hippolytus to life. He was the hero of several
Renaissance medical manuals, but contributed nothing to medical knowledge (Gale, p. 3a).

ll. 23–24 *Rheubarbe . . . Agarick to purge his flegme.* Rhubarb was administered as either a 'simple' or a 'compound' (Llwyd, f 8ᵛ), and was well reputed
for purging 'downward choler' and for possessing an 'opening qualitie' to
reduce first, fever, next, the anger-producing choleric humour, and lastly,
even the humour of phlegm (Gerarde, p. 318). For its part, agaric, an Italian
mushroom, was prescribed as a 'simple' to purge the head and breast (Llwyd,
f8ᵛ, Elyot Yiᵛ), and was expected to release the body of a surcharge of the
lethargy-producing phlegmatic humour (*Physical Dictionary*, B3ᵛ–B4) and
to lower fevers. Rhubarb and agaric automatically reduced a fever by lower-
ing the level of choleric and phlegmatic humours: rhubarb by bringing
down 'the temperature of all the body' and agaric by clearing 'the liquid
matter out of the head' and 'exulcerating' the lungs (Elyot, pp. 78–78ᵛ).

ll. 24–26 *Tertullian saies . . . God was beholden to Man, for growing in his
garden.* Tertullian, *Apologeticus* (for Christianity), in I, *Writings* (*Anti-Nicene
Christian Library*) (Edinburgh, 1869), p. 103. Donne is quoting Tertullian's
attack on man-made gods loosely.

PAGE 42

l. 8 *his tongue.* The semi-colon in *tong*; in 1624(1) is a contemporary con-
traction for -ue, and was probably introduced by the printer because the
word occurs at the end of the last line on page 182. The logical punctuation
after the word is a comma.

ll. 16–17 *thou who gavest Augustus the Empire . . . so had Julian.* Augustine,
De Civitate Dei, V, xxi, p. 219.

PAGE 43

l. 16 *S. Lewis in France.* The life of Louis IX of France (b. Poissy, 1215; d.,
Tunis, 1270), canonized by Boniface VIII in 1297, was popularized by a
biography by John of Joinville, a close member of his retinue. The biography went through many editions in the late sixteenth and seventeenth

centuries. Two vivid accounts of Louis' numerous charitable acts towards lepers in Joinville's biography probably formed the basis of Donne's connection of Louis and the British Maud (*Saint Louis*, trans. by Rene Hague from the text edited by Natalis de Wailly, London, 1955, pp. 28–29, 688).

l. 16   *our Maud is celebrated.* Donne calls Matilda (1080–1118), daughter of Malcolm III, King of Scots, and of Saint Margaret, and first wife of Henry I of England, 'our Maud' to distinguish her from both the French Queen of William the Conqueror and the Burgundian wife of Stephen, King of England, who bore the same name. Sparrow (p. 155) notes the description of her in the *D.N.B.* (London, 1894), Vol. 37, p. 53: she devoted herself 'especially to the care of lepers, washing their feet and kissing their scars, besides building a hospital for them at St. Giles-in-the-Fields, London', translated from a record of Matilda's life in the *Chronica Majora* of Matthew of Paris in *The Chronicles and Memorials*, II, p. 144, edited by H. R. Luard, London, 1874.

ll. 21–23   *Shee would send in that capacitie . . . with them.* Placilla is a variant form of the name of Flacilla (d. 385), the wife of Theodosius the Great (346–395). It appears in the Latin translation of her Greek funeral oration by Gregory of Nyssa (*Opera*, II, Paris, 1615, p. 940), in the *Ecclesiasticae Historiae* of Theodoretus (*Opera Omnia, Coloniae Agrippinae*, 1617, II, ii, p. 205), and in the English translation of this work as *The Ecclesiasticall History of Theodoret* (London, 1612), p. 362, from which Donne probably gets his story about Placilla's visits to the sick. The 'P' spelling in Flacilla's name appears in Sparrow (p. 45), Alford (*Works*, III, p. 532) and all seventeenth-century editions of the work, and is retained here. It may have originated with the translation of the Greek phi as 'ph' in the Latin. Donne quotes Flacilla's answer to her courtiers very loosely, but keeps intact the spirit of her reputation for charity.

PAGE 44

ll. 10–11   *when I asked, perchance, a stone, he gave me bread.* An inversion of the sense in Matt. 7:9: 'Or what man is there of you, whom if his son ask bread, will he give him a stone'; or in the first part of Luke 11:11, reporting the same incident.

l. 12   *a Scorpion, he gave me a fish.* An inversion of the nouns in either the second part of Luke 11:11, 'Or if he ask a fish, will he for a fish give him a serpent'; or in 11:12, 'Or if he shall ask an egg, will he offer him a scorpion?' Donne's memory may have simply failed him and led him to substitute fish for egg, or serpent for scorpion, in either one of the verses.

ll. 12–14 *when I asked a temporall office . . . hee had rather I took this.* Bald believes that Donne is referring to his plea to the Earl of Somerset to intervene with James for a secular post in his behalf (pp. 291–93). Donne may also be summing up the general record of his attempts at secular preferment and James' repeated encouragement for his entry into the ministry (Walton, pp. 16, 27).

l. 30 *we see thee heere in a glasse.* 1 Cor. 13:12.

PAGE 45

ll. 17–18 *him, or his Son, or his sonnes sonnes.* The 'him' is James I, and the 'Son' is Charles, Prince of Wales; Charles was not yet married to Henrietta Maria (May 1, 1625).

l. 19 *their faithfull Stewardship, and dispensation.* The latter word in the sense of spending, perhaps inspired by the parable of the steward in Luke 16:1–9.

ll. 20–22 *distempers of his body . . . sadness of soule.* The memoir drawn up by the royal physician, Sir Theodore de Mayerne, in December 1623, the very month when Donne began composing *Devotions*, describes how James was struck by an 'excessive' fit of diarrhoea, accompanied by his usual symptoms of 'incredible sadness' and bronchial congestion; 'at the end of autumn, it lasted for two or three days . . . After this arthritis, and after this, after an interval of three weeks, he was able to walk without help, while before for months he had had to sit in a chair and be carried or be helped along by the support of others.' In a later passage de Mayerne writes: 'Thrice in his life he was seized with most severe pains of the thigh, very recently on October 28, 1623, as if by a spasm of the muscles and tendons bending the left leg by a vapourous influence' (Norman Moore, pp. 101–2, 104).

PAGE 46

ll. 3–4 *God presented to David three kinds, War, Famine, and Pestilence.* 2 Sam. 24:13.

ll. 4–5 *fires from heaven, and windes from the wildernes.* Jer. 2:15, 24.

ll. 9–10 *the Plurisie . . . the falling sicknes is so.* Pleurisy, a 'swelling of the membrane . . . about the ribs,' from the Latin 'pleuras' (*Physical Dictionary*, L1). The 'falling sickness' was epilepsy; its causes were believed to be humours stopping 'the ventricles of the braynes' (Llwyd, Dii).

l. 13 *the Wolf, and the Canker, and the Polypus.* The wolf, canker, and polypus described types of cancer (the latter two still do). The first, 'a kernel or round bunch of flesh . . . groweth and increaseth' with the voraciousness of the wolf and was known principally as a disease of animals (Turberville, p. 23), but also as a human affliction (Jones, 16b). The 'canker', a word in use at the same time as cancer in the seventeenth century and possibly its origin, was 'a melancholy impostume' like the flower-eating canker worm ('they eateth the partes of the body', Paynell, p. 118), and was spoken of with great fear (Gabelhover, p. 248/2). The polypus tumour was a growth that stuck tenaciously to its place of origin on the body, usually in the nose, and got its name from the polypus or octopus that clung inseparably to its victims (Gerarde, p. 854; Lyte, CXII, p. 219).

l. 14   *whether there be more names or things.* In 'Variety in the Number', *Essays*, p. 55, Donne discusses the validity of the signification of a thing by more than one noun or 'name'. He concludes that the worth of a second 'name' depends on whether it continues to express the honour of God initially implanted in a creature under its original noun.

ll. 21–22   *the names of severall Fevers; how intricate a worke.* The number of fevers in the canon of contemporary medicine was very great, and the argument about what constituted the kinds was pronounced. According to Barrough, p. 213, the only factor common to the fevers was their 'unnatural heate' which took its 'beginning at the heart' and spread 'by the arteries and veins into the whole body'. But to harness the variants of fevers into some intelligible form, Barrough followed the practice of organizing them into a table under two main branches, simple and compound: the simple variant constituted an illness of a single febrile disorder, while the compound variant was made up of a number of fevers, or was a fever complicated by another kind of illness (p. 217).

ll. 32–33   *Martial law ... executions upon the people.* Martial law was a general term for military ordinances outside the jurisdiction of common law and therefore had an abrasive effect in a civil cause because of its extrajudicial character. It was often executed by the constable and marshal of a town by royal order (William Rastell, *Collection in English, of the Statutes now in force*, London, 1615, p. 56; Cowell, Vu3).

l. 34   *an accident of the maine disease.* Accident, in the scholastic sense of a nonessential quality of a substance.

PAGE 47

ll. 2–3   *cholerick man ... must I goe about to purge his choler, or to breake the blow.* The choleric man was overcome by an abundance of the 'unnatural' variety of black humour formed artificially in the head by a 'fome of bloud' (Paynell, p. 138), which left him 'with a dangerous disposition' and the 'violence to kill' (Elyot, 9B). As a cure, contemporary science books recommended a 'downward' purgation of the humour with a variety of oral herbal remedies (Llwyd, X7ᵛ; Elyot 58a).

PAGE 48

ll. 4–5 *the heavens should have bin disposed in a better order, then they are.* Donne is in error. The king Alfonsus in question was king of Castille (1221–1284), not Aragon. Prof. John E. Keller of the University of Kentucky, informs me that the legend of Alfonsus is recorded in *Historia de Espana de Mariana, Libro 30, Cap. 20, BAE* 30, p. 396: 'Don Alonso, rey de Castilla era persona de alto ingenio pero poco recalada sus orejas roberbias, su lengua desenfrenada más a propósito para las letras que para et gobierno de los vasallos; contemplaba al cielo y miraba las estrellas; mas en el entretanto perdio la tierra y el reino'. Prof. Keller discusses this legend briefly in his *Alfonso X, El Sabio* (New York, 1967), p. 13. Sparrow points out (p. 155) that Donne gets Alfonso's title right elsewhere in an undated sermon (V *Sermons*, 15, p. 299).

PAGE 49

l. 21 *Lamb.* Rev. 5:6, 7, where the Lamb, a figure of salvation, breaks the seven seals on the book containing the prophecy of the end of the world. Donne appears to use 'the book of the Lamb' to refer to the whole text of Revelation.

PAGE 50

l. 7 *the eye of a Serpent.* The serpent that kills as soon as it sees may have been the 'dry asp' of Renaissance books of serpents. The dry asp had 'eyes flaming like fire, or burning coals', and, unlike the lethargic, sightless varieties of other serpents, it possessed 'a vehement strong sight' enabling it to spot a victim and kill it by spitting poison (Topsell, p. 631).

l. 8 *thine Eye, O Lord, does so.* The image recurs a number of times in the Bible, for example: I Pet. 3:12; Prov. 7:2, and Ps. 32:8.

PAGE 51

ll. 6–8 *And all these are Concentrique; the common center . . . is decay . . . that is Eccentrique, which was never made.* Donne describes the general concept of material decay in an image of the earth's centre and he makes this image the axis for the figurative rotation of all earthly things. He is elaborating on the contemporary dictum in astronomy that the centre of the earth was the focal point for the concentric revolutions of all other planets (Burton, 2, 2, 3, p. 421). By contrast to these concentric revolutions, anything 'eccentric' was an astral body without fixed centre for its orbit, and therefore without a fixed point in the earth (Recorde, *Castle*, p. 247). In the Copernican system that supplanted Ptolemaic astronomy in the first half of the seventeenth century, the terms 'concentric', 'centre', and 'eccentric' were merely transferred to orbs fixed or unfixed about the mid-point of the sun.

l. 9 *imagine, but not demonstrate.* Donne uses *demonstrate* in the archaic sense of outward exhibition (counterbalancing his use of 'imagine'), rather than in the still current scientific sense of showing by proposition.

ll. 13–16 *All other things ... move upon the same poles ... to this center, Annihilation.* Donne's image of salvation reflects the principles of Ptolemaic cosmology and contemporary medicine. He depicts created things (angels included) as moving around the north and south poles along an orbit fixed in the earth's centre. Paradoxically, in the earth's centre chaos, out of which all earthly things were created, still reigns beneath the ordered shell of the world's outer layers (Recorde, *Pathway*, Bii^v). In Donne's image, nature's laws sustain created things in their figurative revolutions. The laws of 'preservation' or preventative medicine (Cogan, 1584, p. 263; Moryson, p. 166) keep them from falling out of their orbits into the chaotic magnetic centre of the world. In 'Goodfriday, 1613,' the same complex imagery recurs, though with different shades of meaning. Man's soul is a sphere, the orbital intelligence marks its path, and though threatened, nature's laws eventually prevail (11:1–3; 11–15).

l. 20 *The Heavens have had their Dropsie.* Gen. 7:4.

l. 21 *their Fever, and burn the world.* Rev. 8:5.

ll. 22 *a foreknowledge 120 yeares before it came.* Gen. 6:3.

l. 23 *provision against it, and were saved.* Gen. 6:14.

ll. 23–24 *the fever shall ... consume all.* Probably Rev. 8:7, although no passage of this book describes the entire created world destroyed all at once.

l. 26 *it did not quench those heates.* Gen. 7:19.

l. 27 *those heavens, that breath it out.* Rev. 8:12.

ll. 28–30 *the Dog-Starre have a pestilent breath ... wee shadow our selves to a sufficient prevention.* Sirius or Canicula, the dog-star, was the brightest of the fixed stars, and hung in the constellation of the Greater Dog. It was renowned for spreading illness mainly through its influence on the choleric humour, and by exerting tremendous heat on the earth during the dangerous set period of its astral influence known as the dog-days, when the sun was in Leo (Moore, *Hope*, 58b). According to some accounts, this period lasted from the fifteenth or last Kalends of August and, according to others, from the sixth or last Kalends of July till the fourth or last Kalends of September (Arnold, *Chronicle*, p. 172; *Bible*, C4, C5). The star exerted its influence on the heart, arteries, and back through a powerful conjunction of Leo and the sun, which held sway over these parts of the body (Salmon, *Synopsis*, pp. 6, 11). The combined 'hot' and 'dry' qualities of Leo and the sun put pressure on the delicate balance of the humours, causing heart passions and violent fevers among other illnesses. However, since the dog-star was fixed, and its influence regularly dated, provisions—as Donne suggests—could easily be taken to avoid its effects.

l. 31–ll. 1–2, PAGE 52   *Comets and blazing starres . . . no Almanack tells us . . . in secret.* Donne's reference to comets and blazing stars is intelligible in terms of their development as meteors. Like all meteors (which included earthquakes and all kinds of precipitation), comets were thought to be pseudo-astral bodies formed in, on, or about the earth, rather than in the heavens. Their effects could therefore not be gauged by the genuinely astrally oriented techniques of the almanac (Fulke, 2a). Most meteors were formed by the solidification of a number of 'vapours' in the bowels of the earth. However, the comet or blazing star was created by the sun drawing both the 'vapours' of water immediately surrounding the earth, and the 'exhalations' of the earth itself, upwards to any one of the three regions of the air. By a series of causes astronomically impossible to follow and hence beyond the scope of an almanac (as Donne says, 'in secret'), these vapours and exhalations were liquified and solidified into comets and blazing stars through the influence of fire in the third and outermost region of the air from the earth, where they eventually rested. In 'A Feaver', Donne used the vapours and fiery qualities of meteors metaphorically to describe passion (ll. 8–21). He depicted the arousal and fruition of passion in the development of the meteor.

PAGE 52

ll. 3–5   *Astrologer tels us . . . is most dangerous.* Formed in the third region of the air out of the 'thin exhalations' of the earth, blazing stars were consequently of a more portentous and far more secretive nature than the general run of meteors formed in the various shapes of precipitation in the middle and first regions of the air closer to the earth (Fulke, pp. 6a, 13a). The third region of the air was cradled in the 'hollow' of the element of fire which made up the 'highest sp[h]ere' or layer of any of the four elements in the series of layers encircling the earth. Consequently, blazing stars came into being in the hollow of the very element of fire that provided God with elemental heat as his instrument in the act of creation. Their portents were commensurately greater and less decipherable than those of other astral phenomena, and, their occurrence being unpredictable (Fulke, p. 16b), they were naturally referred to by Donne as dangerous: 'there be foure elements, Earth, Water, Ayre, and Fire, one encompassing another round about. . . . The highest is the sp[h]eare of Fire, which toucheth the hollownesse of the Moones heaven: the next is the ayre which is in the hollownesse of the fire: the ayre within his hollownesse, comprehendeth the water and the earth, which both make but one spheare or Globe, or as the common sort may understand it, one Ball. So each element is within another, as the skales of a perie are one above another: or (to use a grosse similitude) as the peeles of an onion are one within another. . . . But for this present purpose let it be knowne, that the aire is divided into three regions, the highest, the middle and the lowest. . . . In the highest region be generated . . . blazing stars' (Fulke, pp. 5a, b, 6a).

l. 12 *murmuring in their hearts.* Exod. 16:12.

ll. 16–17 *My forces are not enfeebled.* Because Donne has already said that he has lost some of the use of his senses and that he is shivering badly (in the second and fifth devotions respectively), he contradicts himself here, but only in terms of the gravity of his illness. He is speaking relatively. He seems to have been suffering from what medical books would have so far described as a 'quotidien' fever. This fever belonged to the category of 'simple' fevers which gave little cause for worry (Barrough, 1613, pp. 244, 239).

ll. 22–23 *Arcana Imperii, secrets of State. Arcana Imperii* was a term describing the right of the king to act without the advice of his ministers and without informing his people. The theory behind it originated in the writings of ancient Rome (Tacitus, *Annalium*, II, 36, *Opera*, Vol. I, London, 1821, p. 321), and, by Donne's time, the term described generally the royal prerogatives of the king (Cowell, Ddd 3^v, under *prerogative*). Donne discusses the Roman origins of the term with derogatory connotations elsewhere too, in *Sermons* (1640), 64, and *V, Sermons*, 15, p. 299. Donne and his contemporaries were much concerned about the significance of the term because of the current constitutional argument about the right of the king to act in private, and to the dramatic reversal of the political position of the parliamentarian, Sir Edward Coke. In 1621 Coke defended *arcana imperii* on behalf of the monarchy, but had altered his stand completely by 1628 under the menace of the king's ever-widening power (M. A. Judson, *Crisis of the Constitution*, New Brunswick, N.J., 1949, p. 32). Donne's use of the term relies on the contemporary fear of *arcana imperii* for its effect. He was surely not attacking James in any way, but his use of the term is nevertheless remarkable in the light of his friendship with him. At the height of the public argument, the king felt bound to justify his right to private political action (*Political Works of James I*, Cambridge, Mass., 1918, pp. 331–32).

l. 26 *examiners.* In the general sense of medical consultants.

ll. 29–31 *thy servant Nazienzen, that his Sister . . . with a pious impudencie.*
Sparrow points to an obscurity in the meaning of 'by relation' and the phrase
'that did it' in all seventeenth-century editions of *Devotions* (p. 156), which an
examination of Donne's source clears up. Donne is paraphrasing a section of
the funeral oration by Gregory of Nazianzus (Cappadocia) (329–389) for his
sister Saint Gorgonia (c. 326–c. 372) (*Opera Omnia*, Paris, 1569, p. 74;
Funeral Orations of St. Gregory Nazianzen and St. Ambrose, in Vol. 22, *The
Fathers of the Church Series*, New York, 1953, p. 113). The word 'relation'
may be a misprint for 'oration', but more likely means simply Gregory's
narration of the sermon for his sister. In his sermon, Gregory referred to the
occasion of her illness; Gorgonia placed her head on an altar and refused to
remove it until she was cured. Donne also reiterates the incident at the beginning of his sermon on Ps. 6:4, 5 (V, *Sermons*, 18, p. 364) in much greater
detail.

ll. 32–ll. 1–2, PAGE 53 *Augustin, wisht . . . Christ might not have died. Against
Two Letters of the Pelagians*, IV, 6, in III of *The Anti-Pelagian Works*, pp.
334–35. Donne paraphrases Augustine's argument loosely.

PAGE 53

ll. 1–4 *if the Serpent before the tentation of Eve . . . went upright.* Flavius
Josephus (A.D. 37/38—c. 100), the Jewish historian, writes that the serpent
shared a common tongue with all creatures before the fall, but lost his power
to speak after it; he supposes that the serpent had feet and that God cut them
off as a penalty for successfully tempting Eve (*Jewish Antiquities*, I, i, 4, in IV,
Josephus, trans. by H. Thackery, New York, 1930, pp. 21–25). Donne used
the story liberally with the century's usual scepticism towards it, to support
his own passing wish that the serpent still talked and stood upright. A gloss
to Josephus' passage in the *marginalia* of a contemporary translation of his
work, says he misunderstood the account of the serpent in Scriptures (*Famous
and Memorable Works of Josephus*, trans. by Thomas Lodge, London, 1609,
p. 4).

ll. 25–26 *we conceive them in the darke . . . We doe them in the light.* Ps. 36:4, 5.

ll. 28–31 *August. confesses . . . he should be unacceptable to his sinfull companions.*
Confessions, II, iii, 7, p. 53.

PAGE 54

ll. 9–11 *As Phisicke works so . . . carry that humour away.* The medical theory
of purgation for 'an over-abundant humour' was based on the complex

operations of all the humours. The purgation had to draw the 'one peculiar and proper humour' that was in excess and no other, or risk endangering the health of the purged person by reducing his healthy quantity of another humour (Moore, *Hope*, p. 56b). The purgation collected 'the superfluous humour' and drew it down the 'open . . . conduites and vessels of the body' (p. 59b), according to a process which imitated the natural crisis of an illness: 'the Humours being drawn together' in a crisis, 'and burthening Nature, by their own weight, break out and expell themselves' (Salmon, *Synopsis*, pp. 175–76).

ll. 21–24 *Thou hast forgiven me those sinnes . . . Mercy he calls a Pardon.* Confessions, X, xxx, 41–42, pp. 225–27.

l. 30 *hee knew not the day of Judgement.* Matt. 24:36.

PAGE 55

ll. 11–20 *If the naming of Sinnes . . . reach not home to all mine.* Donne is satirizing the scholastic categories of sins, for example, the division of actual sin into sins of omission and commission; sins of malice, into sins of ignorance, passion, and infirmity; sins according to their activities, into sins of thought, word, and deed (*Summa*, I–II, Q. lxxii, a3–a9, pp. 277–91). Donne 'names' such sins in the sense of affixing titles to things uselessly proliferated by the ignorance of fallen man (*Essays*, p. 46), due to the loss of the more general concept of sin in Eden as the destruction of the personal relationship between man and God (*Articles*, IX–XVII, pp. 7–12).

l. 24 *a pardon in thy preventing grace.* Preventing grace was the transient divine help given to fallen man without his actually willing it, to start him back on the road to sanctifying or permanent grace. It was a post-scholastic term developed by the thinking of both the Fathers of the Council of Trent in their answer to the predestination of some of the Reformers (Trent, Session VI, 'Justification', V), and by the writers of the Book of Common Prayer ('thy special grace preventing us', Easter Collect, B6) and *The Thirty-Nine Articles* (No. X, p. 8).

ll. 29–30 *The Lyon of the Tribe of Judah.* Rev. 5:5.

l. 30 *that Lyon, that seekes whom hee may devoure.* 1 Pet. 5:8.

l. 31 *Wisedome of the Serpent.* Matt. 10:16; or possibly a reference to Christ (John 3:14), rather than to Moses' serpent (Num. 21:8).

l. 32 *the Malice of the Serpent.* Rev. 12:9.

ll. 33–34 *Thy Dove with thy Olive, in thy Arke.* Gen. 8:11.

PAGE 56

l.4   *to keep the venim.* Venom was not a specific illness, but a word grouping all illnesses afflicting the body from the outside ('Venom is a thing, which being taken at the mouth, or applied outwardly, doeth overcome our bodies, by making them sicke, or by corrupting of them, or by killing them', Monardes, 1580, Fol. 115).

ll. 9–12   *subsistence, then from the heart of man? . . . with all that they have.* Donne is drawing on a number of scholastic ideas (some occur in Aquinas' discussion of the essence of the human soul). The first, 'subsistence', meant a substance capable of existing by itself. The second and third, *'Action* and *motion'*, were terms suggesting being and becoming. Action was the act of being of a thing, its very act of living, so to speak; and motion meant to pass from potentiality to actuality. The fifth and sixth terms, 'powers' and 'faculties', were the sources of action in the soul operating through mind and body (*Summa* I, Q. LXXV, a2, p. 5; al, p. 3; I, Q. LXXVII, a2, p. 57). Donne used the adapted forms of these terms which were found in contemporary psychology books (Bright, pp. 39–47).

Donne may also have in mind William Harvey's discovery of the circulation of the blood and the perpetual motion of the heart. Although Harvey did not publish his findings in his *De Motu Cordis* until 1628, four years after the first edition of *Devotions*, he announced them to the public in the first series of lectures he gave on his appointment as Lumleian lecturer at the College of Physicians in London in 1615, twelve years earlier. Donne could have heard a report of these lectures, and since Harvey was appointed physician extraordinary to James I in 1618, he might have become familiar with his discovery from individuals in the royal circle in which both moved. However, a lot of Donne's vocabulary of the heart—'action', 'motion', and other words in the meditation—is coloured by the language of the less scientific medical treatises contemporary with Harvey's discoveries (Crooke, *Description*, VI, 8, p. 359), as well as by Harvey's vocabulary (*De Motu Cordis*, pp. 61, 167). It suggests Aristotle's description of the heart (*De Partibus Animalium*, 647.a.25–647.b.9) from which contemporary descriptions of an unscientific nature sprang (Crooke, p. 367; Bright, p. 46).

ll. 15–16   *an unnatural heat, a rebellious heat, will blow up the heart.* The 'rebellious heat' in question was the heat caused by any of the illnesses that increased the warmth of the heart artificially, and must not be confused with the great natural heat of the heart. The heart was known as 'the fier and hearth' of the body, and its natural heat was the 'elemental heat' by which God had forged all created things (Jones, B ii^v, Aiiii^v). The other bodily heat was merely generated by illness. This heat raised the natural warmth of the body higher than its normal level, and was a major symptom of a whole group of diseases categorized under the illness of the 'over-heated' heart (Culpepper, p. 31). These afflictions included sudden death by heart failure, to which Donne alludes (Llwyd, a7; Crooke, p. 420).

ll. 21–22   *the eldest is oftentimes not the strongest.* Aristotle's belief about the comparative weakness of the heart (*De Partibus Animalium*, III. 4, 667a. 32–667b. 14; IV. 2, 667b. 4), which Donne here shares, was disseminated in contemporary medical treatises (Crooke, I, Quest. 2, p. 39).

ll. 22–23   *the Braine, and Liver, and Heart, hold not a Triumvirate in Man, a Soveraigntie.* The tradition of the primogeniture of the heart that Donne alludes to originated in Aristotle's *De Partibus Animalium* III. 4, 666a. 10, 20–23 ('For the heart is the first of all the parts to be formed . . . For no sooner is the embryo formed, then its heart is seen in motion as though it were a living creature, and this before any of the other parts, it being, as thus shown, the starting point of their nature in all animals that have blood'). But the question of the supremacy of the three powers, namely, the brain, liver, and heart, springs from the Renaissance argument about the body's number of 'principal' or vital parts. Donne's list of principal parts is in Crooke's tradition which named three, but outside this tradition in the sense that he rejected equal power for them. The Crooke tradition stipulated that the heart merely pre-existed the brain and liver, without extra power (I, Q.4, pp. 44–45). Donne's list is also anti-Galenist, for Galen (*De Locis Affectis*, V, 1, p. 50^v) and Elyot after him (p. 10a) believed in the existence of four principal parts. However, it follows Galen in that it accepts the primacy of the heart.

l. 24   *the foure Elements doe, for his very being.* None of the four elements in the body held priority over the others. All were altered into a new unique substance in the process of making it up. Consequently, none was sovereign. Man's body consisted 'of the fower Elementes being commixed by nature' but 'none of the elementes is to be seen . . . simplie or separatly . . . there appeareth evidentlie a substaunce commixed and made of the elementes, which substaunce retayneth in it the qualities of them, and yet is like none of them' (Moore, *Hope*, pp. 5a, 5b). This theory conditioned Donne's use of 'cunningly' to describe the elements in his body in Holy Sonnet V (l. 1). Its influence is even more apparent in 'The second Anniversary': 'so though the Elements and Humors were/In her, one could not say, this governes there' (ll. 135–36).

ll. 25–26   *the Heart alone is in the Principalitie, and in the Throne, as King, the rest as Subjects.* Donne's description of the heart as a 'principality' in the human body resembles that of the physician, Thomas Vicary, p. 56, closely enough to be derived from it: 'fyrst of the Hart, because he is the principal of al other members and the beginning of life: he is set in the middest severally by him selfe, as Lord and King of al members. And as a Lorde or King ought to be served of his subjectes that have their living of him, so are al other members of the body subjectes to the Hart, for they receyve their living of him, and they doo service many wayes unto him agayne.' Vicary's passage in turn appears to be derived from a number of sections in Aristotle, *De Partibus Animalium*, III, 4; 666a, 10–22; *De Generatione Animalium*, 738b, 16: 'for the heart or its analogue is the first principle of a natural body'.

PAGE 57

l. 1   *Discourse*. The process of time, actions, or circumstances.

ll. 2–3   *the Law of Nature, and yet not the primarie Law of Nature*. Donne's distinction between the primary law of nature and its secondary laws reminds us of Hooker in the *Laws*, pp. 6–7: 'that part of it [eternal law] which orderth naturall Agents, we call usually *Natures* Law', 'those things are termed most properly naturall Agents which keepe the Law of their kind unwittingly'; 'God did then institute a Law natural to be observed by creatures, and therefore according to the manner of Lawes.'

l. 4   *To give every one his owne*. With the moral connotations, perhaps, of Rev. 2:23, and 22:12.

ll. 5–6   *Proprietie, no Meum & Tuum*. Terms of property in civil and ecclesiastical law. The first denoted ownership rights of the fruits of land belonging to someone else, hence the associated Latin terms of 'mine' and 'yours' to signify a partition of rights between both parties (Cowell, D3^v, Fff 4^v; Barnabé Brisson, *De Verborum Quae ad Jus Pertinent Significatione*, Paris, 1596, Fol. 398^v).

ll. 10–11   *the very first dictates of Nature ... looke first to our selves*. Donne is alluding to a proverbial belief that it is better to know how to stay healthy than how to be cured once sick (Coghan, 1584, p. 2). The belief implied the need of a deep knowledge of one's self and of health and sickness (Gale, p. 1).

ll. 32–33   *if they be often taken ... extraordinary operation*. Renaissance books of medicine contained numerous examples of medicines that lost their effect by over-use or achieved unexpected results. Baker (p. 50) speaks of honeysuckle water taken for dropsy that turned people barren, while an overdose of an ivy cordial appears elsewhere as a danger to sanity (Lyte, p. 281).

PAGE 58

ll. 11–13   *forraine poysons ... intestine poysons bred ... by pestilentiall sick-*

nesses. Donne is talking about an 'inward' disease of the intestines afflicting the heart, as opposed to an illness inflicted by some outside 'venemous' agent. A number of intestinal illnesses (like choler and the gall-stone, Crooke, pp. 106, 109), were believed capable of sending fatal vapours up to the heart, after the fashion of a pestilence that, by contrast, spread from the outside through 'an infected ayre' into the pores of its victim (Woodall, p. 324). Donne images the development of the intestinal illness in the evolution of a plague.

l. 19 *a Filiation*. The condition of being a son, in the sense here of a spiritual descendant. The word has connotations of adoption absent in Donne's use of the word in VI, *Sermons* (1640), p. 56.

l. 27 *I the Lord search the Heart*. Jer. 17:10.

PAGE 59

ll. 13–14 *hearts that burne like Ovens*. Hos. 7:6.

l. 15 *Hearts in which their Masters trust*. Prov. 28:25.

PAGE 60

ll. 5–7 *Thou, O Lord, hast given mee Worme wood . . . thou hast cleared a Morning to mee*. Donne's use of wormwood refers to the bitter taste of the plant divinely inflicted on the Israelites as punishment (Lam. 3:15). He also uses it in this punitive sense in the third of his poems for 'The Lamentations of Jeremy' (l. 197). Wormwood also suggests the herb highly recommended as medication in his day to clear away a humour like phlegm out of the organic system (Gerarde, p. 938; Elyot, p. 79ᵛ).

ll. 21–24 *in thy upper house, the Heavens . . . then in others*. Donne is punning on the biblical and astrological meanings of mansions and houses. The biblical meanings are fairly obvious. The upper house refers to a spiritual heaven, and the mansions to the abundance of rooms in God's house in Christ's statement in John 14:2. The astrological meanings are less obvious. The paradoxical 'lower house' (the created universe of Donne's reference) was divided into twelve houses. Each house represented the place of one sign of the zodiac in the heavens (Salmon, *Synopsis*, A3). Superimposed upon these twelve houses were the 28 parts of the ecliptic (the ecliptic was the apparent orbit of the sun). Each part of the ecliptic was occupied by the moon on a separate day of its journey around the sun's orbit. The importance of the mansions in the moon's path depended on the house of the sign of the zodiac through which it passed. The four most important houses, for example, were the four points of the zodiac (two on the horizon, and two on the meridian), whichever these were, according to the time of the year and the position of the earth (Blundeville, I, xxxvi, p. 493). To Donne, the measure of God's influence on the earth would seem to vary as though by his own design, from room to room or mansion to mansion, along the path of the ecliptic.

PAGE 61

l. 2 *Job made a Covenant with his Eyes.* Job 31:1.

l. 4 *Thy Sonne himselfe had a sadnesse in his Soule to death.* Matt. 26:38; Mark 14:34.

l. 5 *deprecation.* A prayer for the removal of evil.

l. 6 *Yet not my will, but thine bee done.* Matt. 26:39; Mark 14:36; or Luke 22:42.

l. 13 *even the flesh of Vipers.* The viper belonged to the serpent family and possessed all of the pejorative characteristics attributed to this family in books on snakes. The writers of these books found it difficult to conceive anything good coming out of a family of beasts responsible for the fall of man (Topsell, pp. 591, 799). Nevertheless, the viper, like the serpent, possessed a great range of medicinal qualities. Its flesh, raw, burnt, pickled, or dried, was one of the constituent elements for numerous compound medicines for all sorts of human ailments (pp. 808–10).

l. 17 *why hast thou forsaken mee.* Matt. 27:46; Mark 15:34.

PAGE 62

l. 5 *if a vapor will.* The official definition of a 'vapor' was a gas that ascended 'into the head like the steam we see ascend from a boiling pot' (*Physical Dictionary*, o1). It came in two forms. Either the vapour was some outside agent that stifled its victim, or else, as Donne depicts it in 'The Canonization', it originated in an imbalance of the humours in the body, and sent a sometimes fatal steam shooting up to the head. In his poem, Donne indicates that this latter 'heat' or 'vapor' was not viral in origin but self-generated.

ll. 5–6 *how great an Elephant, how small a Mouse destroyes.* W. Milgate attributes Donne's familiarity with the threat of the mouse running up the elephant's trunk, in this passage of *Devotions*, in *Paradoxes and Problems* (London, 1923), p. 58, and in *The Progresse of the Soule* (ll. 388–95), to Garcia de Orta's *Aromatum, et simplicium aliquot medicamentorum apud indos nascentium Historia* (Antwerp, 1567), p. 70 (*Notes and Queries*, Vol. 211, 1966, pp. 12–14).

l. 8 *single money.* Small change.

ll. 9–11   *the Ayre is condensed . . . almost made stone.* Donne is writing in both
the Hermetical tradition and the pseudoscientific, mystical tradition of the
early sixteenth-century figure, Paracelsus. In these traditions, stones were
made by the formation of the elements of the air into new compounds by
violent elemental forces like thunder, both in the atmosphere and in the
earth. In human hands such forces could be made to produce the philosopher's
stone which gave men power over matter and spirit (*Paracelsus His Aurora,*
and *Treasure of the Philosophers*, London, 1659, pp. 52–54; *Aureoli Theo-
phrasti Paracelsi Archidoxorum*, Basel, 1582, pp. 81–83; J. B. Van Helmont,
Oriatrike Or, Physick Refined, London, 1662, pp. 90–91).

l. 20   *Plinie hunted after the vapor of Aetna.* Pliny the Elder (Gaius Plinius
Secundus, b. Comum, A.D. 23) died on the shore of Stabiae at the foot of
Vesuvius, investigating the nature of smoke emitted by the volcano in the
destruction of Pompei in A.D. 79. His nephew, Pliny the Younger, writes in
a letter to Tacitus that his uncle left the safety of Misenum, fascinated by a
cloud rising from Vesuvius in the distance, and that he was overcome by an
unusually large puff of smoke at the foot of the volcano (*Letters*, edited with
trans. by William Melmoth, London, 1915, Vol. I, VI, xvi, pp. 475–83).

l. 28   *the Myne that spues out this . . . dampe.* Donne is referring to the second
or 'fiery' sort of the three kinds of 'damps' or fog-like gases (the other two
being 'common' and flameless 'suffocating'), which, according to seventeenth-
century science books, appeared as smoke, usually with fire, killing the
miners it caught in a colliery (Power, *Experimental Philosophy*, p. 181). The
imagery of the murderous 'myne' and the 'dampe' appeared earlier in
Donne's poetry, first in the opening stanza of 'Loves Alchymie' in which the
lovers find night instead of gold at the bottom of the mine, and secondly in
'The Dampe' in which the lover's friends dissect his body, and find that
he was killed by a love-fog (ll. 1–8).

PAGE 63

ll. 5–8   *Fevers . . . over-bending our naturall faculties.* One of the chief causes of
fevers was considered to be 'irregular Eating and Drinking' (Salmon, *Systeme*, IV, I, 11, p. 13.1); of consumption ('ptisicke' of the lungs or tubercu-
losis) 'immoderate drinking' of cold water and strong wine (p. 271.2); and
of 'madness' (a feverless 'mania'), the reason's loss of control over the 'animal
spirits' lodged in the brain (p. 56.1; Barrough, p. 44).

ll. 10–13   *But what have I done . . . to breath these vapours? . . . It is my study.*
Donne's rhetorical question about breeding and breathing in vapours cuts
across the two main branches of melancholy, the 'unnatural' and the 'natural'. Unnatural melancholy was caused by an alteration in the brain 'en-

gendered' by the brain itself (Bright, pp. 2, 24). By contrast, natural melancholy came about through some melancholic humours settling into it from other parts of the body (Barrough, p. 45). Donne concedes having 'unnatural' melancholy: he writes that he 'bred' and 'infused melancholy into himself too much by 'study' and 'thoughtfulness', from which it was reputed often to develop (Bright, p. 194). The over-contemplative man was thought to produce choleric vapour directly in his head. On the other hand, 'natural' melancholy was more physical in character than mental, and was 'breathed' or 'drunk' straight into the head from the vapours of the black choleric humour rising out of the stomach or other parts of the body (Salmon, *Systeme*, 38.1).

ll. 21–22 *strangled himself . . . by crushing his throat between his knees.* Sparrow, p. 157, correctly traces the allusion to IX, xii, *De Mortibus, Non Vulgaribus; Externa*, i, in (we must add) *Dictorum Factorum Memorabilium* (Hanover, 1614), pp. 321–22. The *Dictorum* was a popular educational manual, the only surviving work of the Roman historian, Valerius Maximus, who lived in the reign of Tiberius at the birth of the Christian era. Valerius identifies the 'Coma' whose name appears in Donne's *marginalia* as a brother of the fifth-century B.C. Athenian leader, Cleon.

ll. 29–30 *That which is fume in us.* Donne uses 'fume' in its usual derogatory sense as a synonym for the general class of 'vapor' that rose to the head from the stomach (Vicary, p. 24), rather than in its medical sense as a type of purgative (*Guydos*, Fol. 136 a, b).

l. 32–l. 2, PAGE 64 *The Heart in that body is the King . . . these Noble parts.* The principal parts of the body to which most medical thinkers accorded nobility, were the heart, brain, and liver. However, in his analogy, Donne replaces the liver with the sinews. The sinews of the body, which were synonymous with what medical science today calls nerves, originated in the brain and executed its commands. By the time he wrote *Devotions*, Donne had already in his poetry long committed himself to the idea of their magistracy. The whole imagery of 'The Funerall' relies on the belief that the sinews tie and keep the body together in a coherent organism. However, unless one thinks of them as an integral section of the brain, the sinews were not commonly considered a principal part of the body.

Burton shares Donne's idea of the magistracy of the sinews ('*Nerves*, or sinews . . . proceed from the brain, and carry the animal spirits for sense and motion' I. i. II. iii, p. 130). So do Banister in *The History of Man* (I) (sinews are 'the immediate organs of sence'), and Woodall (sinews generate 'the sense and motion,' p. 86). But none of these statements possesses the suggestiveness of Donne's analogy in *Devotions*. In addition to establishing three principal parts of the body, the analogy attributes to the heart a spiritual primacy that the other contemporary descriptions, being purely physiological, attributed to the brain (Bright, p. 46). Donne's view of the primacy of the heart is evidently due to his emphasis on the human heart as the seal of the Conscience, and as the highest form of human sensibility (*Pseudo-Martyr*, p. 84). The conscience bestowed on the heart a physiological primacy over the brain and sinews.

PAGE 64

ll. 6–7 *what channell ... what vault.* By 'channel' Donne may mean a gutter; by 'shambles', almost certainly a slaughterhouse, a prevalent contemporary meaning for the word; by 'dunghill', a heap of animal refuse; and by 'vault', a covered drain or sewer. All four words suggest sources of material decay, and therefore the vapours that spread illness (Vicary, App. III, p. 154, described an official visitation to a house to consider the dangerous state of its 'comen sewer or vawt' for cleaning).

ll. 12–13 *the Flea ... does all the harme hee can.* Santis Ardoyni Pisaurensis Medici et Philosophi Praestantissimi Opus De Venenis ... Basiliae, N.D. [1562], p. 506. Sante Ardoinus or Arduino as he was known in his native Italy, was a celebrated doctor practising in 1430. The *De Venenis* (a book on drugs) is his chief known work.

l. 15 *a good Pigeon to draw this vapor from the Head.* The fact that Donne was given pigeon to draw vapour from his head suggests that his doctors thought he was suffering from an excess of either the phlegmatic humour, or 'pure' melancholy, or both (Elyot, 21a). Pigeon, possessing 'hot and moist' qualities, was an excellent antidote for the 'cold and dry' excesses of melancholic and phlegmatic humours (Coghan, 1584, 161, p. 134). However the method of the application of the pigeon to Donne's feet as a poultice is unusual. Medical tracts suggested pigeon was to be eaten. Simpson records another incident of pigeon poultice, by Pepys, later in the century (*Study*, p. 243).

PAGE 65

ll. 11–12 *Thou canst punish us by those things, wherein wee offend thee.* Jer. 21:14.

l. 33 *thy blessed spirit too, who descended in the Dove.* Matt. 3:16; Mark 1:10; Luke 3:22, and John 1:32.

PAGE 67

l. 2 *hee that hath cleane hands.* Ps. 24:4.

ll. 13–14 *there are more stars . . . then under the Southern Pole*. According to a commonly accepted count (Recorde, *Castle*, p. 254) there were roughly 1,000 fixed stars, sometimes more, sometimes less (Blundeville, I, xxiii, p. 327), distributed among the forty-eight 'images' of the heavens: about 350 in the twelve images of the signs of the zodiac (I, xxiiii, p. 330), about 328 in the twenty-one images of the North, and the remainder, a little less, about 298, in the fifteen images of the South (I, xxv, xxvi, pp. 331–34). An image was the likeness of the stars to things like 'men, women, beasts . . . and to some things without life, having artificiall shape' (I, xxiii, p. 328).

ll. 17–18 *he livd under a perpetuall Equinoctial*. An equinoctial period in both Ptolemaic and Copernican systems was one of the two times of the year, spring and autumn, when day and night are of equal length, because the sun is crossing the equator equidistant from the two poles (Blundeville, p. 293). While the vernal and autumnal equinoxes are today fixed at 20 March and 22 or 23 September, in Donne's time—according to the religious calendar at the beginning of the King James Bible—they occurred on 13 March and 15 September (A$_2$, C$_5$). Donne's image of an hypothetical perpetual equinox recurs in a variety of forms in the century. John Keill uses it to describe the condition of the earth before the fall (*Examinations, Reflections* [1698], 1734, p. 229) and William Whiston, to conjecture about the state of nature in a planet possessing only one revolution per year (*A New Theory* [1696], 1708, p. 58).

ll. 24–27 *In this accident . . . the Phisicians see more cleerely*. 'Accidents' were symptoms, that is, 'nothing else but the effects of the disposition of the disease', which enabled doctors to identify an illness. They revealed the 'Pathognomonicke' signs that indicated the place of an illness in the general categories of diseases (Hart, pp. 19–20).

PAGE 68

ll. 3–4 *confessions upon the Rack*. Confessions upon the rack were commonly ordered through the Privy Council by royal prerogative, in the reigns of Elizabeth and James I, for purposes of information (i.e. *Acts of the Privy Council, 1598–99*, p. 428). However, having no precedent in the courts of Common Law, they were invalid before a judge in a superior court of law, as Donne recognizes here (David Jardine, *A Heading on the Use of Torture in the Criminal Law of England*, London, 1837, pp. 62–63).

ll. 30–31 *no spotted sacrifice*. The unspotted sacrifice in the Bible is Christ of Heb. 9:14, who is obviously in the foreground of Donne's thoughts throughout this thirteenth expostulation.

l. 32–l. 1, PAGE 69 *the soule of this body, as he is thy Spouse*. Song of Sol. 4:8.

PAGE 69

l. 28   *thou diddest prosper his Rodds.* Gen. 30:39.

PAGE 70

ll. 6–7   *thou hast not left thy holy one in Hell, thy Sonne is not there.* Acts 2:31.

ll. 18–20   *That the house is visited . . . and thy tokens are upon the patient.*
Donne is using metaphorically the passage in Ezek. 9:4–7, describing God's
vengeance on the bad Israelites, and the survival of the good Israelites who
were marked by an avenging angel with a sign of salvation on their fore-
heads. More literally, his statement describes the visitation of the house by
a doctor to certify the presence of a patient in a time of plague.

l. 21   *Wayve.* More commonly spelt 'waive'; a woman outlaw.

l. 27   *reversion.* A legal term describing the return of an estate to a donor.

l. 29   *conveyance.* The legal transference of property from one person to
another by some form of deed.

PAGE 71

l. 3   *the criticall dayes.* The fourteenth meditation and expostulation are a
contemplation on the 'criticall dayes' or crisis of Donne's illness. The arrival
of this crisis is indicated in the previous meditation by the 'accidents' of the
red spots on his body. Donne's description of his crisis is largely metaphoric
rather than literal, serving as the occasion for a meditation on the role of time
in human happiness.

ll. 9–10   *false Happinesses . . . their Critical dayes.* Donne is using metaphorically
an astrological diagnostic term to describe the condition of human happiness.
The three kinds of general 'critical' days of an illness were the 'Critici,
Judicarii, or Decretorii', that is, the critical (a more specific term than the
former), indicatory, and decretory days. These were *'the days wherein a man
may judge, discern, or pass sentence of a Disease'* according to the conjunction of
its symptoms with the position of the planets (Salmon, *Synopsis*, p. 175).
The foreordained path of the disease became obvious in the motions of the
astral bodies from one general 'critical' day to the next.

ll. 12–14   *if Tyme . . . be an essential part of our hapiness.* Augustine, *Confessions*, X. xx. 29, and xxi. 30, pp. 219–20).

ll. 15–17   *the next hollow Superficies . . . of Ayre.* In medical treatises like *A
Physical Dictionary* (N3), a superficies was 'the out-side of any-thing.' But
Donne seems to be using the word figuratively less with medical than with
geometrical and astronomical connotations in mind (like those attached to

its definition in John Rastell's *Book of Purgatory*, London, 1530, II. xx. e2b: 'that which hath but length and brede and no maner of thyckenes'). Donne argues that space, which appeared to be infinite, was really finite in comparison to infinity itself; space was a mere thin shell bounding air, and was figuratively a substance as thin as the air it encompassed. Even though the connection between the images here in *Devotions* and in 'A Valediction: forbidding mourning' is otherwise weak, Donne's reader will certainly remember the 'ayery thinnesse' of the latter part of the poem (l. 24). Astrologically, the position of the superficies in *Devotions* is interesting, following as it does on his reference to the crisis of an illness, and on his prefiguration of the four elements in human happiness. For, to begin with, the four elements made up the matter of 'Elemental Bodies' which naturally included the human body, and it was through such bodies that the stars caused a crisis. The air was the one and only element through which the astral bodies could bring this crisis about. A 'rarification' of air like a superficies by a seasonal change, enabled the stars to bring on some of their greatest alterations possible in the state of human health (Salmon, *Synopsis*, p. 176).

l. 18   *Tyme to be but the Measure of Motion.* Augustine, *Confessions*, XI, xxiv, 31, pp. 262–63.

ll. 20–21   (*one is not, now, & the other is not yet*). Ibid., XI, xviii, 23, p. 257.

ll. 23–24   *now, the present, & the Now is past.* Ibid., XI, xxvii, 34, p. 264.

ll. 24–25   *Tyme, be of the Essence of our Happinesses.* Ibid., X, xxv, 36, pp. 223–24.

l. 29   *Tyme is as a short parenthesis in a longe period.* Donne is punning on 'period'; the word refers both to a long rhetorically constructed sentence and to an indefinite interval of time, and it contrasts with his use of 'eternity' later in his text.

PAGE 72

l. 4   *yet how little of our life is Occasion.* Donne is using the word 'occasion' with its obvious connotations of opportunity, but he may also be punning on its infrequent contemporary astrological sense as the setting of the sun. Sunset figures recur in his analogy in the preceding and following lines.

l. 16   *Youth is their Criticall Day.* In his meditation on the value of time in human happiness, Donne transposes the 'Criticall Day' of astrology analogously to the field of philosophy. In his analogy, youth is the 'Criticall Day' of people who measure happiness in terms of the period of human life alone. The 'critical day' in astrology was the moment in an illness when the transitory character of life seemed most apparent.

l. 20 *as a Pardon, when the Head is off.* The church bell is already ringing out for the death of the man—any new medicine like the cordiall is useless, as is the royal pardon for the stay of an execution which arrives after the execution has already been carried out.

l. 25 *Birdes . . . who can change the Climate.* Donne is punning on two meanings of 'climate'. The word refers to the alteration of the seasons of the year, which the bird of his imagery escapes by flying south to avoid winter; and secondly, to the influence exercised by the astrological bodies through the alteration of the seasons. As the seasons passed, a change of climate involved an increase in the heat or cold of the air in the body, and altered the 'quality' of its humours—that is, it upset their natural level of heat or cold (Salmon, *Synopsis*, p. 176).

PAGE 73

ll. 8–9 *fix our selves, at . . . stationary times.* The temporary or 'periodicall' time of a planet was the moment when it seemed to be 'fixed' in its 'stationary' place on its orbit. Donne uses this moment as a metaphor to describe dwelling at length on an aspect of his life in his meditation. A planet reached its stationary moment regularly when it completed the 'periodicall' time of its orbit, and appeared to exercise a constant rather than a changing influence on the earth. In Donne's text, the planet in question may be the moon whose stationary time under fixed signs was reputed to induce the crises and trials which he mentions (Salmon, *Synopsis*, p. 157).

ll. 10–12 *the Crisis, the triall, the judgment . . . to a spirituall recovery.* The 'crisis' of an illness was the period covering its turning point to either good or bad. It did not so much describe the condition of the patient as the state of the illness itself when it brought the patient to a point of either recovery or death (Salmon, *Synopsis*, p. 175). The astral bodies forced the illness into one direction or the other by acting upon the 'Elemental Body' and humours of the patient with 'Heat, Light, Motion, Position, or Configuration' (p. 177). The foreordained direction of an illness, after its crisis, was made clear by the relation of the patient's symptoms to the astral bodies.

l. 20 *S. Joh. wishes to Gaius.* The identity of Gaius is unknown beyond John's terms of endearment in his epistle to him. Biblical scholars have attempted to identify him with the Caius of the *Apostolic Constitutions* (vii, 46, a book of church orders of the late fourth century), whom John appointed bishop of Pergamum; and less successfully with other men bearing the name of Gaius in the New Testament.

l. 21 *the Soule be leane.* Ps. 106:16.

l. 25 *Climactericall yeares.* A 'climacterical year' in a man's life was a multiple of seven, or nine, or of both, and denoted an astrological period of crisis. It was particularly conducive to death (Butler, *Feminine Monarchie*, London, 1623, E2ᵛ).

ll. 28–29 *Adam . . . died in his climactericall yere.* Gen. 5:5. Adam lived to nine hundred and thirty years.

ll. 29–30 *Sem the eldest son of the next world.* Sem, the less common name of Shem (Gen. 6:10 and Luke 3:36), the first of Noah's three sons (Gen. 6:10, 10:1) who lived six hundred years (11:10–11). By the 'next world' Donne means the world after the flood, the first world being, by inference, the earth between the creation and the deluge.

ll. 30–31 *Abraham the father of the faithfull, in his.* Abraham, who lived one hundred and seventy-five years (Gen. 25:7), was 'the father of the faithful' in the sense that he received the Covenant of the faith directly from God (17:7), with the divine promise that it would be exclusively disseminated through his children (17:8).

ll. 31–32 *the blessed Virgin Mary . . . in hers.* The particular tradition of Mary's death to which Donne is alluding is impossible to specify. According to a number of apocryphal gospel writings, she died variously, two, twenty-two, and twenty-four years after Christ's Ascension. As far as the 'climacteric' character of her death is concerned, Donne is easier to pin down. The time of Mary's death is traditionally also the period of her bodily assumption into heaven.

PAGE 74

l. 10 *evident Indications, and critical Iudicatures.* The 'Indications' of a disease appeared on the 'Indicatory' days, the second of the three kinds of critical days in the crisis of an illness, when the moon came into her semi-sextile, that is, when it was at a 30-degree angle and a twelfth of its zodiac distance away from the earth. The 'critical indicatures', on the other hand, appeared on the 'decretory' or 'judicatory' days making up the third and last kind of critical days of a crisis, when the moon came to her quarter, and was 20 degrees or one eighteenth of its zodiac distance away (Salmon, *Synopsis*, pp. 179, 15).

l. 13 *they came to tempt him in the dangerous question of Tribute.* Matt. 22:17.

l. 14 *the Critical day to the Saduces.* Matt. 22:36.

ll. 27–28 *Religion is in a Neutralitie in the world.* Donne may have in mind the fragile 'neutralitie' between the elements and the humours in the healthy human body. In 'The first Anniversarie' he points out that physicians believed this 'neutralitie' to be really the only form of health possible (ll. 91–92). At other times, the elements and the humours were warring. His image may also be intended to picture religion as a neutral party between contending political forces, as though religion made no claims on his political allegiance. As is evident in *Pseudo-Martyr* (pp. 83–84), however, Donne did not believe in a separation of church and state.

ll. 33–34 *a Crisis, a Judgment upon my selfe this day.* A probable reference to the confinement imposed on Ahaziah by Eli as by divine decree in 2 Kings 1:4.

PAGE 75

l. 1 *judge my selfe, that I be not judged by thee.* 1 Cor. 11:31.

l. 2 *First, this is the day of thy visitation.* The series of the seven days in the expostulation begins the development of the astrological crisis of an illness. It describes the progress of Donne's spiritual regeneration in terms of the maturation of a disease under the influence of the astral bodies. Although the development of the spiritual crisis over seven days also imitates the stages of creation at the beginning of time, it corresponds more exactly to the course of a *crisis judicata*, that is, the second part of the crisis of an illness, which lasted for a week. The *judicata* was influenced on the fourth or fifth day, with either good or evil effects, by the motion of the moon and ended on the seventh day with sufficient clear signs in the body of the patient to indicate the direction of the disease (Salmon, *Synopsis*, p. 178). Donne may not necessarily have gone through a *crisis judicata*—there are indications to the contrary—but he is using the term or a crisis with its identical characteristics as a metaphor to describe spiritual regeneration.

ll. 9–10 *the light, and testimony of my Conscience.* For Donne, conscience gives testimony of right and wrong in that it furnishes saving knowledge to the souls of Christians enrolled in the mystical Register of the Elect (*Essays*, p. 7). It dictates right and wrong according to the knowledge intuitively and divinely deposited in the saved Christian.

ll. 11–14 *rising of thy Son . . . the day of a Conscience dejected.* The second day of Donne's spiritual crisis is a black mood induced by an examination of conscience. Although he images his spiritual crisis in his own acute physical crisis, he does not depict the latter literally, as he relates it to the sun. An acute crisis was always determined by the moon, and he writes to the contrary, purely for the sake of paradox, that his crisis was determined by the sun. It was impossible for Donne not to know that his crisis was governed by the moon. The onslaught of his illness was rapid, and the crises of acute diseases were always determined by the moon, rather than by the sun that determined the crises of chronic illnesses (Salmon, *Synopsis*, p. 177). Donne puns on 'son' to find liberation from his black mood in the metaphoric light of the Son of God. The role of the moon in his astrological crisis is demonstrated by his medical treatment in an earlier meditation. He was given a 'hot and moist' pigeon remedy that would have suitably balanced the phlegmatic coldness induced by the moon (*Synopsis*, 1671, p. 11).

PAGE 76

ll. 10–12 *The day of Judgement . . . the Critical, the Decretory day.* Donne is referring to the concluding 'Decretory' or 'judgment' days of the crisis of an illness (Salmon, *Synopsis*, pp. 175, 179; Hart, p. 21). But he is also punning on the meaning of 'decretory', since the word refers to the 'decrees' of the Last Judgment that he is at that point discussing. Donne uses the astrological 'decretory' day of the judgment as a metaphor for the Judgment of the Second Coming.

l. 29 *called an overshadowing.* Luke 1:35.

PAGE 77

l. 4 *the God of consolation.* Rom. 15:5.

PAGE 78

ll. 8–10 *his Melancholique fancying out . . . death which is so like sleepe.* Donne writes that melancholy provoked dreams through what Thomistic philosophy called the hallucinatory fancy. The fancy was the outlet in sleep for the 'figures' that the mind was too frightened to face when it was awake. In this case in *Devotions*, the 'figures' are those images of death feared by the melancholic mind (Bright, p. 101).

l. 33 *my continuall waking . . . bee a parasceve.* Friday, the day of preparation for the Jewish Sabbath, in Mark 25:42.

PAGE 79

Margin *1 Thes. 5:6.* Sparrow (p. 90) says this note appears three pages too soon in 1624(1) on p. 378 and relocates it to p. 381 where it already occurs correctly to refer the reader to a direct quotation from the biblical verse. However, the note also fits on p. 378 as a reference to Donne's paraphrase of part of the original text ('as do others [sleepe]').

PAGE 80

ll. 29 *watchfulnes . . . this inabilitie to sleepe.* Watchfulness, or insomnia, was a classic symptom of the illness of melancholy (Barrough, p. 46; Salmon, *Systeme*, 37:1).

PAGE 81

l. 3 *such defensatives.* Medical antidotes.

ll. 11–12 *by wilfull absteining from thy Congregations.* By congregation Donne means a local assembly of believers (as in Tindale's translation of the Bible, 1 Cor. 16:19, London, 1537). Its meaning was otherwise normally covered by the word church. Donne's use of 'congregation' might be deliberate preference. To the English Protestant, 'church' was sometimes tainted with connotations of the Roman hierarchy, in both its senses as a local and international institution (Tindale, *Answer to More*, London, 1530, Fol. VIᵛ; *Articles*, No. 19, p. 13).

l. 27 *From the bels of the Church adjoyning.* The sixteenth devotion is the first of three devotions on bells. Each devotion deals with one of the three bells recommended to be rung by the minister for his ill or deceased parishioners in the section on 'Ministers to Visit the Sick' in *Constitutions and Canons* of the Church of England (H4). However, Donne does not deal with the bells in their logical canonical order, which is the passing bell, the death knell and the funeral bell, but begins with the third and then returns to the first and second. The section in the canons reads: 'When any man is dangerously sicke in any Parish, the Minister or Curate (having knowledge thereof) shall resort unto him or her, (if the disease be not knowen or probably suspected to be infectious) to instruct and comfort them in their distress, according to the order of the Communion booke, if hee be no Preacher: or if he be a Preacher, then as he shal thinke most needefull and convenient. And when any is passing out of this life, a Bell shalbe tolled, and the Minister shall not then slacke to doe his last duetie. And after the parties death (if it so fall out) there shall bee rung no more but one short peale, and one other before buriall, and one other after the buriall.'

ll. 30–31 *Author, who writ a Discourse of Bells . . . Prisoner in Turky.* Hieronymus Magius, or Gerolamo Maggi (b. c. 1523, Anghiari da Paolo; d. 1572, Constantinople), wrote his treatise on bells, *De Tintinnabulis*, in Constantinople while a prisoner of the Turks, who captured him in the sack of Famagusta in Cyprus. As Sparrow points out (p. 158), Magius was an engineer in the service of Venice, whose chief works therefore dealt with the fortification of cities, but who wrote his treatise on the history and the use of bells from memory, as he tells us in his preface, to compensate having been denied all books by his jailors.

PAGE 82

ll. 3–4 *the Turkes . . . melted the Bells into Ordnance.* Angelo Rocca, bishop of Tagaste (b. Rocca Contratta, in Ancona, 1545; d. Rome, 1620) refers to the Turks melting the bells down for armaments in his treatise on bells, *De Campanis*, p. 2. Donne mentions his work in his *marginalia* a little later.

ll. 5–6 *I have lien neere a steeple . . . more than thirty Bels.* Bald conjectures that Donne was in Antwerp in 1612 during his continental tour in the service of Sir Robert Drury (p. 261). Donne himself mentions the possibility of passing through Antwerp on his way to England in a letter to Sir Henry Goodyer, dated August 16 of that year (*Letters*, p. 252; Bald, p. 260). The church with the 'more than thirty Bels' was the Cathedral of Notre Dame which had thirty-three bells in its highest tower (Rocca, *De Campanis*, p. 81). The harmoniousness of their sound was reputed throughout Europe.

ll. 7–8 *one so bigge, as that the Clapper . . . weigh nore than six hundred pound.* The bell in Donne's reference is the Georges-d'Amboise (named after its donor), which stood in the Tour de Beurre of Rouen Cathedral. It was melted down for cannon material in 1793, and its huge clapper was fixed into the wall of one of the principal houses of Déville, on the road from Rouen to Le Havre. Donne could have heard the bell on a journey out of Amiens during his period of service with Sir Robert Drury in the winter of 1611–12 (Bald, p. 261). The bell was ordered cast by Cardinal d'Amboise in 1500 and completed in 1501, weighing 36,000 pounds, 710 pounds for its clapper alone (Donne is out by 110 pounds) ([Jean François Pommeraye] *Histoire de L'Église Cathédrale de Rouen*, Rouen, 1686, p. 49).

l. 9 *the Bells . . . solemnise the funerall of any person.* A disquisition on the funeral function of bells occurs in both Donne's sources: Maggi on p. 46 and his editor, Sweertius, on p. 91 of *De Tintinnabulis*; and Rocca on pp. 133–35 of *De Campanis*.

ll. 17–18 *a story of a Bell in a Monastery.* The event supposedly occurred in a monastery for preaching friars in Salerno, Italy (Rocca, pp. 66–67).

l. 35 *Mortification by Example.* Mortification was a medical term describing the deadening of any part of the body, usually by gangrene, and was used by doctors in lessons in anatomy (Jacques Guillemeau, *The French Chirurgerye*, London, 1597, 2ᵛ; *Physical Dictionary*, I, 8).

PAGE 83

l. 29   *the Triumphant Church.* The 'triumphant' church is the communion of saved souls in eternity.

ll. 32–33   *Trumpets, at the Resurrection.* Matt. 24:31.

PAGE 84

l. 9   *Vaunt.* The van of an army.

l. 10   *extends.* Literally, troops drawn out to reach one or more certain points.

l. 18   *repetition Sermon.* The repetition sermon was usually a school and university exercise. The student gave the sermon in Latin from notes that he took down during its original delivery in English. The purpose of the exercise was to lodge the sermon's message in his memory (W. F. Mitchell, *English Pulpit Oratory*, London, 1932, pp. 74–75). In another tradition, the repetition sermon was delivered in English or Latin once a year at the University Church in Oxford, for divines and learned men (D. Glanville, *The Remains*, Surtees Society Publications, Edinburgh, 1840, p. 43).

l. 21   *Deaths-head in a Ring.* The death's head ring contained the representation of a human skull as a symbol of death. In the seventeenth century it was worn for mourning (*Devout Communicant*, 1688, p. 8), and by procuresses (Dekker, *Northward Hoe*, London, 1873, III, *Works*, IV, p. 50). In the latter case it had very specific religious rather than physical connotations. In shapes other than the ring, the death's head image always retained the general connotations of mortality as a reminder of death (for example, in 2 Henry IV, 2, 255; and at least twice in Donne's *Songs and Sonnets*, 'A Valediction: of my name in the Window,' ll. 21–22, and Elegy IX, 'The Autumnall', l. 44).

PAGE 85

ll. 6–7   *Temples of the holy Ghost.* 1 Cor. 6:19.

l. 18   *Thou hast sent one from the dead to speake unto mee.* Luke 16:24.

PAGE 86

l. 5   *for whom this Bell tolls.* The 'passing' bell for the dying in the English Church's liturgy for the sick. The image of this bell occurred earlier in Donne's writings, in an extended reference to contemporary medical manuals in 'The Will'. The lover of the poem bequeathed his 'physick bookes' to 'him for whom the passing bell next tolls' (ll. 1–2).

ll. 6–8 *I may thinke . . . have caused it to toll for mee.* Donne's inspiration may come from a passage in Rocca's *De Campanis*, pp. 133–34: 'Comitatus autem ille ad opus sepeliendi, ex septem operibus misericordiae corperalibus unum, referri potest. Quae sane institutio, et consuetudo perantiqua, valde pia, et valde necessaria consetur, quia (ut ait Guillelmus Bernardus) citra hunc usum pulsandi Campanas, morte multorum à multis ignorata, Defunctorum animae precibus Fidelium non iuvarentur, nec Viventibus ob huius generis opera praemium apud Deum merendi daretur occasio. Hinc, ut sentio, laudanda videtur consuetudo illorum locorum, in quibus ad sonitum, seu tinnitum funebrem expressius indicandum, Companae non utramque, sed ad unam tantum partem paulatim, aut sensim pulsantur, quasi moerorem quemdam, vel humanam viventium imbecillitatem quodam modo repraesentantes.'

l. 23 *contention.* Suit of law.

l. 25 *which of the religious Orders.* Donne satirizes a contemporary dispute over the Catholic canon law that restricted the ringing of church bells to persons specified by the rector of a parish. Canon law (Nos. 1184–1186) reads that the rector of a church bestows the right to ring bells on a fit candidate. His choice prevails unless it is challenged by someone on the basis of local traditions (*Traité de Droit Canonique*, Vol. III, edited by Charles de Clercq, Paris, 1947, pp. 23–24).

PAGE 87

ll. 29–30 *drawing light out of darknesse.* 2 Cor. 4:6.

l. 32 *confirmation.* The ratification of a bishop in his post.

PAGE 88

l. 23 *I goe to prepare a place for you.* John 14:3.

ll. 26–31 *Thy legacies in thy first will, in thy old Testament . . . the joies and glories of heaven.* Plenty, Gen. 41:29; victory, Ps. 98:1; wine and oil, Jer. 31:12; milk and honey, Exod. 3:8; friends, Prov. 14:20; ruin of enemies, Ps. 89:40; peaceful hearts and cheerful countenances, Prov. 15:13. Numerous other passages in the Old Testament might be pointed out to support Donne's list with varying degrees of precision. The items in his list of divine benefits make up the 'galleries' (Ezek. 41:15) lining the way to the Chamber of Sacrifice in the temple of the Israelites, in Ezekiel's vision (42:13).

PAGE 89

ll. 8–9 *art made of no substances . . . are made of none of these circumstances.* The scholastic argument about God stated that he was uncreated and that in reality he possessed no 'substance' at all in an ordinary sense, because his 'being' made up a 'genus' all by itself. This 'being' distinguished God from all created things as he existed singly and no created 'substance' existed 'singly', but rather in 'multiples' with a lot of other like substances in its genus. By analogy, the same originality held true for God's experience as for his being. Experiences like joy and glory were not 'circumstantial' in him; that is, they were not mere accrued 'accidents' distinguishing his 'being' from that of a creature. Rather, his emotions were absolute, 'substantial', 'essential', and 'eternal', without beginning or end, or variation in intensity (*Summa*, I, Q. CIV, a2, 'Treatise on Man', p. 384; I, Q. III, a6, pp. 39–40, and a3, p. 34; I, Q. XX, a1, pp. 284–285).

ll. 19–20 *speechlesse Creatures, in Balaams Asse*. Num. 22:28.

l. 20 *unbeleeving men, in the confession of Pilate*. Matt. 27:24.

ll. 21–22 *the Devill himselfe, in the recognition . . . of thy Sonne*. Matt. 4:6; Luke 1:3.

l. 27 *death is the wages of sinne*. Rom. 6:23.

ll. 30–31 *I commend my spirit*. Luke 23:46.

PAGE 90

ll. 22–23 *My God, my God, Why hast thou forsaken me*. Matt. 27:46.

PAGE 91

l. 5 *The Bell rings out*. A meditation on the death knell in the English Church's canon for the dead. In 'The second Anniversary' written eleven years earlier, the death knell had the additional significance of summoning Elizabeth Drury into the Triumphant Church of the dead and the saved (ll. 99–101).

ll. 13–15 *it is nothing, but . . . Elements in the body*. An argument held by one kind of Renaissance atheist, attributed, for example, to Sir Walter Raleigh by his accusers in the Royal Commission against atheists held at Cerne Abbas, 21 March, 1594, in Appendix III, *Willobie His Avisa* (Edinburgh, 1926), pp. 256, 260, 266–67. The argument was earlier enunciated by the Italian thinker Peter Pomponazzi in *Tractatus de Immortalitate Animae* (N.p., 1534), p. 76, and refuted in England by, for instance, Bishop John Woolton in *A Treatise of the Immortalitie of the Soule* (London, 1576), Fol. 5–6; and by Sir John Davies, in the second part of *Nosce Teipsum*, 1697, XXXII–XXXIII, pp. 92–106.

l. 19 *if my soule were no more than the soule of a beast*. Donne is raising a stock objection to the scholastic argument about the independent existence of the soul from the body. He is following the fashion of Aquinas in the *Summa* of bringing up an objection himself before giving his proof. Donne's proof for the immortality of the human soul is based on its differences from the animal soul, and is the one which Aquinas himself provided for the same objection (*Summa*, I, Q. LXXV, a3, pp. 7–8).

l. 27 *I shall finde some.* Donne is imitating Augustine's method of disputation in his letter to Jerome on the origin of the human soul (IV, *Letters*, 166, XII–XIV, pp. 17–19). Like Augustine, Donne has no particular individuals in mind when he refers to 'some' believing certain things about the soul and to some holding 'others'. He is merely personifying certain philosophical positions under repeated usage of the impersonal pronoun. His purpose is to single out a number of points, many of them dealt with by Augustine (including the origin of the soul of a child in the bodies of its parents). The question of the independent existence of the soul is Donne's first point and is likewise Augustine's (III, pp. 8–9).

l. 30 *derived with the body from Mortall parents.* Augustine, *Letters IV*, No. 166, X, pp. 15–16.

PAGE 92

ll. 2–3 *That they attend an expiation . . . in a place of torment.* Trent, Session VI, 'On Justification', Canon XXX; Session XXV, 'Decree Concerning Purgatory'. Donne rejects the existence of the Catholic Purgatory. His references to it in both his prose (*Conclave*, p. 9) and his poetry (Satyre III, l. 3) are invariably derogatory.

ll.3–4 *they attend the fruition of the sight of God . . . but of expectation.* Calvin, *Institutes*, 1961, Vol. I, III, v, 10, pp. 683–84; *Psychopannychia*, in Vol. III, *Tracts and Treatises of the Reformed Faith*, edited by T. F. Torance, trans. by H. Beveridge (London, 1958), pp. 435–36; also, Richard Hooker, 'A Learned Sermon on the Nature of Pride', *Works*, edited by John Keble (Oxford, 1888), Vol. III, p. 640.

l. 5 *that they passe to an immediate possession of the presence of God.* Zwingli, 'Of Purgatory', *Exposition of Faith*, in *Zwingli and Bullinger* (London, 1953), Vol. XXIV, Library of Christian Classics, p. 54; 'Concerning Prayer', *Book of Homilies*, II, 7, 3 (London, 1563), fol. 135ᵛ–36.

ll. 7–8 *to Saint Hierome.* IV, *Letters*, 166, I, p. 6; II, p. 7.

ll. 9–11 *Let the departure of my soule . . . bee to my reason.* Donne is paraphrasing Augustine's comment on his own letter to Jerome concerning the immortality of the soul (No. 166) in his next letter to him (IV, *Letters*, 167,

II, p. 33). He condenses Augustine's already abbreviated thought into an aphorism.

l. 33 *a kennell.* The surface drain of a street, or a gutter.

PAGE 93

l. 4 *Rubbidge.* Variant of rubbish.

l. 6 *a clocke.* A variant spelling of cloak.

ll. 10–11 *when this soule departs . . . no more vegetation, no more sense.* Donne is following the scholastic argument that a human being had three souls, vegetative, animal, and rational, and the third animated the other two (*Summa*, I, Q. LXXVIII, a1, pp. 73–76). At death, the rational soul passed out of the body, killing off the other two; but by contrast, at birth, the existence of the vegetative and animal souls seemed to precede the creation of the rational soul (I, Q. LXXV, a3 and a6, pp. 7–8, 14–16).

ll. 11–12 *Mother in law.* Stepmother.

l. 17 *prophane.* In the sense of not sacred because unconsecrated.

l. 24 *Controller.* A house or state steward in charge of keeping a check on expenditures.

l. 25 *(as that was) any convenient reason is enough.* Donne refers to the discussion of God's injunctions to Moses, Lev. 21:2–4, which he introduced at the beginning of the expostulation.

ll. 31–32 *the Pictures of some dead persons.* Wisd. of Sol. 14:15.

PAGE 94

l. 1 *statues, and pictures contracted an opinion of divinity, by age.* Wisd. of Sol. 14:16.

ll. 5–6 *60. yeeres after it is made.* Donne is probably making an error and means forty and not sixty years. By the 'law of prescription' the Roman Church considered that something in its possession which was not protected by civil or common law became its sacred property after forty years (E. Taunton, *The Law of the Church*, London, 1906, pp. 501–2). Donne is extending the Roman principle of prescription to the veneration of images in the possession of the Church.

ll. 16–17 *God will not suffer his holy officers . . . to see them.* Lev. 21:11.

l. 26 *It is a second death.* Rev. 20:14.

ll. 30–31 *we are all dead men.* Exod. 12:33.

PAGE 95

l. 19 *Commination.* Threat of divine vengeance or retribution.

l. 24 *to a plurall.* By plural, Donne means that Christ repeats his thoughts twice, in identical language in the King James translation of the Bible.

PAGE 96

l. 31 *his last office, the office of a Judge.* John 5:22.

l. 32 *societie of humane bodies in heaven.* Rom. 8:11.

PAGE 97

l. 17 *any indication of concoction in these waters.* Donne is describing a late stage of his illness, some indeterminate time past its crisis, when the bad humours were expected to leave the body through a kind of secretory function known as 'concoction'. Concoction was a general term in physiology referring to digestion (*Physical Dictionary*, D4ᵛ; Crooke, p. 164). The particular 'concoction' in question was the third of three kinds of digestion, and it accompanied the closing stages of certain illnesses with a number of secretions like 'sweat and tears' (Burton, I, i, 2. ii). Thus, Donne's doctors are looking for what Hart calls (p. 21) 'the signes of concoction, after the beginning of the disease is past over, and the humours by meanes of the naturall heate, well concocted, sequestred, and separated from that which is putrid and corrupt, [that] do appear about the time of the increasing or vigour of the disease, in the *urine*, spittle . . . as also in other excretions'.

PAGE 98

l. 6 *preventions, nor anticipations, nor obligations.* Three legal terms which Donne uses to describe impossible interferences with nature: 'prevention', in canon law, being the privilege of a superior to prevent one of his subordinates from exercising a right that was legally his as an inferior (Edward Hall, *Chronicle*, 1550, 'Henry VIII', 184b); 'anticipation', taking possession of something before it actually became yours (*Chronicle*, 1548, 672); and 'obligation', being a legal restraint imposed on someone by contract (William Bedwell, *Discovery*, London, 1615, N4ᵛ). Nature would admit none of these in her workings. Donne had earlier in *Conclave* (p. 7) treated 'prevention' satirically as a characteristic of Kepler's and Brahe's rules of astronomy.

l. 18 *syndicated with Commissions.* Censured by certain orders (by comparison, *Pseudo-Martyr*, p. 154: 'his Vicar shall . . . Syndicate . . . Princes on earth').

PAGE 99

ll. 14–18 *such a height of figures ... so perswading commandements.* Writing perhaps with tongue in cheek, Donne lists a number of poetic 'figures' common in the language of Renaissance manuals of rhetoric and poetry. For example, he echoes Puttenham's description of the 'figure' in *The Arte of English Poesie*, III, iii (London, 1589), p. 119, as an ornament 'inwardly working a stire to the minde' and then his list of figures, III, VII, 128–29: a metaphor, 'an inversion of sence by transport'; an allegory, 'a duplicitie of meaning or dissimulation under covert and darke intendments'; and an hyperbole, an 'incredible comparsion giving credit'. (The third heaven in his description of the hyperbole is the paradisal visionary state described in II Corinthians XII, 2). The 'harmonious eloquution' at the end of Donne's catalogue is defined by Wilson in *The Arte of Rhetoric* (London, 1585), p. 6, as the application 'of apt wordes and sentences to the matter' of the figure of speech; while his concluding statements about 'commanding perswasions' echo the figurative descriptions of the general categories of poetic language in the manuals (Puttenham, III, ii, p. 118). Donne had already dwelt on the figurative language of the Scriptures in two sermons, the first in 1618: 'There are not so eloquent books in the world, as the Scriptures: Accept those names of Tropes and Figures, which the Grammarians and Rhetoricians put upon us, and we may be bold to say, that in all their Authors, Greek and Latin, we cannot finde so high, and so lively examples, of those Tropes, and those Figures, as we may in the Scriptures' (II, *Sermons*, 7, pp. 170–71); and the second sermon in the spring of 1623 itself (VI, *Sermons*, 1, pp. 55–56).

PAGE 100

ll. 1–2 *Hierome and Augustine call upon persons.* Augustine, I, *Letters*, 28, p. 98; and 72 (Jerome to Augustine), p. 332. The correspondence between the two saints had become rather heated because Augustine pointedly questioned Jerome's methods of biblical interpretation and translation. Both appealed literally to unlearned as well as learned authorities to lower the temperature of their debate and to pursue their arguments.

l. 10 *Circumcision carried a figure of Baptisme.* Perhaps inspired by Acts 10:44–46, where the baptismal rite bestows the benefit of the circumcision of the Jews on Gentiles.

ll. 11–12 *perfection in the new Jerusalem.* Heb. 4:1–4.

l. 33 *the first life ... was in waters.* Gen. 1:20.

l. 35–page 101, l. 1. *thou callest Gennezareth ... a Sea.* Gennesareth or Chinnereth, Num. 34:11, Deut. 3:17, Josh. 13:27.

COMMENTARY

PAGE 101

ll. 1–2 *thou callest the Mediterranean Sea, still the great Sea.* Num. 34:6, Josh. 1:4.

l. 17 *that red Sea, drownes none of thine.* Exod. 14:29.

ll. 27–28 *Neverthelesse thou wouldest not . . . be idle.* Wisd. of Sol. 14:5.

PAGE 103

ll. 2–3 *the raine-bow, that secured the world for ever.* Rev. 4:3.

l. 9 *they saw a little cloud rising out of the Sea.* 1 Kings 18:44.

l. 10 *presently they had their desire of raine.* 1 Kings 18:45.

ll. 10–11 *Seven dayes . . . have we looked for this cloud.* Gen. 7:4.

ll. 19–20 *thou hadst perfited . . . and rest of a Sabbath.* Gen. 2:2.

ll. 26–27 *Thy Priests came . . . by steps in the Temple.* Ezek. 40:49.

ll. 27–28 *Thy Angels came downe to Jaacob, by steps upon the ladder.* Gen. 28:12.

ll. 28–29 *thy selfe camest to Adam in Paradise.* Gen. 2:16.

l. 29 *nor to Sodome in thine anger.* Gen. 19:24.

PAGE 104

l. 20 *fatnesse.* The superior and most rewarding part of a thing.

PAGE 105

ll. 5–6 *the seale of an Armie set to them.* Neither the English army nor any of its branches had distinct seals, but the orders for a corps might be sealed with the insignia of the nobleman or the general in charge.

ll. 8–9 *Hermes . . . the head and shoulders of a man.* Donne should be using the more exact term, 'Herma', the Latinized form of the Greek Hermes, describing a kind of statue, of head and bust without arms, surmounted on a block, originally of Hermes or Mercury himself. The statue was reserved for renowned individuals in ancient Rome and Greece, meriting to be portrayed in Hermes' figure as messengers of the gods for their service to the state (Plutarch, *Moralia*, trans. by P. Holland, London, 1603, p. 401; Cicero, *de Legibus*, ed. by Georges de Plinval, Paris, 1959, II, xxvi, 65, p. 78).

ll. 20–21 *against the having of Children.* Augustine, *The Good of Marriage*, trans. by C. T. Wilcox, M.M., in Fathers of the Church Series, Vol. 27 (New York, 1955), Chap. V, p. 15. The question of a childless marriage is one of the first Augustine raises in his study of matrimony.

l. 23 *The arts and sciences.* One contemporary tradition of education lumped the arts and sciences together synonymously under one branch of learning (for example, by Robert Recorde in *The Ground of Arts: Teaching the Perfect Worke and practise of Arithmeticke*, London, 1618, A5ᵛ, A6).

l. 24 *the head; that is their proper Element and Spheare.* Donne is punning on some fairly refined Renaissance terminology. The head was the proper element of the arts and sciences because it was the seat of the reason and furnished them with their 'elemental' material of ideas. The head was also the proper sphere of the arts and sciences, because it is round and symbolically suggests the orbital spheres of the seven planets that, according to Ptolemy, lay immediately beyond the elemental area of the earth (Recorde, *Castle*, pp. 7–8). However, in astrological terms the head was neither an element (which was 'simple'), nor a sphere (which was a trajectory), but was compound (made up of the four elements) and planetary (composed of a solid complex mass).

ll. 26–27 *a fist, and this by a hand enlarged.* 'Over and over again in logical and rhetorical treatises of the English Renaissance, logic is compared to the closed fist and rhetoric to the open hand, this metaphor being borrowed from Zeno through Cicero [*De Finibus*, II, 6] and Quintilian to explain the preoccupation of logic with the tight discourses of the philosopher, and the preoccupation of rhetoric with the more open discourses of orator and popularizer' (Howell, p. 4).

PAGE 106

ll. 5–6 *of providing strength, by increasing weaknesse.* Donne's disquisition on purgation reflects the concern of doctors first, with its extremely 'hot' character (Barrough, 1617, p. 242), and secondly, with its phenomenally heat-producing effect as it reduced the 'quality' of a body back to normal. A 'quality' was the hotter, colder, thicker, or thinner consistency of one of the four elements of a body beyond its usual level (Elyot, 59a, 51a; Culpepper, p. 94). As in Donne's case, doctors often waited to apply the correct purgation until the crest of an illness was passed and the patient had regained some strength, out of fear of misdiagnosing the 'quality' and inducing a relapse (Moore, *Hope*, pp. 57b–58a).

ll. 10–11 *over-watchfull, over-diligent ... misery of man.* The illness which Donne is apostrophizing is a bout of melancholic sadness. Over-watchfulness and great diligence to his fears were standard symptoms of the melancholic person, and 'cunningness' and 'sociability' were suitable descriptions of the treacherousness and contagiousness of the disease (Barrough, 1617, pp. 45–46; Bright, pp. 125–29).

ll. 14–15 *attenuation . . . evacuation . . . exinanition and annihilation.* Donne's analogy describes the three steps in purgation and concludes epigrammatically with an alchemical concept. Attenuation, the first step in purgation, was a process for slimming a patient down of his excess humorous fats; it was followed by evacuation, an expulsion of material from the body (Elyot, 52b), and finally by the exinanition or complete emptying of the patient's venomous humours (Moore, *Hope*, pp. 56b, 57; Elyot, p. 53a), until, in Donne's analogy, the body suffered alchemical annihilation by evaporating out of existence (Joseph Mede, *A Paraphrase and Exposition of the Prophesie of Saint Peter*, 2, Peter, 3:7, London, 1638). The metaphoric use of these terms was common enough (Donne, *Essays*, p. 54; Montaigne, *Essays*, trans. by Florio, [1603] 1632, p. 522).

ll. 21–22 *faith or repentance . . . and works.* The priority of faith over penance and works was at the core of the theological debates of the Roman Church and the Protestant Reformers (*Trent*, Session XIV, 'Penance', VI; Session VI, 'Justification', VII; *Thirty-Nine Articles*, 11–13).

ll. 22–24 *The head and the hand too . . . perfitly spirituall.* Donne builds up a series of analogies between three kinds of men, first, a 'natural' man in a primitive state symbolized by the head and hand that represented rational potential and action (Howell, p. 4; George Downame, *Doctrine of Christian Liberty*, London, 1609, p. 36); secondly, a man who was 'civil' not in the sense of Renaissance courtesy books, but in the tradition of the heathen formed into a state without the guiding light of Judaeo-Christian revelation (William Sclater, *An Exposition with Notes . . . Epistles to the Thessalonians*, I, London, 1630, second edition, p. 40); and thirdly, the Renaissance Christian who was gifted with reason, revelation, and faith, and who was obliged to perform good works for salvation. In *Pseudo-Martyr*, pp. 83–84, Donne distinguishes between all three kinds of men for the same reasons; the 'savage' lived in a company which developed into a commonwealth and finally into a Christian community.

ll. 26–27 *(for who sees that, who searches those Rolls.)* The 'Rolls' were the Register of the Elect, the 'Decrees and Rolls of God' in *Essays* (p. 7), containing metaphorically the list of souls saved throughout the history of the world. The Rolls could not be read according to mere principles of logic, and could be understood only by revelation at the end of time. The existence of the Rolls was a fact demonstrable to mankind by the intuitive urgings of the conscience which resided metaphorically in the human heart.

PAGE 108

l. 1 *finde out the same center.* It was an axiom of text books in astronomy that the centre of a circle was the key to retracing its circumference (Recorde, *Pathway*, B).

ll. 5–6 *evacuation of my soule by confession.* Donne's analogy between a confession of sins and a purgation of the body should not strike us as being far-fetched. Galen, one of the foremost authorities of the Renaissance, recommended purgation as a cure for a number of spiritual ills originating in the imbalance of the humours (*Hippocratis De Humoribus*, II, XVII, *Opera*, Vol. XVI, p. 266). Sparrow says Donne may have been quoting Galen from memory (p. 160). He may also be referring to Galen through the medical commentaries, like Elyot's *Castle*, which relied on him heavily.

ll. 8–9 *To take physicke ... is dangerous.* Galen, *Hippocratis De Acutorum Commentarius* XI, p. 539, in Vol. XV, *Opera*; and *Hippocratis de Humoribus* XII, p. 107, in Vol. XVI. These are only two of the places where Galen talks about the dangers attending the taking of medicine.

ll. 11–12 *thou hast put the power of absolution.* Donne is referring to the first or 'declaratory' form of the three kinds of absolution in the Book of Common Prayer (B, Bᵛ). This form of absolution resided in the power of the church and clergy by divine ordinance, and was administered by the presiding minister to a congregation at the general confession during the Daily Offices (*Prayer Book Dictionary*, eds. G. Harford and M. Stevenson, London, 1625, p. 237).

ll. 12–14 *Physicke may be made so pleasant ... extinguished.* Galen, *De Sanitate Tuenda, Liber IV*, in II, *Operum*, p. 294, Cols. A–B; *De Simplicium Medicamentorum Facultatibus, Liber IV*, X, in XI, *Opera*, p. 652.

ll. 18–20 *To minister many things ... no harme.* Galen, *De Compositione Medicamentorum*, p. 817, Col. a, in V, *Operum*.

ll. 28–29 *a Cup of Stupefaction, to take away the sense of his paine.* For the tradition of the Jewish offering of a stimulant to a prisoner on his way to execution, Donne had a number of immediate sources: several biblical passages, Mark 15:23, noted in his text, and Matt. 27:34 (in these verses the wine is a different potion from the vinegar given Christ on the Cross in Matt. 27:48 and Luke 23:36; *Dictionary of the Bible*, Edinburgh, 1902, edited by J. Hastings, Vol. IV, under 'vinegar'); and the Babylonian Talmud, 'Sanhedrin' tractate, 43a (edited by Seder Mezikin, London, 1935, Vol. I, pp. 279–80).

PAGE 109

ll. 5–6 *one soule so, as that they might maintaine a simpathy in their affections.*

This theory of the affections and the union of souls is also referred to in 'The Exstasie', ll. 41–44, and *passim*:

> When love, with one another so
> Interinanimates two soules,
> That abler soule, which thence doth flow,
> Defects of lonelinesse controules.

ll. 6–7 *the accidents of this world.* Donne is using the word 'accident' in the scholastic sense of the inessential quality of some existing thing. Scholastic vocabulary was used currently in the description of emotional states, cosmography, and diseases in seventeenth-century books of medicine and psychology (Monardes, 1596, Fol. 118; Aquinas, *Summa*, I, Q. XC, a2, pp. 251–52.

PAGE 110

l. 11 *GOD saw that Man needed a Helper.* Gen. 2:18.

PAGE 111

ll. 3–4 *an abhorring is there in Nature, of vacuity.* Vacuity was an emptiness in nature created by the annihilation of matter. It was purely theoretical since such a void was impossible. The physicist, Powers, wrote a generation later than Donne that matter might be 'great or little, yet never shrink by sub-division into nothing'. To conceive of 'Vacuity in Matter' was as vain as considering the possibility of rest in 'Nature' (*Experimental Philosophy*, b3ᵛ).

l. 16 *an under-value.* A contemporary term for the reduction of a market price below standard (Randel Cotgrave, *A Dictionarie*, London, 1611, under 'non-prix').

ll. 24–26 *few Circles . . . Epicicles, and other lesser Circles, but yet Circles.* The 'few Circles' refer either to the orbits of the seven known planets in the Ptolemaic system, or to the orbs of the heavenly elements (eleven according to some accounts) that surrounded the earth (Burton, 2, 2, 3, p. 421), or to both. The epicycles include both the circles formed by the planets rotating on their poles, and the circles formed by planets rotating on orbits about points other than the earth. The 'lesser Circles', for their part, probably refer to the circles traced by the revolution of subordinate spheres about the planets, and to the coloured halo-like circles of vapour about the sun, moon, and other stars (Fulke, *Garden*, 1634, p. 34).

PAGE 112

l. 2 *glasse of the next World.* 1 Cor. 13:12, and 2 Cor. 3:18.

ll. 3–4 *Art . . . to carry the Species.* Art: reading the Book of Creatures. Species: the outward appearance or image of a thing.

l. 9 *Resurrection of my body . . . Resurrection of my soule.* This section is probably a paraphrase of the passage comparing the earthly to the risen glorified body, in 1 Cor. 15, with a specific elaboration of verse 49: 'And as we have borne the image of the earthly, we shall also bear the image of the heavenly.' Verses 20 to 58 of the chapter appear prominently in the service for the burial of the dead in both the 1549 and 1552 versions of the Book of Common Prayer (F. E. Brightman, *The English Rite*, II, London, 1915, pp. 866–71).

ll. 10–11 *Martyrs under the Altar.* Rev. 6:9–10: 'And when he had opened the fifth seal, I saw under the altar the souls of them that were slain for the word of God.' In Sermon CCXXI (1), *Patrologia Latina*, Vol. 39, Col. 2154, which Donne may also have in mind, Augustine cites this passage to justify the placing of relics beneath Christian altars. The practice is still held in the Roman Church, having originated with the construction of the first altars on top of the sarcophagi of Christians in the catacombs.

ll. 17–18 *where Lazarus had beene foure daies.* John 11:17.

l. 22 *all these loud Names.* Exod. 19:16.

l. 22 *Winds.* Jer. 4:11–12, and 30:23; Ezek. 1:4.

l. 23 *Chariots.* Jer. 4:13; Zech. 6:1.

l. 23 *falls of waters.* Isa. 49:10; Rev. 22:1.

l. 31 *not of a Whisperer.* Matt. 3:3; Mark 1:3; Luke 3:4; John 1:23.

PAGE 113

ll. 17–18 *Cains murther did so.* Gen. 4:10.

l. 19 *waters are afflictions.* 1 Kings 22:27; 2 Chron. 18:26.

PAGE 115

l. 3 *thy measures and degrees.* A 'degree' was a three-hundred and sixtieth part of the flat zodiac circle representing the motions of the planets. By contrast, the 'measure' was the three hundred and sixtieth part of the year (a fraction more than a day) represented by each degree in the zodiac (Recorde, *Castle*, p. 29).

l. 6 *the Messenger of Satan, to humble him.* 2 Cor. 12:7.

PAGE 116

l. 30 *propensnesse to diseases in the body.* The idea of the body's natural inclination to illness recurred often in Renaissance texts of medicine. It usually found its expression in either a defence or an apology for medicine. The inclination of the body to infirmity was considered the result, however indirectly, of the fall of Adam (Barrough, 1617, A5ᵛ; Coghan, 1584, inverted PP 1). Donne is referring to an internal illness caused through no apparent 'venomous' or outside agency.

PAGE 117

ll. 2–5 *the distempers and diseases of soiles, sourenesse, drinesse, weeping . . . hanger of a hill.* Donne lists a number of soil diseases and then a cure for each. Sourness was a bitterness of soil (Googe, p. 17b) remedied by some chemical action in the earth itself; dryness, a kind of aridity (Fulke, *Meteors*, p. 19) which a 'hanger', the wood on the side of a hill, might cure by shedding on it its natural moisture; 'weeping', 'wet', or swampy ground which a heat treatment made drier and more arable (Googe, p. 17a).

l. 7 *health from cauterizing.* The definition of a cauterization in *Guydos Questions* is 'an operation made with fire artificially in the body of man for certain utilyties' (Fol. 47 [appearing wrongly as 48]), usually with a red hot iron (gold or silver in the case of the more delicate operations) to purge it of cold and moist 'dispositions' (Fol. 48), like the 'malignant moisture' Donne describes as ruining the land. Cauterization was believed to destroy evil physical 'dispositions' by drying or burning them up, but had come into a certain amount of ill repute by the end of the sixteenth century as not being very effective through indiscriminate use.

ll. 13–14 *Marle . . . or from slimie sand in other shoares.* Marle was sandy earth imported into England by ship particularly from France, and was reputed to produce the best kind of soil to fertilize farm land; the '*slimie sand in other shoares*' is probably 'marga' from Germany, of a much 'fattier' substance than marle (Googe, p. 19b).

ll. 17–18 *it might preserve a sound part.* Doctors recommended amputation under comparatively sophisticated conditions, but regularly enough, usually in the hope of preventing the spread of gangrene and other infections to the rest of the body (Woodall, p. 387). The technique was used frequently to compensate for the lack of effective antidotes, but with complete ignorance of the rules governing the spread of germs (Woodall, 'A Treatise of Gangrena,' pp. 381–86).

l. 28 *marish.* An obsolete variant of marsh.

ll 33–34 *specifique forme . . . the sharpe accidents of diseases.* In scholastic thought, a 'substance' was the essence and pith of a thing, made up of matter and form. A thing shared this matter and form of its substance with all other things in the same genus as itself; its 'specific form' to which Donne refers was the individual occurrence of the general form of the substance in itself (*Summa*, I, Q. XC, a2, pp. 251–52; II, i, Q. VII, a1, pp. 104–5; I, Q. CV, a5, pp. 400–1).

PAGE 118

l. 2   *glorifying these bodies.* 1 Cor. 15:39–42.

ll. 5–6   *What Hypocrates.* The Greek physician (b. c. 460 B.C.), with Galen, Avicenna, Averroes, and Aquinas, one of the chief authorities of medical manuals, particularly through his often quoted 'Aphorisms'.

ll. 14–15   *my actuall sinne . . . another fuell, originall sinne.* Actual sin: a transient fall from sin by a deliberate act of the will of fallen man, described in the scholastic tradition (*Summa*, I–II, Q. lxxxvii, a6) and in No. 9, *Thirty-Nine Articles* (pp. 7–8); Donne's diction echoes the vocabulary of the latter.

l. 28   *That sinne tooke occasion by the Law.* Rom. 7:8.

PAGE 120

ll. 6–7   *Ezechias lease for fifteene yeeres.* Isa. 38:5.

l. 7   *Lazarus his lease, for a time.* John 11:43.

PAGE 121

l. 9   *propriety, a Meum & Tuum.* Legal terms in the division of rights over property.

PAGE 121

l. 29   *into one naturall, unnaturall day.* In the Ptolemaic system, a 'natural day' was the fixed period of twenty-four hours from a given point like noon or sunset on one day to the same point on another. It was made up of intervals of light and darkness created by the rotation of the universe about the fixed point of the earth. Donne's 'natural unnatural day' was a purely imaginary day thirty-six impossible hours long. Its intervals of light and darkness were made up of the longest night of the year (Dec. 12) and the longest light period (June 11), each almost 18 hours long, an impossible 36 hours in all, according to the movement of the sun first into its winter tropic and, six months later, into the summer tropic, in conjunction with the meridian (Recorde, *Castle*, pp. 11–12, 24–25).

PAGE 123

l. 6 *they fall into relapses.* For example, the adoration of the Golden Calf in Exod. 32:4; the lust of the Israelites for flesh and manna in Num. 11:4; and their incest in Judg. 3:6.

l. 9 *murmurings against thee.* Exod. 16:2, 7; Num. 14:27; Ezek. 20:8.

ll. 10–11 *embracing the Idolatries of their neighbours.* Ezek. 20:16.

PAGE 124

ll. 14–17 *if ye do in any wise goe backe . . . thornes in your eies, till ye perish.* Josh. 23:13.

l. 30 *there went a Prince of every Tribe.* Josh. 22:14.

l. 32 *is the iniquity of Peor too little for us.* Josh. 22:17.

PAGE 125

l. 1 *professe themselves to bee of the same profession.* Josh. 22:28.

l. 2 *the Army returned without bloud.* Josh. 22:30.

ll. 12–13 *if he returne to his sinne, hee decrees for Satan.* Tertullian, 'Conversion and Relapse,' *On Penitence,* 5, in *Treatises on Penance* (Ancient Christian Writers Series XXVIII), trans. by William P. Le Saint, S.J., London, 1959, pp. 21–23.

l. 35 *to pardon my brother seventy times seven.* Christ's injunction to Peter to forgive his enemy in Matt. 18:22. As 1624 (1) reads, 'seventy seven times,' Donne misquoted the Bible, or the printer copied his manuscript wrongly.

PAGE 127

l. 7 *aboard with Hymeneus.* Donne may be referring to Haemon, who slew himself beside the body of his betrothed Antigone whom his father, Creon, had executed for burying the body of her own executed brother, Polynices, against his orders. However, Donne may also have in mind Hymen or Hymenaeus, supposedly a son of Apollo and a Muse of Greek song lore. According to one story, Hymen was killed by the collapse of his house on him on his wedding day, and he became a patron of betrothed persons.

Selective Bibliography

The following is a list of works referred to more than once in the Commentary, mostly Renaissance texts on theology, medicine, and astrology. Some were originally referred to by Donne. The presence of several dates after an entry means that more than one edition was used, according to availability.

ALEXIS, OF PIEDMONT. *The Secretes of the reverend Maister Alexis of Piedmont: containyng excellente remedies against diverse diseases, woundes, and other accidentes*, translated by William Warde. London, 1580.

ARISTOTLE. *De Generatione Animalium*, ed. by Arthur Platt, and *De Partibus Animalium*, ed. by William Ogle, in Vol. V, and *Physica*, ed. by R. P. Hardie and R. K. Gay, in Vol. II of *The Works of Aristotle Translated into English*, ed. by J. A. Smith and W. D. Ross. Oxford, 1908–52.

ARNOLD, RICHARD. *Customs of London, Otherwise Called Arnold's Chronicle*. London, [1502] 1811.

Articles, Whereupon it was agreed, in 1562 . . . of the Churche of England [The Thirty-Nine Articles]. London, 1571.

AUGUSTINE OF HIPPO. *Augustine: Confessions and Enchiridion*, Vol. VII of *The Library of Christian Classics*. London, 1955.

————. *De Civitate Dei*, Vol. I; *Homilies*, Vol. X; and *Against Two Letters of the Pelagians*, IV, 6, Vol. III of *The Anti-Pelagian Works*, Vol. XV of *The Works of Aurelius Augustine*, edited by Marcus Dods. Edinburgh, 1871.

————. *Letters*, V Vols., translated by Sister Winifred Parsons, S.N.D., in *Fathers of the Church Series*, Vol. 12–16. New York, 1955.

BAKER, GEORGE. *See* Generus.

BANISTER, JOHN. *The Historie of Man, sucked from the sappe of the most approved Anathomistes*. London, 1578.

————. *The Workes of the famous Chyrurgian, Mr. John Banister; By him digested into five Bookes.* London, 1633.

BARROUGH, PHILIP. *The Method of Physick, Containing the Causes, Signes, and Cures of Inward Diseases.* London, [1583] 1613, 1617, 1639.

The Holy Bible, Conteyning the Old and the New ... Imprinted at London by Robert Barker, Printer to the Kings most Excellent Majestie. anno. Dom. 1611.

BLUNDEVILLE, THOMAS. *M. Blundevil His Exercises, Contayning Eight Treatises ... Cosmographie, Astronomie, and Geographie.* London, [1594] 1636.

Book of Common Prayer, printed by Robert Barker, fol. London, 1611.

BRIGHT, THOMAS. *A Treatise of Melancholy.* London, 1586.

BURTON, ROBERT. *Anatomy of Melancholy*, edited by F. Dell and P. Jordan-Smith. New York, 1955.

BUTLER, CHARLES. *The Feminine Monarchie: or The Historie of Bees.* London, [1609] 1623.

CALVIN, JOHN. *The Institution of the Christian Religion*, trans. by Thomas Norton. London, [1561] 1611; [Vol. XX in *Library of Christian Classics*] 1961.

COGHAN, THOMAS. *The Haven of Health.* London, 1584.

Constitutions and Canons Ecclesiasticall agreed upon, 1603 [of the Church of England]. London, 1604, 1612.

COWELL, JOHN. *The Interpreter.* Cambridge, 1607.

CROOKE, HELKIAH. *A Description of the Body of Man ... Collected and Translated Out of all the Best Authors of Anatomy.* London, [1615] 1631.

CULPEPPER, NICHOLAS. *Galen's Art of Physick* [A Commentary]. London, 1671.

DAVIES, SIR. JOHN. "Of the Soule of Man, and the Immortalitie thereof," *Nosce Teipsum.* London, [1599] 1622, 1697.

DAY, R. *The Key of Philosophie ... how to ... calcine.* London, 1580.

DODOENS, D. REMBERT. *See* Henry Lyte.

DOLAEUS, JOHN. *See* William Salmon.

ELYOT, SIR THOMAS. *The Castle of Health*. London, [1539] 1541.

FORESTUS, PETRUS. *See* James Hart.

FRAMPTON, JOHN. *See* Monardes.

FULKE, WILLIAM. *A Most Pleasant Prospect Into the Garden of Naturall Contemplation, to behold the naturall causes of all kinde of Meteors.* London, [1563] 1634.

GABELHOVER, OSWALD. *The Boock of Physicke*, trans. by A. M. Dorte, 1599.

GALE, THOMAS, trans. "briefe Declaration," *Certaine Works of Galens.* London, 1586.

GALEN, CLAUDIUS. *De Compositione Medicamentorum Per Genere, Liber I,* and *De Sanitate Tuenda Liber IV*, in *Galeni Operum.* Basle, 1542.

———. *De Simplicium Medicamentorum Facultatibus, Liber IV*, in Vol. XI; *Hippocratis De Acutorum Morborum Victu Liber*, in Vol. XV; and *Hippocratis de Humoribus Liber et Galeni in Eum Commentarii Tres*, in Vol. XVI of *Medicorum Graecorum Opera*, trans. from the Greek into Latin by C. G. Kuhn. Leipzig, 1829.

GENERUS, DOCTOR. *The newe Jewell of Health. . . . by Doctor Generus,* trans. by George Baker. London, 1576.

GERARDE, JOHN. *The Herball or Generall Historie of Plantes.* London, 1597.

GOOGE, BARNABY. *The Whole Art and Trade of Husbandry.* London, 1614.

GUIDO, DE CAULIACO. *Guydos Questions, Newly Corrected.* London, 1579.

GUILLEMEAU, JACQUES. *The French Chirurgerye.* Dorte, 1579.

HART, JAMES. *The Arraignment of Urines* [trans. from the work of Petrus Forestus], and *The Anatomie of Urines.* London, 1623–25.

HARVEY, WILLIAM. *De Motu Cordis*, Latin text with English trans. by K. J. Franklin. London, 1957.

HERBERT, GEORGE. *Works*, edited by F. E. Hutchinson. Oxford, 1941.

HOOKER, RICHARD. *Laws of Ecclesiastical Polity*. London, [1594] 1617.

HOWELL, W. S. *Logic and Rhetoric in England, 1500–1700.* New York, 1961.

JONES, JOHN. *A Briefe, Excellent, and Profitable Discourse, of the naturall beginning of all growing and living things*, with *The benefit of the Auncient bathes of Buckstones*. London, 1574–72.

KEYNES, SIR GEOFFREY. *Bibliography of Donne*. Cambridge, 1958.

LANGLEY, THOMAS. *An Abridgement of the notable worke of Polidore Vergile*. London, 1546.

LLWYD [LLOYDE], HUMPHREY [HUMFRE]. *The treasury of health . . . by one Petrus Hispanus . . . translated into English by Humfre Lloyde*. London, 1585.

LYTE, HENRY. *A New Herbal, Or Historie of Plants . . . in the Dutch . . . by . . . D. Rembert Dodoens . . . translated out of French . . . by Henry Lyte*. London, 1619.

MAGIUS [MAGGI], HIERONYMUS. *De Tintinnabulis liber postumus. F. Sweertius . . . notis illustrabit*. Hanover, 1608.

MERCATOR, GERARD. *Atlas, Containing his Cosmographicall Description of the Fabricke and Figure of the World*, trans. by W. Saltonstall [Generosus]. London, 1635.

MONARDES, NICHOLAS. *A Booke which treateth of two medicines . . . the Bezaar stone, and the Herbe Escueronera. . . . compyled by Doctor Monardes of Sevill. 1574. Translated . . . into English by John Frampton. Published with Frampton's translation of Monardes' Joyfull Newes.* London, 1577, 1580, 1596.

MOORE, NORMAN. *History of the Study of Medicine in the British Isles*. London, 1908.

MOORE, PHILIP. *The hope of health*. London, 1565.

MORYSON, FYNES. *An Itinerary*. London, 1617.

NORTON, THOMAS. *See* Calvin, John. *The Institution of Christian Religion*.

PAYNELL, THOMAS. *Regimen Sanitatis Salerni*. London, [1528] 1597.

A Physical Dictionary: OR, An Interpretation of such crabbed Words and Terms of Arts . . . in Physick, Anatomy, Chirurgery, and Chymistry. London, 1657.

POWER, HENRY. *Experimental Philosophy . . . Microscopical, Mercurial, Magnetical*. London, 1664.

RECORDE, ROBERT. *The Castle of Knowledg, containing The Explication of the Sphere*. London, 1556.

———. *The Pathway to Knowledge, Containing the First Principles of Geometrie.* London, 1551.

ROCCA, ANGELO. *De Campanis Commentarius.* Rome, 1612.

SALMON, WILLIAM. *Systema Medicinale, A Compleat Systeme of Physick . . . Translated . . . out of the most Learned John Dolaeus . . . by William Salmon.* London, 1686.

———. *Synopsis Medicinae.* London, 1671.

SALTONSTALL, W. *See* GERARD MERCATOR.

STEVENSON, BURTON. *Proverbs, Maxims and Familiar Phrases.* London, 1949.

Thirty-Nine Articles. See *Articles.*

THOMAS AQUINAS. *Summa Theologica,* edited by the Fathers of the English Dominican province. London, 1912.

TOPSELL, EDWARD. *The History of Four-footed Beasts and Serpents.* London, 1658.

Trent, Canons and Decrees of the Council of. London, 1888.

TURBERVILLE, GEORGE. *Turbervile's Booke of Hunting, or The Noble Art of Venerie or Hunting.* Oxford, [1576] 1908.

VICARY, THOMAS. *A Profitable Treatise of the Anatomie of mans body* [1577], edited by F. J. Furnivall. London, 1888.

VIRGIL, POLIDORE. *See* Thomas Langley.

WALTON, ISAAC. *Lives.* London, 1951.

WARDE, WILLIAM. *See* Alexis of Piedmont.

WOODALL, JOHN. *The Surgeons Mate. . . . with A Treatise of the Cure of the Plague, Surgical Mate.* London, 1639.

WRIGHT, THOMAS. *The Passions of the Minde.* London, 1621.